With illustrations by
P Endsleigh Castle ARAeS
J Goulding
K Broomfield
R Ward

Aircraft in Profile

Volume 1/Part Two

General Editor **Charles W Cain**

Profile Publications Ltd Windsor Berkshire England
Doubleday & Company Inc Garden City New York

© Profile Publications Limited 1965

Doubleday & Company Inc. edition 1965

First published in England in 1965
by Profile Publications Limited
Coburg House Sheet Windsor
Berkshire England

Revised (4th) edition 1976

ISBN 0 85383 411 3

ISBN (USA) 0 385 05428 9

Acknowledgements
Credit where credit is due. The authors, artists,
the general editor and the publishers, Profile
Publications Ltd., take this opportunity of
acknowledging with sincere and grateful thanks
the immense amount of invaluable assistance
rendered unstintingly by government
departments, military bureaux, the aerospace
industry, learned bodies, historical associations
and museums—not least, people as people who
have opened up their own private archives
simply because of their real affection for
aviation in one form or another. In the case of
the more recent parts of *Aircraft in Profile*,
authors have been invited to make
'Acknowledgements' an integral facet of their
overall work. To everyone who has helped in
the past and will feel free to do so in the
future. . . . Thank you! from the team that
makes up *Aircraft in Profile*.—CWC.

Note to readers
Authenticated additional or corrected
information, together with appropriate
photographic or other material evidence, will
be welcomed by the Editor, the specific author
will be notified accordingly.—CWC.

Uniform with this volume

Aircraft in Profile Series *3rd Edition*
AFVs of the World Series *1st Edition*
Locomotives in Profile Series
Warships in Profile Series
Small Arms in Profile Series
Cars in Profile Series

Printed in England by Edwin Snell Printers, Yeovil, Somerset

Foreword

To the many who have already added to their book collection *Aircraft in Profile* Volume 1/Part One, what more can be added to the Foreword which is repeated below for newcomers? That you have now acquired this companion part is sufficient proof that you value the series. What you really want to know now is: Will there be more parts of successive volumes to come? The answer is a resounding yes!; and that's got to be good news for the discerning reader.

This is a unique experience. Never before has anyone attempted to produce such a great aviation library series. The original objective was to create a wide variety of aircraft monographs aimed to satisfy the most discerning of aviation buffs, fans and enthusiasts in every part of the world.

What has resulted from the original concept of reaching out for the highest standards is a product unique in the annals of aviation publishing. Today, the collected works total well in excess of 1,000,000 words and more than 250 individual Aircraft Profiles.

Undeniably, there is an insistent demand for warplane subjects and essentially civil aircraft are in the minority. But *Aircraft in Profile* as a series is prepared by historians who are more concerned with the accuracy of their researching than presenting the reader with less exacting popular histories.

This first volume sets the style for subsequent volumes by ranging over aviation's horizons from World War One through the years to the Second World War and on into the 1950s. In fact, some more recent Profiles are concerned with aircraft of the 1970s. To help the newcomer find his way around, this volume contains a quick-reference section called 'Aircraft Profile Finder'.

Finally, for those who like to know what is between these hard covers statistically-speaking, there are no fewer than 296 black and white photographs, 24 pages of full-colour artwork views (140 separate drawings) and about 50,000 words.

March 1976   **Charles W Cain**

Contents

Corrections and Additions
No work of such dimensions can be totally free from errors and omissions.
Page 26 (Heinkel He 111 H) For 'Edelweis' read 'Edelweiss'.
Pages 29 & 36 (He 111 H) For Boelke' read 'Boelcke'.
Page 36 (He 111 H) Transport in background with Italian civil registration I-DOUL is now positively identified as a tri-motor Savoia Marchetti S.M.73 at
    Maison Blanche, November 8, 1942.
Pages 136 & 143 (Hawker Hurricane IIC) For 'Kuttlewascher' read 'Kuttelwascher'.

Index to Volume One   Part Two

Key: (c) colour drawings; (p) photographs

► Country of Origin and Period of Use.

(1) ■□□□ World War 1 :1914-18	(3) □□■□ World War 2 :1939-45
(2) □■□□ Post-W.W.1 :1920s-1930s	(4) □□□■ Post-W.W.2 :1950s-1970s

Austria-Hungary (1914-18)

Ö. AVIATIK (BERG)
No.	Period	Aircraft
151	■□□□	Berg D I

PHÖNIX
| 175 | ■□□□ | Scouts (D I-IV) |

Australia

COMMONWEALTH
| 178 | □□■□ | Boomerang |
| 154 | □□■□ | Wirraway |

Canada

CANADAIR
| 186 | □□□■ | Sabres (Mks. 1-6; see also U.S.A./North American F-86 Sabre) |

Czechoslovakia

AVIA
| 152 | □■□□ | B-534 |

France

AEROSPATIALE/BAC
| 250 | □□□■ | Concorde |

BLOCH (see M. BLOCH)

BREGUET
| 157 | ■□□□ | †Breguet 14 (Type XIV) |

DASSAULT (M. DASSAULT)
| 230 | □□□■ | †Mirage III-5 (& Milan) |
| 143 | □□□■ | M.D. 450 Ouragan |

DEWOITINE
| 135 | □□■□ | D.520 |

HANRIOT
| 109 | ■□□□ | †HD-1 |

LIORE ET OLIVIER
| 173 | □□■□ | LeO 45 Series |

MARCEL BLOCH
| 201 | □□■□ | (M.B.) 151 & 152 |

MORANE SAULNIER
| 147 | □□■□ | M.S.406 |

NIEUPORT
| 49 | ■□□□ | †N.17C-1 |
| 79 | ■□□□ | †N.28C-1 |

POTEZ
| 195 | □□■□ | Potez 63 Series |

SPAD
| 17 | ■□□□ | †S.P.A.D. XIIIC.1 |

SUD-AVIATION
| 180 | □□□■ | Caravelle 3 & 6 |

Germany

ALBATROS
| 127 | ■□□□ | †D I-D III |
| 9 | ■□□□ | †D V |

ARADO
| 215 | □□■□ | Ar 234 Blitz |

AVIATIK (see Ö. Aviatik: Berg D I, Austria-Hungary)

BÜCKER
| 222 | □□■□ | Bü 131 Jungmann |

DORNIER
| 164 | □□■□ | †Do 17 & 215 |

FIESELER
| 228 | □□■□ | †Fi 156 Storch |

FOCKE-WULF
3	□□■□	†FW 190 A
94	□□■□	FW 190 D/Ta 152 Series
99	□□■□	FW 200 (Condor)

FOKKER
25	■□□□	†D VII
67	■□□□	†D VIII
55	■□□□	†Dr I (Triplane)
38	■□□□	†Monoplanes (Eindeckers)

GOTHA
| 115 | ■□□□ | G I-G V |

HEINKEL
15	□□■□	He 111 H
203	□□■□	†He 162 (Salamander)
234	□□■□	He 177 (Greif)
219	□□■□	He 219 Uhu

HENSCHEL
| 69 | □□■□ | Hs 129 |

JUNKERS
177	□□■□	Ju 52 Series (Ju 52/3m)
76	□□■□	Ju 87 A & B ('Stuka') ('A'—'Anton'; 'B'—'Berta')
211	□□■□	†Ju 87 D Variants ('Stuka') ('D'—'Dora')
29	□□■□	Ju 88 A
148	□□■□	Ju 88 Night Fighters
187	■□□□	Monoplanes ('Blechesel')

L.F.G. (see ROLAND)

MESSERSCHMITT
40	□□■□	†Bf 109 E ('E'—'Emil')
184	□□■□	Bf 109 F ('F'—'Friedrich')
113	□□■□	Bf 109 G ('G'—'Gustav')
23	□□■□	†Bf 110 (Day Fighters)
207	□□■□	Bf 110 (Night Fighters)
225	□□■□	†Me 163 Komet
161	□□■□	†Me 210/410 Series
130	□□■□	†Me 262 (Schwalbe/Sturmvogel)

PFALZ
| 43 | ■□□□ | †D III |
| 199 | ■□□□ | †D XII (& D XIV) |

PHÖNIX (see AUSTRIA-HUNGARY)

ROLAND (L.F.G.)
| 163 | ■□□□ | †C II ('Walfisch') |

SIEMENS-SCHUCKERT
| 86 | ■□□□ | †D III & IV |

UDET
| 257 | □■□□ | U-12 Flamingo |

Great Britain

AIRSPEED
| 227 | □□■□ | Oxford Mks. I-V |

ARMSTRONG WHITWORTH
| 153 | □□■□ | Whitley (Mks. I-VII) |

AVRO
†Avro 707 (see Avro Vulcan)
65	□□■□	†Lancaster I
235	□□■□	Lancaster Mk. II
243	□□□■	Avro (Hawker Siddeley) Shackleton Mks. 1-5
162	□□□■	†Vulcan (& Avro 707)
168	□□□■	York (Mks. I & II)

BAC/AEROSPATIALE
| 250 | □□□■ | BAC/Aerospatiale Concorde |

B.E.
| 133 | ■□□□ | B.E.2, 2a & 2b |

BOULTON PAUL
| 117 | □□■□ | Defiant (Mks. I-III) |

BRISTOL
193	■□□□	Bristol M.1 (M.1A-M.1D)
137	□□■□	Beaufighter Mks. I & II
93	□□■□	Blenheim I
218	□□■□	Blenheim Mk. IV (& R.C.A.F. Bolingbroke Mks. I-IV)
6	□□■□	Bulldog (Mks. I-IV)
21	■□□□	†Fighter ('Brisfit')
237	□□■□	F.2B Fighter (see No. 21) (RAF: 1918-30s)
139	■□□□	†Scouts C & D

DE HAVILLAND
91	■□□□	D.H.2
26	■□□□	†D.H.4 (see also AMERICAN DH-4)
181	■□□□	D.H.5
62	■□□□	D.H.9
248	□■□□	D.H.9A (RAF:1918-30)
145	□■□□	D.H.10
108	□□□■	Comet Srs. 1-4 (now Hawker Siddeley Comet)
174	□□□■	Hornet (& Sea Hornet)
52	□□■□	Mosquito I-IV
209	□□■□	Mosquito Mk. IV
144	□□■□	†Rapide (Dragon Rapide)

| 132 | □□■□ | †Tiger Moth |
| 48 | □□□■ | †Vampire Mks. 5 & 9 |

ENGLISH ELECTRIC/BAC
| 54 | □□□■ | †Canberra Mks. I & IV |
| 114 | □□□■ | †P.1 & Lightning 1 |

FAIREY
44	□■□□	Fairey III F
240	□□■□	Barracuda Mks. I-V
34	□□■□	†Battle Mks. I-V (and Trainer)
56	□■□□	Flycatcher
254	□□■□	Fulmar Mks. I & II
212	□□■□	†Swordfish Mks. I-IV

GLOSTER
33	□■□□	†Gamecock (Mks. I-III & Grebe Mk. I)
10	□■□□	Gauntlet (Mks. I & II)
98	□□■□	†Gladiator (Mks. I & II, also Sea Gladiator)
179	□□□■	†Javelin 1-6
78	□□■□	Meteor F.IV (F.4)
12	□□■□	Meteor F.8

HANDLEY PAGE
11	□□■□	†Halifax B.III, VI, VII
58	□□■□	Hampden (Mks. I & II, also Hereford)
182	□■□□	†Heyford (Mks. I-III)

HAWKER
198	□□□■	P.1127 and Kestrel (now Harrier)
140	□■□□	Audax & Hardy
57	□■□□	†Hart (& Hart Trainer)
4	□□□■	Hunter F.6
167	□□□■	Hunter Two-Seaters
111	□□■□	Hurricane I (& Sea Hurricane Mk. IA)
24	□□■□	†Hurricane IIC (& Sea Hurricane Mks. IC & IIC)
126	□□■□	Sea Fury (& Fury)
71	□□■□	†Sea Hawk
197	□□■□	Tempest I-VI
81	□□■□	†Typhoon

HAWKER SIDDELEY (see AVRO & DE HAVILLAND)

MARTINSYDE
| 200 | ■□□□ | Elephant |

R.E.
| 85 | ■□□□ | †R.E.8 |

S.E.
| 103 | ■□□□ | S.E.5 |
| 1 | ■□□□ | †S.E.5a |

SHORT
74	■□□□	Short 184
84	□■□□	Empire Boats ('C' & 'G'-Class; also 'Mercury-Maia' Composite)
142	□□■□	Stirling (Mks. I-V)
189	□□■□	Sunderland (Mks. I-V)

SOPWITH
121	■□□□	†Sopwith 1½ Strutter
31	■□□□	Camel F.1
169	■□□□	†Dolphin (5.F.1)
13	■□□□	†Pup
50	■□□□	†7F.1 Snipe
73	■□□□	†Triplane

SUPERMARINE
39	□■□□	†S.4-S.6B (Schneider Trophy Racers)
221	□□■□	Seafires (Merlins) (Mks. I-III)
41	□□■□	†Spitfire I & II
166	□□■□	†Spitfire V Series
206	□□■□	†Spitfire Mk. IX (& Mk. XVI)
246	□□■□	Spitfire (Griffons) Mks. XIV & XVIII
224	□□□□	†Walrus I & Seagull V (RN variants)

VICKERS (-ARMSTRONG)
66	□□□■	†Valiant (Mks. 1 & 2)
5	■□□□	†F.B.27 Vimy (Mks. I-III)
72	□□□■	†Viscount 700
229	□□■□	Warwick Mks. I-V
256	□□■□	Wellesley Mks. I & II
125	□□■□	Wellington I & II

WESTLAND
159	□□■□	†Lysander (Mks. I-III)
32	□■□□	Wapiti (Mks. I-VII)
191	□□■□	Whirlwind (Mk. I)

Italy

ANSALDO (see S.V.A.)

CAPRONI REGGIANE
- **123** □□■□ **Re. 2000 (Falco I)**
- 244 □□■□ Re. 2001 (Falco II), Re.2002 (Ariete) & Re.2005 (Sagittario)

FIAT
- 110 □□■□ B.R.20 (Cicogna)
- 22 □□■□ C.R.32
- **16** □□■□ †**C.R.42 (Falco)**
- 188 □□■□ G.50 (Freccia)
- 119 □□□■ G.91

MACCHI
- 64 □□■□ M.C.200 (Saetta)
- **28** □□■□ **C.202 (Folgore)**

S.V.A (ANSALDO)
- 61 ■□□□ Scouts (S.V.A 4-10)

SAVOIA MARCHETTI
- **89** □□■□ **S.M.79 (Sparviero)**
- 146 □□■□ S.M.81 (Pipistrello)

Japan (*Allied code names)

AICHI
- 241 □□■□ D3A ('Val') & Yokosuka D4Y ('Judy') Carrier bombers

KAWANISHI
- 233 □□■□ Four-motor Flying-boats : H6K 'Mavis'* & H8K 'Emily'*
- 213 □□■□ Kyofu ; Shiden & Shiden KAI Variants ('Rex'* ; 'George'*)

KAWASAKI
- 105 □□■□ †Ki-45 Toryu ('Nick'*)
- 118 □□■□ Ki-61 Hein ('Tony'*)

MITSUBISHI
- 129 □□■□ A6M2 Zero-Sen ('Zeke'* & 'Rufe'* floatplane)
- 190 □□■□ A6M3 Zero-Sen ('Hamp'*)
- 236 □□■□ †A6M5/8 Zero-Sen ('Zeke 52*') (see Nos. 129 & 190)
- 160 □□■□ G3M ('Nell'* & Yokosuka L3Y 'Tina'*)
- 210 □□■□ G4M 'Betty'* (& Ohka Bomb —'Baka'*)
- 172 □□■□ Ki-21 ('Sally'* & Ki-57/MC-20 'Topsy'*)
- **82** □□■□ **Ki-46 ('Dinah'*)**

NAKAJIMA
- **141** □□■□ **B5N 'Kate'***
- 46 □□■□ Ki-43 Hayabusa ('Oscar'*)
- 255 □□■□ Ki-44 Shoki ('Tojo'*)
- 70 □□■□ Ki-84 Hayate ('Frank'*)

YOKOSUKA
D4Y ('Judy') (see AICHI D3A)

Netherlands

FOKKER
- 87 □■□□ C.V
- 63 □■□□ D.XXI
- 134 □□■□ G.1 ('Faucheur')
- 176 □□■□ T.VIII

Poland

LUBLIN
- 231 ■□□□ R.XIII Variants

P.Z.L.
- 75 □□■□ †P.11 ('Jedenastka')
- 104 □■□□ P.23 Karas
- 170 □■□□ P.24
- 258 □■□□ P.37 Los

Sweden

SAAB
- 138 □□■□ J 21 A & R
- 36 □□□■ †J 29

Yugoslavia
- 242 □■□□ IK Fighters (IK-1 to IK-3, & IK-5)

U.S.A.

AMERICAN DH-4
- 97 ■□□□ DH-4 ('Liberty Plane')

BELL
- **165** □□■□ **P-39 Airacobra**

BOEING
- 192 □□□■ Boeing 707 (& 720 ; C-135/VC-137)
- 77 □□■□ B-17E & F Flying Fortress
- 205 □□■□ B-17G Flying Fortress
- **101** □□■□ **B-29 Superfortress**
- 83 □□□■ †B-47 (Stratojet)
- 245 □□□■ B-52A/H Stratofortress
- 27 □□■□ F4B-4
- 2 □□■□ P-12E
- 14 □□■□ †P-26A ('Peashooter')

BREWSTER
- 217 □□■□ Buffalo (Brewster F2A & Export Models 239-439)

CHANCE (& LTV) VOUGHT
- **47** □□■□ †**F4U-1 Corsair (also as Brewster F3A, Goodyear FG)**
- 150 □□■□ F4U-4 to F4U-7 Corsair (also AU-1 & Goodyear F2G)
- 239 □□■□ LTV A-7A/E Corsair II
- **90** □□□■ **F-8A to E Crusader (now LTV F-8)**
- 251 □□■□ OS2U Kingfisher (Vought-Sikorsky OS2U & NAF OS2N)

CONSOLIDATED
- **19** □□■□ **B-24J Liberator**
- 183 □□■□ PBY Catalina ('Dumbo' ; also PBY-5A/6A Amphibian Canso)

CURTISS
- 37 ■□□□ JN-4 ('Jenny')
- 45 □■□□ †Army Hawks (P-1 & P-6)
- 116 □■□□ †Navy Hawks (BFC & BF2C ; F6C & F11C & F11C-2 Goshawk)
- **80** □□■□ **Hawk 75 (R.A.F. Mohawk)**
- **136** □□■□ †**P-40 Kittyhawk (Mks. I-IV ; R.A.F. only, U.S.A.A.F. Warhawk)**
- **35** □□■□ **P-40 Tomahawk (Mks. I-II)**
- **124** □□■□ **SB2C-1 Helldiver (also U.S.A.A.F. A-25 Shrike)**
- 194 □□□■ SOC Seagull
- 128 □■□□ Shrike (A-6, A-8 & A-12)

DOUGLAS
- 102 □□□■ †A-4 Skyhawk
- 202 □□■□ A-20 (7A to Boston III) (also R.A.F. Havoc ; not U.S.A.A.F. models)
- **96** □□■□ **DC-3 (to Dec. 1941 only)**
- 220 □□■□ †Dakota Mks. I-IV (1941-,70 ; R.A.F. & Dominion/Commonwealth air forces only)
- 249 □□■□ †R4D variants (U.S.N's DC-3/C-47s)
- 196 □□■□ †SBD Dauntless
- 171 □□■□ TBD Devastator
- **60** □□■□ **Skyraider (ex-AD-1 to AD-7 now A-1E to A-1J)**

FORD
- 156 □■□□ Tri-motors ('The Tin Goose' series)

GEE BEE (GRANVILLE BROTHERS)
- 51 □■□□ †Racers

GRUMMAN
- 252 □□□■ A-6A/E Intruder, EA-6A & EA-6B Prowler
- 92 □■□□ †F3F Series
- **53** □□■□ **F4F-3 Wildcat (British R.N: Martlet I only)**
- **107** □□■□ **F8F Bearcat**
- 214 □□■□ TBF Avenger (also Eastern TBM Avenger)

LOCKHEED
- 120 □□■□ Constellation (L-049/C-69 ; L-1049 Super Constellation/C-121/R7V/WV-2 ; L-1649 Starliner)
- 223 □□□■ C-130 Hercules
- 253 □□■□ Hudson Mks. I-VI (also U.S.A.A.F. A-28/A-29, AT-18 & U.S.N. PBO-1)
- **106** □□■□ **P-38J-M Lightning**
- 131 □□□■ †F-104G/CF-104 (U.S.A./Canadair: Starfighter)
- 204 □□□■ P2V Neptune (now P-2, also Kawasaki GK-210 Turboprop version)

LTV (see CHANCE VOUGHT)

MARTIN
- 247 □□■□ B-57 Night Intruders & General Dynamics RB-57F (U.S.A.F. Canberras)
- **112** □□■□ **B-26B & C Marauder R.A.F. Mks. I-II, also AT-23/TB-26 & U.S.N. JM-1)**
- 235 □□■□ Maryland & Baltimore (R.A.F. Maryland Mks. I-II, Baltimore Mks. I-V, U.S.A.A.F. A-30)

McDONNELL DOUGLAS
- 208 □□□■ †F-4 Phantom

NORTH AMERICAN
- **59** □□■□ **B-25 A to G Mitchell (R.A.F. Mks. I & II, also U.S.N. PBJ-1, U.S.A.A.F. AT-24, RB/TB-25)**
- **100** □□■□ **P-51 B & C Mustang (R.A.F. Mk. III, also U.S.A.A.F. F-6)**
- **8** □□□■ †**P-51 D Mustang (R.A.F. Mk. IV, F-6/-51D, TP/TF-51D)**
- **20** □□□■ †**F-86A Sabre (see also CANADAIR Sabre)**
- **30** □□□■ †**F-100 Super Sabre (F-100A to F & TF-100)**
- 42 □□□■ FJ Fury (FJ-1 to FJ-4)
- 155 □□□■ T-28 (Trojan, also in U.S.A., Nomad & Nomar, France as Fennec)

REPUBLIC
- **7** □□■□ †**P-47D Thunderbolt (R.A.F. Mks. I-II, also P/TP-47G)**
- 95 □□□■ †F-84F Thunderstreak (Also RF-84F Thunderflash)
- 226 □□□■ †F-105 Thunderchief

RYAN
- 158 □□■□ PT/ST Series (PT-16 to PT-25 ; Sport Trainers)

THOMAS-MORSE
- 68 ■□□□ †Scouts (S-4 to S-9)

VOUGHT (see CHANCE VOUGHT)

U.S.S.R.

ILYUSHIN
- 88 □□■□ IL-2 ('Shturmovik')

LAVOCHKIN
- 149 □□■□ †LA-5 & 7

MIKOYAN
- 238 □□□■ †MiG-21 variants ('Fishbed'/'Mongol')

PETLYAKOV
- 216 □□■□ PE-2

POLIKARPOV
- 122 □■□□ †I-16 ('Mosca' or 'Rata')

YAKOVLEV
- 185 □□■□ †YaK-9

---

†Line drawings, with cross sections for accurate model making, are available for these types from 'Plans Service', Model and Allied Publications Ltd, 13-35 Bridge Street, Hemel Hempstead, Herts, England.

The Sopwith Pup

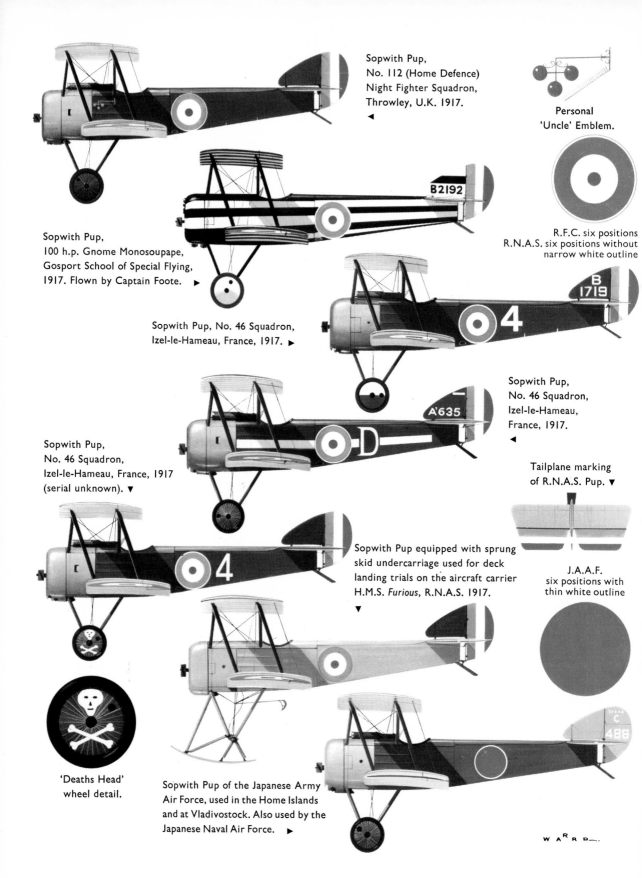

Sopwith Pup,
No. 112 (Home Defence)
Night Fighter Squadron,
Throwley, U.K. 1917.
◄

Personal
'Uncle' Emblem.

R.F.C. six positions
R.N.A.S. six positions without
narrow white outline

Sopwith Pup,
100 h.p. Gnome Monosoupape,
Gosport School of Special Flying,
1917. Flown by Captain Foote. ►

Sopwith Pup, No. 46 Squadron,
Izel-le-Hameau, France, 1917. ►

Sopwith Pup,
No. 46 Squadron,
Izel-le-Hameau,
France, 1917.
◄

Tailplane marking
of R.N.A.S. Pup. ▼

Sopwith Pup,
No. 46 Squadron,
Izel-le-Hameau, France, 1917
(serial unknown). ▼

Sopwith Pup equipped with sprung
skid undercarriage used for deck
landing trials on the aircraft carrier
H.M.S. *Furious*, R.N.A.S. 1917.
▼

J.A.A.F.
six positions with
thin white outline

'Deaths Head'
wheel detail.

Sopwith Pup of the Japanese Army
Air Force, used in the Home Islands
and at Vladivostock. Also used by the
Japanese Naval Air Force. ►

W A R R ___.

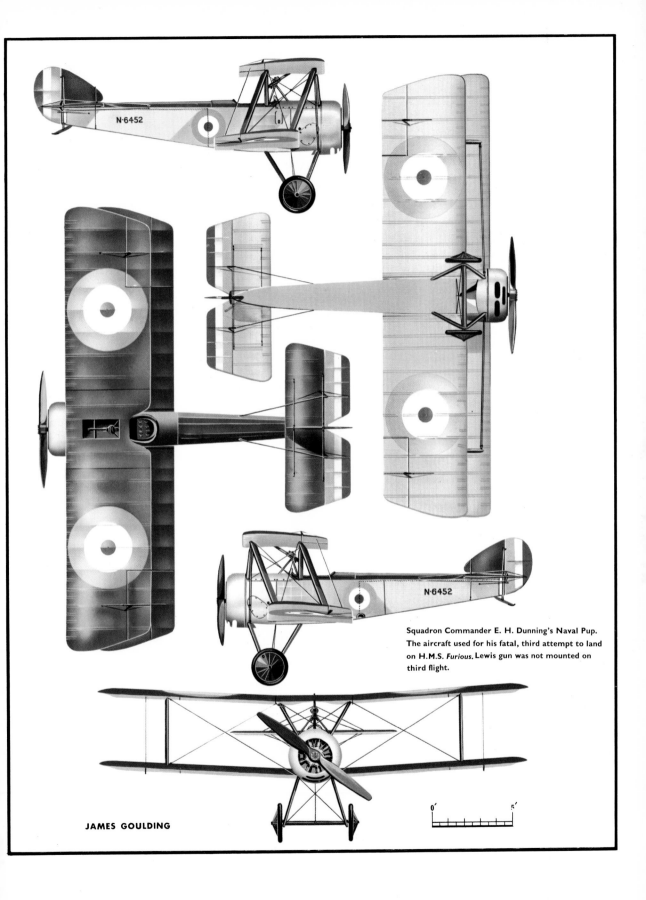

Squadron Commander E. H. Dunning's Naval Pup.
The aircraft used for his fatal, third attempt to land
on H.M.S. *Furious*. Lewis gun was not mounted on
third flight.

JAMES GOULDING

The Sopwith Pup

by J. M. Bruce

The black and white striped Monosoupape-powered Pup flown by Captain Foote of the Gosport School of Special Flying.
(Photo: via K. M. Molson)

ON 9th February 1916 the experimental department of the Sopwith Aviation Co., Ltd., passed the prototype of a single-seat fighting scout that had been designed by Herbert Smith, whose 1½-Strutter two-seater was then in production. The new single-seater bore a distinct resemblance to the 1½-Strutter but was appreciably smaller and was powered by an 80-h.p. rotary engine. It was a military development of a little single-seater that had been built in 1915 as a personal transport and aerobatic aircraft for Harry Hawker, the Sopwith company's test pilot. To the flying services the new scout was so obviously an offspring of the 1½-Strutter that it was unofficially named the Pup.

In his delightful book *The Clouds Remember* Oliver Stewart wrote of the Pup from personal operational experience, and his description of the aircraft is one of the best ever to appear in print. Of its name he has this to say:

A minor comedy of officialism was enacted with the Pup. Those in high places were grieved to observe this name "Pup"; they regarded it as un-dignified, frivolous, slangy, unofficial and Heaven knows what else. So they found time, during the fury and trouble of war, to sit down and pen an order which called upon all officers and men to note that the Sopwith Pup was not the Sopwith Pup, but the Sopwith Scout Mark Something-or-Other, and it demanded that on all future occasions the aeroplane should be referred to under that title and none other. Everybody read the order and marvelled, and then referred to the machine as the Sopwith Pup. So another, more peremptory, order came out drawing the attention of all units to this prevalence of incorrect nomenclature. The aeroplane was in future always to be described as the Sopwith Scout Mark Something-or-Other. So I suppose

that and the perverse state of mind of the fighting forces when it came to language, both good and bad, accounts for the fact that the aeroplane has ever after been known exclusively as the Sopwith Pup.

In 1916 the Sopwith company were contractors to the Admiralty, and the first Pups were delivered to the Royal Naval Air Service. The first prototype was given the official serial number *3691* and five more were built, numbered *9496*, *9497* and *9898–9900*. It

A very early Pup, possibly 3691 itself, at the R.N.A.S. station, Dunkerque. Although a Sopwith-built aircraft, it has the red, white and blue stripes on the elevators that almost invariably distinguished the products of the Beardmore company.
(Photo: E. F. Cheesman)

The first Standard-built Pup, A626, in German hands after its capture on 5th January 1917. The thick-framed windscreen had been removed and replaced by padding on the rear end of the Vickers gun.
(Photo: Egon Krueger)

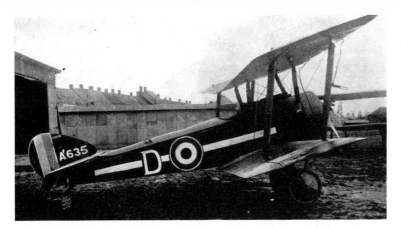

is not known which type of engine was installed in *3691*, but the other five R.N.A.S. prototypes had the 80-h.p. Clerget. A Pup, possibly No. *3691* itself, was sent to Naval 'A' Fighting Squadron at Furnes late in May 1916. It was an immediate success: its performance on only 80 h.p. was remarkable, its handling qualities impeccable.

The Admiralty placed contracts with the Sopwith company and with William Beardmore & Co. From the serial number of the first Beardmore-built Pup the Admiralty took its official designation for the aircraft: Sopwith Type 9901. Like the prototypes, the first eleven Pups of the first Beardmore batch had the 80-h.p. Clerget; but all the remainder had the 80-h.p. Le Rhône, the engine that was to power the majority of Pups.

In construction and appearance the Pup was of classic simplicity. The fuselage was the usual wire-braced wooden box girder that was so typical of the period; the longerons were of ash, the spacers of spruce. The mainplanes had spruce spars and ribs, with the profiles of the wing tips formed of steel tubing; the trailing edges were of special-section steel tubing. In the tail unit steel tubing was extensively used, the fin, rudder and elevators being made wholly of it; all joints were brazed. In the tailplane only the rear spar and tips were made of steel tubing; the leading edge, ribs, riblets and compression members were all of wood.

Tanks for 18½ gallons of petrol and 5 gallons of oil were mounted within the fuselage immediately above and behind the engine. The Pup that was tested at

Below: *A7325 was aircraft 1 of No. 46 Squadron, R.F.C., and is seen here with its pilot, Captain Marchant.*

This Le Rhône Pup of Central Flying School had the lower part of its engine cowling removed. Cable bracing replaced the standard Rafwires, a Lewis gun was mounted on the fuselage, and all fabric surfaces were doped white.

Left: *The installation of the 100-h.p. Gnôme Monosoupape, here seen on a Whitehead-built Pup.* Right: *Fuselage detail of Whitehead-built, Monosoupape-powered Pup. The hydraulic lead and trigger motor of the Constantinesco C.C. synchronising mechanism can be seen.*

Pup with 80-h.p. Gnôme engine, photographed at Martlesham Heath.
(Photo: Imp. War Museum)

Whitehead Pup B5292 fully assembled.

Monosoupape-powered Pup A653 with Vickers gun offset to port.

Central Flying School on 21st October 1916 consumed six gallons of petrol per hour at 8,000 ft. with the engine running at 1,175 r.p.m. Consumption of the castor-oil lubricant was no less than ten pints per hour.

The engine cowling and fuselage panels immediately behind it were of aluminium sheet; the fuselage top decking about the cockpit was covered with plywood. All other parts of the airframe were fabric-covered, but some Pups had parts of their centre sections covered with transparent material to improve the pilot's upward view.

A single Vickers gun constituted the armament of most Pups. It was mounted centrally on top of the fuselage immediately ahead of the cockpit. A padded windscreen was attached to the rear of the gun by four short stays. Some operational pilots preferred to discard this windscreen altogether and padded the rear end of the gun for facial protection; others preferred a wide windscreen at the forward end of the cockpit opening. On the early production Pups the gun was synchronised by means of the Sopwith-Kauper interrupter gear, and was fired by the depression of a short lever that projected horizontally rearwards from the underside of the part of the gun that was inside the cockpit. On later aircraft the Scarff-Dibovski or Constantinesco C.C. synchronising mechanisms were standardised.

The Admiralty specified eight Le Prieur rockets as an alternative to the Vickers gun, but in some instances (e.g., *N5186*) the Pup had both the gun and the rockets. It is doubtful whether the rocket-equipped Pups saw much operational use; certainly no record of any action in which they figured has yet been found.

First deliveries of production Pups went to the R.N.A.S.; aircraft of the Sopwith-built batch *N5180–N5199* were with No. 2 Squadron, R.N.A.S. in September 1916; *N5182* was then with the Dover Defence Flight. Ten had been completed by the end of that month. On 26th September 1916 the first Beardmore-built Pup (No. *9901*) made its maiden flight. The second followed on 23rd October and deliveries continued until 29th June 1917, when the last Beardmore-built Pup, *N6459*, was accepted by the R.N.A.S. The Pups ordered from the Standard Motor Co., Ltd., began to come along in December 1916, those built by Whitehead Aircraft Ltd. in January 1917. The Standard and Whitehead Pups were intended for the R.F.C., but the first Standard-built aircraft, *A626*, was transferred to the R.N.A.S., allocated to No. 8 (Naval) Squadron, and captured intact by the Germans on 5th January 1917. This Pup was exhaustively tested by the Germans and gave

Detail of the Whitehead-built Pup B5292 with cowling not yet fitted to its 100-h.p. Gnôme Monosoupape engine. Dangling between the forward legs of the undercarriage is the cable that held the cowling in place. Right: Cockpit of Whitehead-built Pup.

One of the Beardmore-built Pups of "C" Squadron, R.N.A.S., Imbros, armed with Vickers and Lewis guns.

them an early indication of what they might expect from this type.

The Pups of No. 1 (Naval) Wing at Dunkerque scored some early successes. On 24th September 1916 Flight Sub-Lt. S. J. Goble took off two minutes after German aircraft had bombed Dunkerque, caught an L.V.G. two-seater near Ghistelles and shot it down in flames. No. 1 Wing's Pups and Nieuports shot down eight enemy aircraft between 24th September and 23rd October 1916.

As the bitter struggle on the Somme that had begun on 1st July 1916 dragged into the autumn the R.F.C. found itself in difficulties. Three new squadrons had come from England, but of these No. 19 had the B.E.12, which proved to be virtually useless. Of the five squadrons brought into the Somme area from the north, two had been transferred elsewhere by October; and all the remaining units had suffered many casualties. On 17th October it was decided to form an R.N.A.S. squadron that would be sent to the Somme area to assist the R.F.C.; the new squadron was to be formed from the R.N.A.S. units then at Dunkerque.

The product of this exercise was the celebrated No. 8 Squadron, R.N.A.S., or "Naval Eight" as it came to be called. The personnel went to Vert Galand aerodrome within days of the decision to create the unit; its first aircraft arrived on 26th October, and the squadron's first patrol was flown on 3rd November. Its initial equipment consisted of one flight of Nieuport Scouts, one of Sopwith 1½-Strutters, and one of Pups. The six Pups had come from No. 1 Wing.

Naval Eight proved the Pups to be ideal fighting aircraft and wanted more of them. The 1½-Strutters were replaced by Pups on 16th November 1916, and by the end of the year the Nieuports had also gone. This was achieved by Wing Captain C. L. Lambe, who at that time had overall responsibility for the Dover-Dunkerque group of naval air stations. He had to undertake to provide the 80-h.p. Le Rhône engines for the Pups. Some came from crashed Nieuports; some he begged from the French naval air service; all were overhauled at Dunkerque and sent to Dover to be installed in the Pup airframes.

Between 3rd November and the end of 1917 the Pups of Naval Eight shot down twenty enemy aircraft. Three of these were accounted for by Flight Sub-Lt. D. M. B. Galbraith. The Squadron was withdrawn on 31st January 1917 for re-equipment with Sopwith Triplanes.

Other Pup squadrons were operational by that time. No. 54 Squadron, R.F.C., had reached France on Christmas Eve 1916; No. 3 (Naval) Squadron replaced Naval Eight on 1st February 1917. On 6th March, No. 66 Squadron, R.F.C., arrived on the western front, and No. 46 Squadron exchanged its Nieuport 12 two-seaters for Pups in April. At various times in 1917 the Pup was also flown by R.N.A.S. Squadrons Nos. 2, 4, 9, 11 and 12.

For all its lightness of construction the Pup proved to be a formidable fighter in the early months of 1917. On 11th April Flight Sub-Lt. J. S. T. Fall of No. 3 (Naval) Squadron shot down two Albatross scouts and

Left: *Dunning's second successful landing on* Furious, *7th August. This is the same aircraft (note white tip on lower starboard aileron) but on this occasion it carried a Lewis gun and was fitted with rope toggles under the lower wings and fuselage. (Photo: Imperial War Museum). Right: Dunning's third landing, just before his fatal plunge over* Furious' *starboard bow. Note the aircraft has rope toggles but no Lewis gun; the lower starboard aileron is uniformly doped khaki-green overall. This is in fact N6452.*

Night-flying Pup with partly obliterated national markings, fitted with navigation lights. (Photo: via C. A. Nepean Bishop)

a Halberstadt single-seater in the course of a single fight near Cambrai. The duties of No. 4 (Naval) Squadron consisted of providing offensive patrols and escorts for R.N.A.S. aircraft operating from Dunkerque, and the unit was also responsible for the protection of surface craft against air attack. At 6.25 a.m. on 12th May 1917 seven Pups of No. 4 (Naval) Squadron encountered a formation of Albatros fighters near Zeebrugge and shot down five of them.

Among those who flew the Pup operationally was Lt. (later Major) J. T. B. McCudden during a three-week period of attachment to No. 66 Squadron. He had flown Pups in England, where he had armed his with a Lewis gun on the centre section for the purpose of attacking the Gotha bombers whose attacks on London were starting in the early summer of 1917. McCudden found that a Pup, properly handled, could be a match for the Albatros D III, and wrote:

> I realised that the Sopwith could outmanoeuvre any Albatros, no matter how good the pilot was . . . when it came to manoeuvring, the Sopwith Scout would turn twice to an Albatros' once.

It was because the Pup retained its remarkable manoeuvrability at altitude that it survived in France until the end of 1917. By the autumn of that year its performance and armament had been surpassed. In September No. 66 Squadron added a Lewis gun to at least six of the Pups (*B2162*, *B2168*, *B2176*, *B2182*, *B2185* and *B2221*); and in the following month some pilots of No. 54 Squadron fitted a Lewis gun on the centre section. This had to be discarded, however, for the Pup centre section was not stressed to take the gun.

Although the end of 1917 saw the Pup's withdrawal from the western front, production of the little Sopwith was then only approaching its maximum. The greatest output was reached in the first quarter of 1918, when 500 Pups passed inspection. Most of these late-production Pups went to training units, where the type was immensely popular. Production continued almost up to the time of the Armistice: according to official statistics 32 Pups passed inspection in the final quarter of 1918.

The Pup had been introduced to Home Defence duties in July 1917. On the 10th of that month No. 46 Squadron was withdrawn from France and sent to Sutton's Farm, Essex. This was done in deference to a demand made by the public in England for improved air defences after the second major bombing attack on London of 7th July 1917, when twenty-one Gothas dropped 72 bombs on the capital, killing 57 people and injuring 193. But the Gothas never returned to London in daylight, the Pups of No. 46 Squadron

never engaged one, and the unit returned to France at the end of August.

Pup squadrons were formed specifically for Home Defence purposes: No. 112 at Throwley on 30th July 1917, No. 61 at Rochford three days later. On 12th August sixteen Pups of the latter unit took off to attack ten Gothas that had flown over the east coast, but the bombers had the height of the Pups and only a few of the Sopwiths managed to catch up with the German formation forty miles from the English coast. Owing to petrol shortage and gun troubles such combats as took place were brief and inconclusive.

Flight Lt. H. S. Kerby of the R.N.A.S., flying a Pup from Walmer, attacked a Gotha that was lagging about 4,000 ft. below the main formation and forced it down on to the sea. On 21st August Kerby was again successful. Flying Pup *N6440*, he shot down a Gotha off Margate.

Probably used in experiments in taking off from ships, this Beardmore-built Pup had two grooved wheels under each lower wing.

Below: *The same aircraft on an experimental dummy deck at the Isle of Grain. The wooden troughs were intended to keep the take-off straight. This photograph is dated 7th September 1917.*

Below: *Shipboard use of the wooden troughs seen in the preceding illustration. Believed to be aboard H.M.S.* Pegasus.
(Photo: F. Cable)

This Beardmore-built Sopwith 9901 was flown on its acceptance test on 30th May 1917 by A. Dukinfield Jones; at that time it had engine no. 6683 and airscrew no. 1225. It was delivered to Turnhouse for service aboard H.M.S. Manxman. In this photograph N6443 is seen aboard the battle cruiser H.M.S. Tiger on a small platform built on to a gun turret; its tail skid rests on the Tail Guide Trestle. (Photo: F. Cable)

The official history implies that the Home Defence version of the Pup was powered by the 100-h.p. Gnôme Monosoupape engine, but it is doubtful whether all such Pups had that engine. This variant of the Pup had the bottom segment of the engine cowling removed to assist the flow of exhaust gases, and there were four slots in the starboard upper quadrant of the cowling. A more open cowling was fitted to the Monosoupape engine of Pup *A653*; this aircraft was unusual in having its Vickers gun mounted on the port upper longeron instead of in the usual central position. With the Monosoupape the Pup's rate of climb was improved and 1,000 ft. were added to its ceiling.

A few Pups were fitted with the 80-h.p. Gnôme engine: *B5949*, *B5950* and *B5980*, thus powered, were in use at Cranwell in February 1918; and *N6202* also had this engine. It is believed that a Gnôme Pup was tested at Martlesham Heath, but the test report has yet to be discovered.

On 5th February 1917 the Grand Fleet Aircraft Committee that had been set up by Admiral Beatty presented a report in which, *inter alia*, it recommended that Pups should replace Sopwith Baby seaplanes in the aircraft carrier H.M.S. *Campania*; it had earlier been decided that this change should be made in H.M.S. *Manxman*. The Committee further recommended that certain light cruisers and other ships should be equipped to carry Pups. These recommendations were made with a view to providing the Fleet with a potentially effective anti-Zeppelin weapon. A shipboard version of the Pup was produced; it had a modified centre section with a central opening to permit a machine-gun to be fired upwards. A Lewis gun was mounted on a tripod in front of the cockpit. Alternatively or additionally, eight Le Prieur rockets could be carried.

This association with the Fleet led to a considerable number of modifications to the Pup. The first shipboard aircraft were fitted with an air bag in the rear fuselage to serve as emergency flotation gear. This was not very effective, as Flight Commander F. J. Rutland found on 29th April 1917. He had taken off from *Manxman* to patrol an area where Zeppelins were expected; compass trouble prevented him from regaining his ship before his petrol gave out; after ditching a few miles off the Danish coast his Pup floated for only twenty minutes.

One of the prototype Pups, 9497 (marked N9497) was used in early deck-landing experiments and is here seen with its arrester hook lowered, approaching the dummy deck at the Isle of Grain. The airscrew guard can just be distinguished.

As a result of Rutland's experience the Mark I Emergency Flotation Bags were designed. These were attached to the undersides of the lower wings, against which they lay flat while deflated. They were tested on 23rd June 1917, the subject aircraft being *9901*. The Pup was moored off the Isle of Grain, and after six hours was still afloat.

Ditching trials were conducted at the Isle of Grain with a Pup that had a jettisonable undercarriage. On the first attempt the Pup overturned on striking the water, but later attempts were successful after a hydrovane had been fitted under the fuselage and a duralumin plate on the tailskid.

Rutland pioneered the flying of Pups from small platforms aboard cruisers. In June 1917 he flew a Pup from the light cruiser H.M.S. *Yarmouth*, which had been fitted with a platform above the conning tower and forecastle gun: the platform gave a take-off run of twenty feet. On 21st August Flight Sub-Lt. B. A. Smart made his first take-off from *Yarmouth* to shoot down the Zeppelin L.23. He ditched near H.M.S. *Prince* and was rescued by her boat; as they were in enemy waters his Pup was abandoned.

H.M.S. *Yarmouth* had had to steam into wind to launch her Pup. As an improvement over the fixed platform, Lt. Commander C. H. B. Gowan suggested that a platform built on to a ship's gun turret could be turned into the "felt" wind while the ship maintained her course and the aircraft flown off. This was tried on the battle cruiser H.M.S. *Repulse*, and on 1st October 1917 Rutland flew a Pup from a platform on "B" turret, which was trained 42° on the starboard bow into a felt wind of 31·5 m.p.h. He repeated the feat eight days later, when the platform had been transferred to an after turret. As a consequence, it was decided on 17th October that all light cruisers and battle cruisers should carry fighting aeroplanes, provided that their gun armament was not interfered with.

The Admiralty had been interested in the possibility of launching aeroplanes by catapults before the war began but did not pursue the idea actively until 1916, when tenders were invited for the construction of catapults. To the design of Mr. R. F. Carey a catapult was made by the Waygood-Otis company and erected at Hendon in 1917. Two Pups of the first Beardmore batch, 9948 and 9949, were delivered direct to Hendon for catapult tests; one source states that tests of the Carey catapult, using a Pup, were conducted in October 1917. The official history does not mention the Pup in this connection, but implies that the first successful launch was of the Avro 504H. The catapult was not developed, partly because Pups could be flown from the small platforms on board ship.

When H.M.S. Furious, which had five Pups in her complement, joined the Fleet at Scapa Flow in July 1917, the first wartime attempts at landing-on were made. Furious had at that time only one flight deck, ahead of the funnel and superstructure, which was intended for take-offs only. Landing-on could only be accomplished by an aircraft with the Pup's superb controllability, for it entailed flying alongside, crabbing inboard until the aircraft was over the ship's forward deck, and then touching down.

The first deck landing was made in this way by Squadron Commander E. H. Dunning on 2nd August 1917. This showed that the deck party could assist in bringing down the aircraft manually (the relative speed between Pup and ship was very small), consequently rope toggles were fitted under the lower wings and fuselage. With these handling aids fitted and a Lewis gun mounted, Dunning made a second landing on 7th August, but his Pup was blown back after touching down and damaged its elevators. He changed to N6452 for his third attempt, but this time he was too far forward and waved the deck party away. His engine choked when he opened the throttle; the Pup stalled and fell over Furious' starboard bow; Dunning drowned. On 17th October it was decided to fit Furious with a 284-ft. after landing-on deck.

This led in turn to much experimental work with undercarriages and arrester gears in which Pups were used extensively. The undercarriage wheels were replaced by wooden skids in order to decelerate the aircraft after touch-down; various arrangements of arrester cables, both fore-and-aft and athwartships, were tried.

The work was initiated at the Isle of Grain under Squadron Commander H. R. Busteed, using a dummy deck laid out on the aerodrome. One of the Pups employed was No. 9497, one of the prototypes, which was flown with wheels, airscrew guard, and a large hook designed to engage athwartships arrester cables. At least one Pup had sprung skids and a hook pivoted under the aircraft's centre of gravity; another had fixed skids with a pronounced curve, horns to engage fore-and-aft cables and an aft-mounted hook

Beardmore-built Pup with sprung skids in place of wheels and an arrester hook for athwartships cables.
(Photo: Imperial War Museum)

This Pup had rigid skids with flexible forward extensions, three V-shaped horns for fore-and-aft arrester cables, and a hook for athwartships cables.

Sopwith 9901a Pup aboard H.M.S. Furious, *the arrester cables having been engaged by the horns on the undercarriage.*
(Photo: Imperial War Museum)

for athwartships cables. Ultimately a rigid skid undercarriage was standardised, each skid having two pairs of horns. This version of the Pup had the Admiralty designation Sopwith 9901a; ten were with units of the Grand Fleet on 31st October 1918.

Unfortunately, although the experiments at Grain had been successfully pursued, it was found that landing a lightly-loaded Pup on the after deck of H.M.S. Furious with the ship steaming at something like 30 kt. was almost an impossibility. The funnel and superstructure of the ship created so much turbulence that an alarming proportion of landings ended in crashes, and operational use of Furious' landing-on deck was abandoned.

Better results were obtained in October 1918 with H.M.S. Argus, which had a flush flying deck without any superstructure. A Pup fitted with nine V-shaped horns under the spreader bar of its wheel undercarriage and a curved guard under the airscrew was

Pup with wheel undercarriage, multiple horns under the spreader bar, and airscrew guard cum hydrofoil. Flown by Lt.-Col. R. Bell Davies, V.C., D.S.O., in deck-landing trials aboard H.M.S. Argus, *23rd October 1918.*

One of the Pups given to Australia under the Imperial Gift scheme, A4-9 was originally C530. It is here seen fitted with a camera gun. (Photo: via R. Waugh)

successfully landed on *Argus* by Lt. Arnold and Lt.-Col. R. Bell-Davies, V.C., D.S.O., on 22nd and 23rd October.

An extensively modified version of the Pup was built by Beardmore as the W.B. III; the prototype was the converted Beardmore-built Pup No. *9950*. This had folding wings without stagger and a slightly lengthened fuselage. The undercarriage of the first thirteen production W.B. IIIs (*N6100–N6112*) could fold into the underside of the fuselage to conserve space aboard ship; in this form the aircraft had the official designation S.B.3F. All the other W.B. IIIs *N6113–N6129* and *N6680–N6749*) had a jettison-able undercarriage and were designated S.B.3D. The suffix letters F and D indicated the type of under-carriage fitted, and signified Folding and Dropping respectively. In the R.N.A.S. the W.B. III was usually known as the Beardmore folding Pup. The modifica-tions impaired the handling qualities, however, and the W.B. III was not popular. Some apparently went to Japan.

Away from the main theatre of war the Pup was used operationally only by the R.N.A.S. in the Mediterranean area, where a few were flown by 'C' Squadron at Imbros and 'F' Squadron at Amberkoj and Marian. There can be little doubt that the 79 Pups that were sent to the Middle East Brigade were used for training purposes at No. 5 Fighting School, Heliopolis: *B6043* is known to have been on the strength of that unit.

A late series of trials in which a Pup was used were conducted in the autumn of 1918. A Pup and a Sala-mander were painted in experimental camouflage schemes and, flying at 1,500–2,000 ft., were observed by other aircraft at 5,000–7,000 ft. The record of these trials is in an official Confidential Information Memo-randum dated October 1918.

A few Pups were supplied to some of the Allies. As a gift from the British government *N6204* was sent to Russia in 1917, and in the following year *N6470* and *N6471* were given to the Greek government. The fates of these Pups are unknown. On 1st March 1917 *A6164* made a forced landing in neutral Holland and was used for a time by the Netherlands air service as *La41*, later *S212*.

Two Pups were reported to be on the strength of the U.S. Navy on 1st November 1919. These may have been the aircraft that had the U.S. Navy designating

numbers *A-5655* and *A-5656*, to which the 130-h.p. Clerget engine is improbably attributed in one U.S. document.

The Pup was officially declared obsolete in the R.A.F. in December 1918 and rapidly disappeared. Possibly the last in official service was *B7565*, which was still flying at the R.A.E., Farnborough, in December 1922. In its last months of R.A.F. service the Pup had been so much sought after by officers for use as a personal aircraft that it is surprising that no more than eight were given civil registrations. It seems that in the U.K. none survived later than 1924, when *G-EBFJ* (ex *C242*) was scrapped.

At least eleven Pups were given to Australia as part of the Imperial Gift in 1919. These aircraft, *C521–C528* and *C530–C532*, became *A4-1* to *A4-11* of the R.A.A.F. Another Pup that went to Australia was *C476*, which became *G-AUCK* and *VH-UCK*. It was still flying in 1944, powered by a five-cylinder radial engine, and was finally dismantled on 21st September 1945.

The last word on the Pup is best left to Oliver Stewart:

The perfect flying machine. This is the term which the Sopwith triplane nearly fulfilled and which the Sopwith Pup did fulfil. As a military aircraft it had certain short-comings, but as a flying machine—a machine which gave a high return in speed and climb and for a given expenditure of horse-power, which had well-balanced, powerful controls, which was stable enough but not too stable, which was sensitive enough without being too sensitive, and which obeyed its pilot in a way that eventually secured his lasting admiration and affection—the Sopwith Pup was and still is without superior.

Specification

Power: 80-h.p. Le Rhône 9C; 80-h.p. Clerget; 80-h.p. Gnôme; 100-h.p. Gnôme Monosoupape.

Dimensions: Span 26 ft. 6 in.; length 19 ft. 3¾ in.; height 9 ft. 5 in.; chord 5 ft. 1½ in.; gap 4 ft. 4⅞ in.; stagger 1 ft. 6 in.; dihedral 3°; incidence 1° 30′; span of tail 10 ft. 1 in.; incidence of tailplane 1° 30′ with Le Rhône engine, 2° 30′ with Monosoupape; wheel track 4 ft. 7 in.; tyres, Palmer 700×75 mm.; airscrew diameter 8 ft. 6·4 in. (Le Rhône).

Areas: Wings and ailerons 254 sq. ft.; ailerons, each 5·5 sq. ft.; tailplane 23 sq. ft.; elevators 11·8 sq. ft.; fin 3·5 sq. ft.; rudder 4·5 sq. ft.

Although G-EAVX (ex B1807) had an 80-h.p. Le Rhône engine it was fitted with the Monosoupape-type cowling; it also had a head-rest behind the cockpit. This photograph was taken at Hendon; the occasion was the 1921 Aerial Derby, 16th July 1921.

(Photo: *Flight International*)

Armament: One fixed 0·303-in. Vickers machine-gun with Sopwith-Kauper, Scarff-Dibovski or Constantinesco C.C. synchronising gear, Aldis and ring-and-bead sights. The shipboard version of the Pup had one 0·303-in. Lewis machine-gun on a tripos in front of the cockpit, firing upwards through the centre section, R.N.A.S. Pups could be armed with eight Le Prieur rockets, in addition to or in place of the machine-gun. For ground attack duties R.F.C. Pups could carry a small load of 25-lb. bombs.

Weights and Performance

Engine				Le Rhone	Monosoupape	
No. of trial report	..	..	..	M.31	M.95	M.95A
Date of trial report		..	..	21st Oct. 1917	April 1917	May 1917
Type of airscrew used on trial	..			Lang L.P.1020	Vickers 57	
Weights (lb.):						
Empty	..	..	..	787	856	
Military load	..	..	..	260	260	
Fuel and oil	..	..	..	178	181	
Loaded	..	..	..	1,225	1,297	
Max. speed (m.p.h.)						
At ground level	..		..	111·5	—	110
At 6,500 ft.	..	..	..	106·5	105	107
At 10,000 ft.	..	..	..	104·5	101·5	104
At 15,000 ft.	..	..	..	94	95·5	100
Climb to:				m. s.	m. s.	m. s.
6,500 ft.	..	..	..	8 0	7 10	7 5
10,000 ft.	..	..	..	14 25	13 0	12 25
15,000 ft.	..	..	..	30 6	26 55	23 25
Service ceiling (feet)	..		..	17,500	18,000	18,500
Endurance (hours)	..		..	3	1¾	1¾

Production: Serial numbers were allotted as follows for 1,896 Pups ordered under official contracts:
Sopwith Aviation Co., Ltd., Canbury Park Road, Kingston-on-Thames. *3691, 9496–9497, 9898–9900; N5180–N5199; N6160–N6209; N6460–N6529 (N6480–N6529 not built).*

William Beardmore & Co., Ltd., Dalmuir, Dunbartonshire. *9901–9950; N6430–N6459.*
The Standard Motor Co., Ltd., Cash's Lane, Coventry. *A626–A675; A7301–A7350; B1701–B1850; B5901–B6150; C201–C550.*
Whitehead Aircraft Ltd., Richmond. *A6150–A6249; B2151–B2250; B5251–5400; B7481–B7580; C1451–C1550; C3707–C3776; D4011–D4210.*

Known A.R.D. rebuilds: *B804, B4218.*
Service use: France—R.F.C. Squadrons Nos. 46, 54, 66; Special Duty Flight. R.N.A.S. 'A' Squadron at Furnes; No. 1 Wing, Dunkerque; Naval Squadrons Nos. 2, 3, 4, 8, 9, 11 and 12; Seaplane Defence Flight at St. Pol. *Italy*—One Pup with No. 66 Squadron. *Home Defence*—R.F.C. Squadrons Nos. 46, 61 and 112; R.N.A.S. stations Dover, Manston, Port Victoria, Great Yarmouth, Walmer. *Mediterranean*—'C' Squadron, R.N.A.S., Imbros; 'F' Squadron, R.N.A.S., Amberkoj and Marian. *Shipboard use*—Aircraft carriers *Furious, Campania, Manxman, Vindex* and *Argus;* light cruisers *Caledon, Cassandra, Cordelia, Dublin* and *Yarmouth;* battle cruisers *Repulse* and *Tiger.*

Examples of Pups used by operational units:
No. 46 Sqn. R.F.C.—*A673, A7325* (aircraft 1), *A7348* (3), *B1733, B1795, B1843.*
No. 54 Sqn. R.F.C.—*A639, A672, A6183, A6215, B1730, B1792.*
No. 66 Sqn. R.F.C.—*A6181, A7314, B1710, B1745, B1846.*
No. 112 Sqn. R.F.C.—*B1772, B5910.*
No. 2 Sqn. R.N.A.S.—*N5181, N5187.*
No. 3 Sqn. R.N.A.S.—*N5185, N6160, N6163, N6174, N6203, N6465.*
No. 4 Sqn. R.N.A.S.—*B1818, N6168, N6184, N6185, N6468, N6469.*
No. 8 Sqn. R.N.A.S.—*3691, 9898, N5182, N5190, N5196, N5198.*
No. 9 Sqn. R.N.A.S.—*N6167.*
No. 11 Sqn. R.N.A.S.—*9899, N6167, N6174, N6184, N6192, N6199.*
No. 12 Sqn. R.N.A.S.—*B1816, B1817, N6167, N6182, N6467.*
'C' Sqn. R.N.A.S.—*9942, N6432, N6433* (*9942* and *N6432* known to have been used by 'F' Squadron also.)
H.M.S. *Furious*—*N6452, N6453, N6454.*
H.M.S. *Tiger*—*N6443.*
H.M.S. *Manxman* (allocated)—*9913, 9943, 9945, N6431, N6444, N6455.*
H.M.S. *Vindex* (allocated)—*9921, N6457, N6458.*

The Boeing P-26A

The Boeing P-26A

by Peter M. Bowers

P-26A of the 73rd Pursuit Squadron, one of three (34th, 73rd and 95th) of the 1st Pursuit Group which carried similar squadron designs in different colours.
(Peter Bowers' collection)

To be in the vanguard of progress is a rare achievement; to be part of the rearguard a distinction. To be both first and last is something of a rarity, but this is the unusual claim to fame of the diminutive Boeing P-26, the "Peashooter" to all who flew this attractive monoplane fighter of the mid 'thirties.

The P-26 was one of the best-known U.S. Army Air Corps pursuit aircraft of the years between the two world wars, and in addition to being far more advanced in construction and performance than contemporary service models it can also lay claim to a number of "firsts" and a number of "lasts".

It was the first production, all-metal, American fighter, and also the first production monoplane fighter. It was the last open cockpit fighter accepted for service with the Army; the last with a fixed undercarriage and the last with an externally-braced wing.

For the Boeing Company it was their last production fighter, and it brought to an end a fifteen-year period during which time Boeing was the leading manufacturer of first-line fighters for both the Army and the Navy.

THE DESIGN IS APPROVED

Design of the Boeing Model 248 (P-26) started in September 1931, and was the result of a series of conferences between Boeing and the Army Air Corps. It incorporated many of the features proposed by company technicians and service advisers. The original

The first Boeing 248 before purchase by the Army Air Corps and carrying the designation of XP-936. Note small headrest and wheel pants projecting behind landing gear legs.
(Photo: Boeing)

Left: *Third prototype XP-936 with line-up of Curtiss Hawks in background.*
(Photo: Fred C. Dickey Jnr.)

Below: *Boeing Model 248 photographed while designated YIP-26, still with original headrest.*
(Peter Bowers' collection)

designation of Model 248 was soon dropped in favour of XP-936 (Experimental Pursuit Airplane Design 936) with the signing of an Army Bailment Contract on 5th December 1931. This contract specified that Boeing would construct, at their own expense, three test airframes, for which the Army would provide engines, instruments and other equipment. A contract clause stated that the three airframes would remain the property of the Boeing Company.

The reasoning behind this apparent hard-headed economy by the Army was the latter's reluctance to spend limited funds for a then, radically different aeroplane to those already in service. The Model 248, therefore, was something of a speculative venture for Boeing.

The design progressed rapidly and actual construction of the first prototype began in January 1932, with the first flight taking place on 20th March. This

The Model 248 after redesignation to P-26 and modification to P-26A standard with high headrest. Change from olive drab to blue fuselage paint is evident in that the fuselage colour photographs lighter than the yellow of wings and tail on orthochromatic film.
(Peter Bowers' collection)

remarkably high rate of progress in developing and building a new, experimental design was accomplished by concentration of the company's manpower and production facilities on the project. Aircraft orders were something of a rarity in the "lean" 'thirties, and so determined was Boeing to obtain a production order, that the entire design and engineering teams set up their draughting tables in the factory alongside the three prototypes, ironing out difficulties as they arose.

The second airframe was completed and delivered to Wright Field for static tests before the first machine had made its maiden flight, while the third was delivered to Selfridge Field, Michigan, on 25th April, for service tests with active squadrons.

Shortly after flight tests of the two XP-936s began the Army, satisfied with performance and structural

P-26A with wing flaps lowered and pilot's access door on port side open. Note bomb rack between undercarriage legs.
(Peter Bowers' collection)

Left: P-26A showing open access door and scalloped paint finish on Townend ring. Right: P-26A of the Bolling Field detachment. Colour scheme can be found on page 166. Aircraft was stationed on Bolling Field, across the Potomac River from the White House.
(Photos: A. U. Schmidt and Peter Bowers' collections)

Standard P-26As showing headrest profile. Note that some P-26s did not have radio mast. (Peter Bowers' collection)

durability, purchased the three prototypes under a standard purchase contract signed on 15th June 1932, and assigned the designation of XP-26. This was soon changed to the service test designation of YIP-26 and eventually to plain P-26.

STRUCTURAL DETAILS

The P-26 was an entirely new design venture for Boeing, and while structural features drew heavily on other all-metal models such as the Monomail, the 202/205 fighter and the 218, the use of wire-braced wings and a fixed undercarriage seemed to be a backward step in view of the company's experience with retractable landing gear and cantilever wings.

However, the external bracing allowed a lighter structure and wires produced less total drag than rigged struts. The fixed undercarriage added drag but reduced weight and structural complexity, and provided a low anchor point for the flying wires.

The rear portion of each undercarriage leg consisted of an inverted tubular bipod fastened to the front and rear wing spars. The flying wires were attached to the apex, and the wheel pivoted about the apex on an arm, with the landing loads being absorbed through the oleo shock absorber strut connecting the wheel axle to the front spar. The entire lower portion of the landing gear was enclosed by a streamlined wheel fairing, or "pant". A removable spreader bar was supplied to keep the undercarriage rigid when the aeroplane was in for service with wings removed or wires slack. One of the two flyable XP-936s was converted to a single strut type of undercarriage leg by the Army.

Fuselage was of a semi-monocoque type with aluminium bulkheads, hat-section longerons, skin stiffeners and skin. The nine-cylinder Pratt & Whitney SR-1340G radial, air-cooled engine, was bolted to the firewall and enclosed in a Townend ring.

The wing, low-set on the fuselage, was of low-aspect ratio with a thin section. Two main spars, built up of sheet and angle duralumin, supported dural ribs, to which was riveted closely-spaced spanwise stringers and the metal skin. It was externally braced with

P-26As from the 34th (foreground) and 73rd (second aircraft) Pursuit Squadrons photographed "circa" 1936. Note differences in cowling and stripe colours. Interruption of striping on first a/c caused by replacement cowling panel. (Photo: Gordon S. Williams)

17

Left and right: *P-26As of the 94th Pursuit Squadron, 1st Pursuit Group. Left aircraft was finished blue, the above green.*
(Photos: Fred C. Dickey Jnr.)

Left: *P-26A, standard a/c, lacks radio mast.* Right: *P-26A, 550-h.p. Wasp, of the 20th Fighter Group (Squadrons 55th, 77th and 79th).*
Details of a/c on page 167.
(Photo: Richard Ward)

stainless steel front and rear lift and drag wires attached to the fuselage and undercarriage legs. Tail surfaces, fully cantilevered structures, were of single spar construction with a dural skin attached to a Warren-truss of stamped dural sheet ribs.

PROTOTYPE PERFORMANCE

When undergoing service tests at Wright Field the XP-936 weighed 2,119 pounds empty and 2,789 pounds loaded. Flight tests revealed a maximum level speed of 227 m.p.h. at 10,000 feet; 210 m.p.h. at 20,000 feet and 174 m.p.h. at 27,800 feet, the aircraft's service ceiling. Absolute ceiling was 28,900 feet; initial climb rate 2,300 ft./min., and cruising speed 193 m.p.h.

It is interesting to compare the covered performance of the XP-936 with that of the Boeing P-12F*, the last production biplane for the Army, which was in production at the time the monoplane fighter was delivered. Powered with a slightly later version of the same engine that gave it only a 20-h.p. advantage, the XP-936 was just 39 lb. heavier than P-12F but 27

*See pages 13-24 for the P-12 story

m.p.h. faster. It outclimbed the biplane by 476 feet per minute, but fell 800 feet short of the P-12's absolute ceiling.

PRODUCTION BEGINS

Before service tests of the XP-936 were completed the Army decided to go ahead with it in an improved form. On 7th November 1932 a new specification was issued for a fighter which incorporated the best features of the Model 248 with the improvements found desirable during the test programme. The three prototypes completed the series of acceptance tests but never entered squadron service.

A contract for the modified design, the Model 266A, P-26A, was awarded on 28th January 1934. One hundred and eleven aircraft were ordered, and this was later increased to a total of 136, the additional aircraft being completed as P-26Bs and 26Cs. This was the largest order placed for a single aircraft type since the Boeing MB-3A of 1921.

Outwardly the P-26A differed from the prototypes

Rare photograph shows P-26A on skis. (Fred C. Dickey Jnr. collection)

Above: *P-26A with Wright Field fuselage marking.*

Below: *P-26A of 20th Pursuit Group.* (Peter Bowers' collection)

P-26A of Bolling Field Detachment; one view shows engine mounting, second shows a/c in NACA wind tunnel.

P-26A of the 34th Pursuit Sqdn. in special camouflage used during "War Games". (Peter Bowers' collection)

only in that the wheel spats did not project aft of the undercarriage strut fairing. Originally, the P-26A had the low, streamlined headrests of the prototypes, but these were strengthened and increased in height by eight inches for pilot protection after one of the early production aircraft went over on to its back following a landing on soft ground. The pilot was killed without serious damage to the aircraft. Delivery of later production machines was delayed until the modification was completed.

Internally, the P-26A wing structure was considerably revised and operational equipment such as flotation gear and radio was added. The first production P-26A made its maiden flight on 10th January 1934, and was delivered to the Army on 20th June 1935. Powerplant was a single Pratt & Whitney Wasp R-1340-27 engine rated at 500 h.p. at 2,200 r.p.m. at 7,500 feet. It drove a Hamilton Standard, two-blade, adjustable pitch propeller.

Armament consisted of the standard two 0·30-inch machine guns, or one 0·30-inch and one 0·50-inch machine gun. Provision was made for two 100 lb. or five 30 lb. bombs slung under the fuselage and wings.

The last P-26A of the initial order for 111 was delivered on 30th June 1934, and the unit price per aircraft in such quantities, less engine and government-furnished equipment (GFE) was 9,999 dollars, compared with 10,197 dollars for the P-12E biplane in similar quantities.

With the P-26As in regular service, the Army

Second photograph of ski-equipped P-26A. This unit also had similar skis fitted to their Boeing P-12s. Martin B-10 twin-engined bombers in background also had skis. (Fred C. Dickey Jnr. collection)

P-26A of the 73rd Attack Squadron, kicking mule insignia. Note 17th Attack Squadron insignia below headrest.

(Photo: Fred C. Dickey Jnr.)

became dissatisfied with the relatively high landing speed of 82·5 m.p.h. and, as a result, experimental flaps were developed by the Army and fitted to one aeroplane, reducing the speed to 73 m.p.h. Boeing fitted these flaps to all the P-26As then in service and on the 26Bs and Cs still on the production line. Service models were returned to the Boeing plant for retrofit installations.

All P-26 models had been withdrawn from regular squadron service and relegated to mechanic training schools when World War II began. Most of those stationed overseas were sold to the Governments of the Philippines and Panama, and two were sold to Guatemala. The Philippino P-26As of the 6th Pursuit Squadron went into action against the Japanese soon after Pearl Harbour was attacked, and one is credited with shooting down one of the attacking bombers. Several of the Panamanian P-26s were acquired by Guatemala in 1942/43 and were still in service as trainers in 1957. One was obtained by the

Air Museum of Claremont, California, where it is now on display in its original markings, and a second was obtained by the U.S. Air Force Technical Museum, Wright-Patterson AFB, Dayton, Ohio.

Two of the twenty-five aircraft added to the first P-26A order were completed as P-26Bs (Model 266A), differing only from the 26A in being fitted with fuel injection Wasp R-1340-33 engines and a number of fuel system revisions. The first 26B was delivered to the Army on 20th June and the second on 21st June 1934.

After the fuel injection system had been satisfactorily tested in service, the Army decided to adopt it for the P-26Cs, many of which became P-26Bs upon completion of the modifications. The cost of a P-26B/C was 14,009 dollars, less engine and GFE.

Twenty-three of the 25 aircraft added to the original 111 P-26A order of 28th January 1934, were built as P-26Cs (Model 266) and so little did they differ from the As that the factory model number was not changed. The first P-26C was delivered on 10th

P-26A, serial number 33-136, in a close flight view. Note how headrest would protect pilot.

(Photo: U.S. Air Force)

P-26As of 94th Pursuit Squadron in line abreast formation.

(Fred C. Dickey Jnr. collection)

Line-up of ten Model 281s at Canton, China. The first crashed during a demonstration by an American pilot, and the remaining nine were eventually overcome by superior Japanese forces. Below: Refuelling a Model 281 from drums and hand pumps in China.

(Photos: Herbert Poncetti)

February 1936, and the last on 7th March. After about a year in service many of the P-26Cs were converted to 26B standards by installation of the fuel injection engine and revision of the fuel system and its controls.

THE EXPORT "PEASHOOTER"

The Model 281 was an export version of the XP-936 and P-26A series, differing only in the details of military equipment. First flight of the Model 281 was made on 2nd August 1934, and early tests indicated that the landing speed was excessive for the small and unimproved fields from which the fighter would be expected to operate. Split-type wing flaps were developed and installed, and were also tested by the Army for comparison with the experimental flaps that the Army had installed on the standard P-26A.

Only twelve export "Peashooters" were completed and sold: one to Spain and eleven to China. The first Chinese aircraft reached its destination on 15th September 1934, and the last was shipped on 16th January 1936. One Chinese fighter was supplied with an alternate landing gear using large, low pressure tyres to permit operation from muddy fields.

One Chinese squadron operating the Model 281 was

continuously in action against the Japanese invaders on the Chinese mainland, and a considerable number of kills were registered before the fighter was forced out of service through lack of spares.

The Boeing P-26 served as front-line equipment in its various marks with a number of Army Air Corps pursuit and attack squadrons at home and overseas, before being finally replaced by the Curtiss P-36A and Seversky P-35 in 1940. Among the squadrons equipped were the 3rd, 16th, 17th, 18th, 19th, 20th, 27th, 32nd, 34th, 38th, 55th, 73rd, 77th, 79th, 94th and 95th. In its time the fighter was one of the world's most advanced aircraft and it established several military speed and altitude records.

First Boeing Model 281, export version of the P-26A. This aircraft was used by Boeing to develop a flap design that was eventually fitted to all 26As and Cs.

(Photo: Boeing)

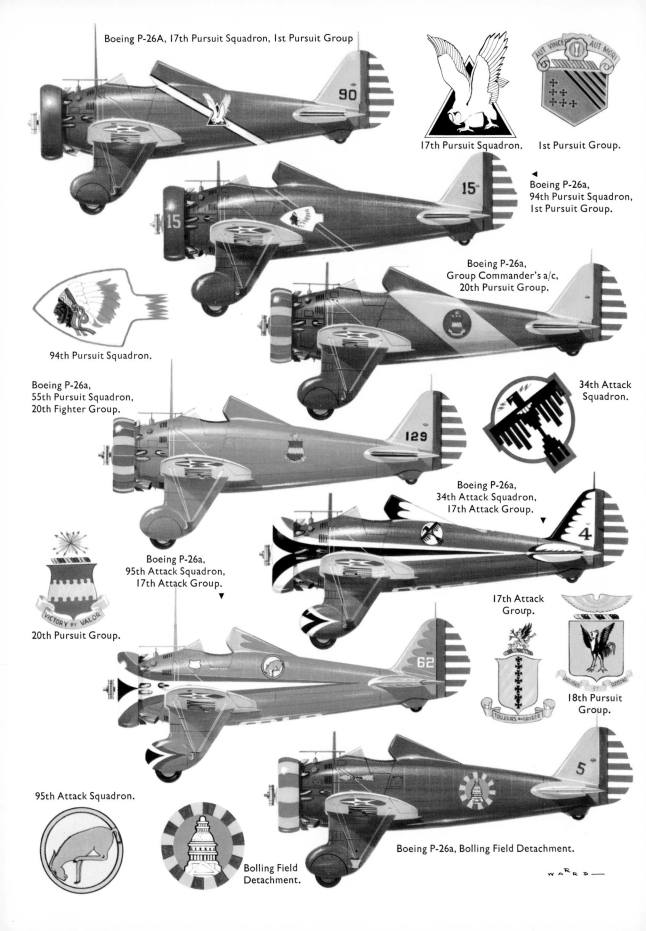

Boeing P-26A, 17th Pursuit Squadron, 1st Pursuit Group

17th Pursuit Squadron.

1st Pursuit Group.

◄ Boeing P-26a, 94th Pursuit Squadron, 1st Pursuit Group.

Boeing P-26a, Group Commander's a/c, 20th Pursuit Group.

94th Pursuit Squadron.

34th Attack Squadron.

Boeing P-26a, 55th Pursuit Squadron, 20th Fighter Group.

Boeing P-26a, 34th Attack Squadron, 17th Attack Group. ▼

Boeing P-26a, 95th Attack Squadron, 17th Attack Group. ▼

17th Attack Group.

18th Pursuit Group.

VICTORY BY VALOR

20th Pursuit Group.

95th Attack Squadron.

Bolling Field Detachment.

Boeing P-26a, Bolling Field Detachment.

WARD

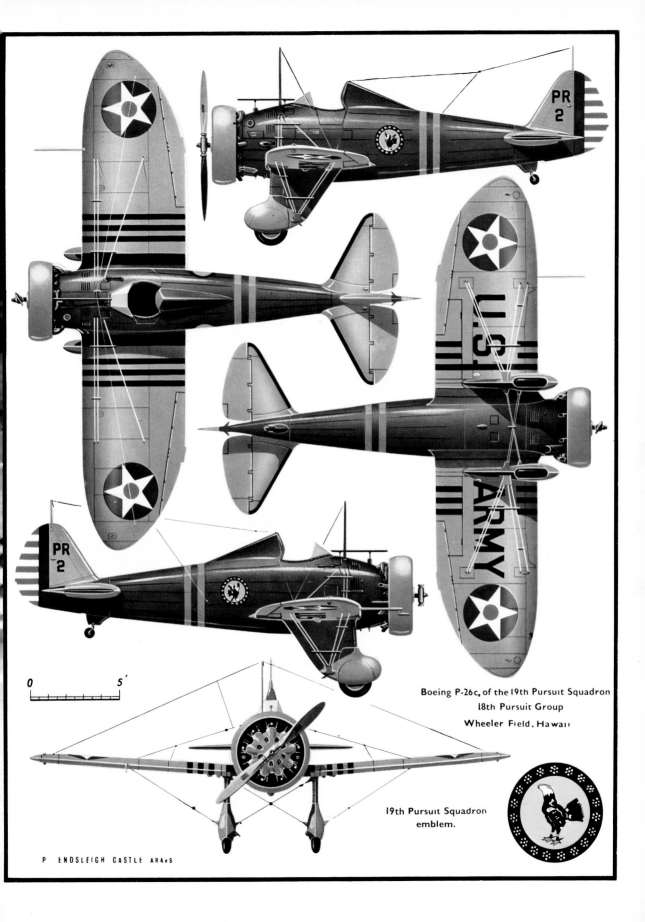

PR
2

U.S.
ARMY

PR
2

0   5´

Boeing P-26c, of the 19th Pursuit Squadron
18th Pursuit Group
Wheeler Field, Hawaii

19th Pursuit Squadron
emblem.

P ENDSLEIGH CASTLE ARAeS

Above: *P-26As recovered from Guatemala by The Air Museum and U.S.A.F. Museum respectively. Left a/c has blue fuselage and red/white striping and Thunderbird insignia of 34th Attack Squadron. Right a/c has black and white striping and olive drab fuselage* (Photos: North American and E. M. Sommerich). Below: *Air Force photo of an actual P-26A of 34th A. Sqdn. shows that true markings were different from those on both restorations.*

Specification

	Dimensions				Performance					Weights		Engine	Fuel
	Wing Span	Length	Height	Wing Area	Max. Speed 6,000 ft.	Cruis-ing	Land-ing	Climb F.P.M.	Service Ceiling	Empty	Loaded	Pratt & Whitney	Gallons
	ft. in.	ft. in.	ft. in.	sq. ft.									
P-26 (XP-936)	27 5	23 9	7 6	150	277	193	82·5	2,230	27,800	2,120	2,789	R-1340-21 525 h.p.	105
P-26A	27 11½	23 10	10 5	149·5	234	200	73	2,360	27,400	2,196	2,955	R-1340-27 500 h.p.	50–106
P-26B	27 11½	23 9	10 5	149·0	235	200	73	2,360	27,800	2,301	3,060	R-1340-33 600 h.p.	107
P-26C	27 11½	23 9	10 5	149·0	235	200	73	2,360	27,800	2,332	3,074	R-1340-27	104
Model 281	27 11½	23 7¼	7 10½	149·5	235	210	68	2,210	28,200	2,354	3,039	R-1340-33	—

Constructor's and Serial Numbers

Boeing Model	Military Designation	Number Built	Boeing Construction No.	Military Serial	First Flight	First Delivery	Last Delivery
248	XP-936	3	1678	32–412	20–3–32	13–3–32	25–4–32
248	XP-26	—	—	—	—	—	—
248	Y1P-26	—	—	—	—	—	—
248	P-26	—	1679 1680	32–413 32–414	—	—	—
266	P-26A	111	1804 to 1914	33–028 to 33–138	10–1–34	16–12–33	30–6–34
266B	P-26B	2	1916 1919	33–179 33–185	10–1–34	20–6–35	21–6–35
266	P-26C	23	1915, 1917 1918, 1920 to 1939	33–186 to 33–203	—	10–2–36	7–3–36
281	None	12	1959 to 1962, 1965 to 1972	None	2–8–34	15–9–34	15–1–36

The Heinkel He 111H

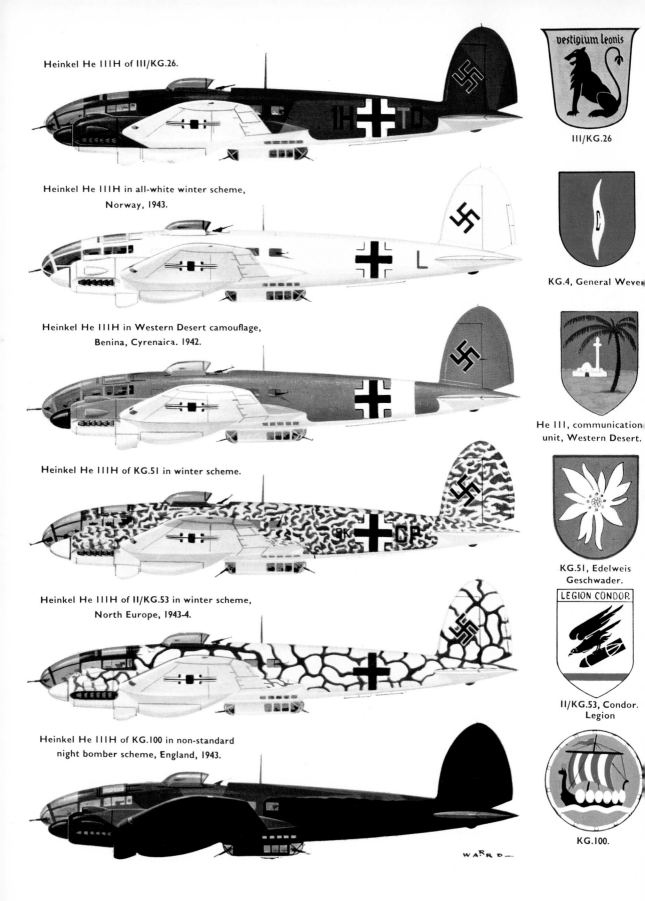

Heinkel He 111H of III/KG.26.

III/KG.26

Heinkel He 111H in all-white winter scheme,
Norway, 1943.

KG.4, General Wever

Heinkel He 111H in Western Desert camouflage,
Benina, Cyrenaica. 1942.

He 111, communication
unit, Western Desert.

Heinkel He 111H of KG.51 in winter scheme.

KG.51, Edelweis
Geschwader.

LEGION CONDOR

Heinkel He 111H of II/KG.53 in winter scheme,
North Europe, 1943-4.

II/KG.53, Condor.
Legion

Heinkel He 111H of KG.100 in non-standard
night bomber scheme, England, 1943.

KG.100.

WARD

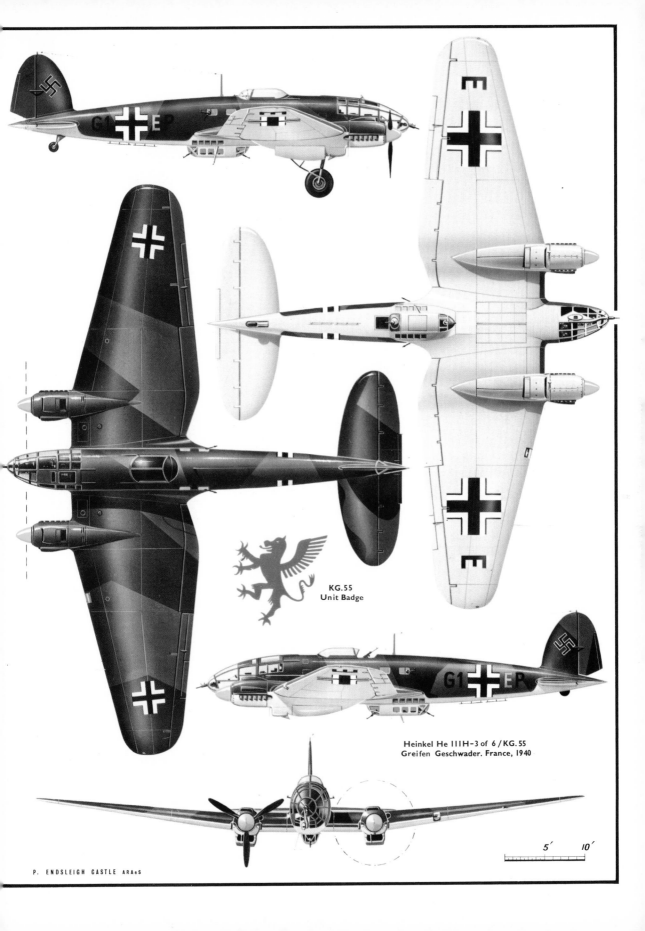

KG.55
Unit Badge

Heinkel He 111H-3 of 6 / KG. 55
Greifen Geschwader. France, 1940

5′   10′

P. ENDSLEIGH CASTLE ARAeS

The Heinkel He 111H

by Martin C. Windrow

HS-?, a Heinkel of KG4 captured in Tripoli by 260 Squadron, R.A.F.   (Photo: Imperial War Museum)

THE final collapse of Germany in the spring of 1945 can be attributed in great part to her inability either to effectively counter the Allied strategic bombing offensive or to mount a significant campaign of retaliation. Eight years previously, the misleading successes of the *Legion Condor* in Spain helped to persuade the leaders of the fledgling *Luftwaffe* that the fast, manoeuvrable medium bomber, used as the spearhead of *blitzkrieg*, was the means by which they would dominate Europe. When the weakness of their chosen weapon was clearly revealed in 1940 and 1941 many pressures (not least that of optimistic apathy) prevented an effective reversal of policy and the foundation of a realistic German strategic bomber force. The Heinkel He 111H and its ageing contemporaries continued to roll from the factories, pitifully vulnerable in a type of war for which they had not been designed.

Born on the drawing-boards of Siegfried and Walter Günther, supposedly in response to a specification issued by *Deutsche Lufthansa* for a high-speed mail and passenger aircraft, the Heinkel He 111 displayed from the first the characteristics of a military rather than a commercial aircraft. In view of the imminent announcement of the re-birth of German military aviation, this was no coincidence. Development of the design was carried out in 1934, the first prototype being completed in the winter of 1934/35. The low-wing monoplane was of metal, stressed-skin construction, with an attractively streamlined fuselage. Power was provided by two B.M.W. VI liquid-cooled engines rated at 660 h.p. The He 111V1 made its maiden flight at Marienehe early in 1935, and initial flight trials were encouraging. With a range of 930 miles and a top speed (214 m.p.h.) comparable to those of contemporary fighter aircraft, the prototype had three provisional gun positions and a bomb-load capacity of 2,200 lbs.

The He 111V2 was the first commercial prototype with ten-seat passenger accommodation and a smoking compartment in place of the bomb-bay. The V3 was the next military machine, and the V4, publicly displayed for the first time at Berlin-Tempelhof in January 1936, was the second civil version. By this time the

first batch of pre-production He 111A-O bombers had already been completed at Heinkel's Rostock plant.

The subsequent development history and *Luftwaffe* acceptance of the pre-war He 111 series does not fall within the scope of this work, but the participation in the Spanish Civil War by He 111B, D, E and F variants serving with *Kampfgruppe* 88 had a very real effect on the career of later sub-types. Out of the virtually unmolested operations of these aircraft over the Government lines in Spain grew the dangerous belief that fast medium bombers with a defensive armament of three rifle-calibre machine guns needed, at the most, only light fighter escort on daylight operations.

DESIGN DEVELOPMENT

The first major changes in the appearance of the basic design came with the He 111P sub-types, which began leaving the assembly lines in 1938. This series embodied the new, straight-tapered wing and streamlined, ventral gondola tested on the He 111V7 and, most striking of all, the re-designed nose-section tested on the He 111V8. Extensively glazed and off-set in the interests of pilot visibility, the new nose formed an unbroken projection of the fuselage contours and was to become the "trade-mark" of He 111s throughout the Second World War.

The He 111H-O and H-1 appeared in the summer of 1939. The prototype for this series was the He 111V19 and the only major difference between the He 111P and early H variants was the switch to Junkers Jumo 211A-1 engines of 1,000 h.p., for there was considerable demand for the DB 601 powerplant used in the P series for Messerschmitt Bf 109 and Bf 110 fighters. The *Kampfgeschwader* began to re-equip with the He 111H, but few had reached the *Luftwaffe* before the invasion of Poland on 1st September 1939.

During the "Phoney War" and the air battles over Norway and France, it became obvious that the defensive armament of the He 111H-1 (three 7·9 mm. MG 15 machine guns) was totally inadequate. The H-2 was fitted with two further 7·9 mm. weapons mounted in the fuselage side windows for beam pro-

The He 111V-8, D-AQUO, which was the test-bed for the "glass-house" nose section.   (Photo: Imperial War Museum)

tection, and the He 111H-3, powered by Jumo 211D-1 engines of 1,200 h.p., sometimes appeared with the nose-cone MG 15 replaced by a 20 mm. MG FF cannon.

OPERATIONAL SHORTCOMINGS

In spite of these modifications, and hard-won experience of combat with modern fighter aircraft, the Heinkel-equipped units which took part in the *Luftwaffe*'s daylight offensive against the British Isles in the summer of 1940 were severely mauled. Contrary to the belief of some German schools of thought, the He 111's speed was no guarantee of safety from the attentions of R.A.F. Spitfires and Hurricanes. Losses in the *Kampfgeschwader* involved in this phase of operations (which included KG 53 "*Legion Condor*" and KG 55 "*Griefen Geschwader*") were heavy, and a feature of this offensive was the high proportion of German bombers which returned to their French bases with dead or severely wounded aircrew. Of the five main crew positions in the He 111H, the ventral gondola was probably the most unpopular; an obvious initial target for interceptors, it earned the nickname "*das Sterbebett*"—the Deathbed—in at least one *Gruppe*.

German fighter protection for the bomber units during the Battle of Britain was of limited value, especially in the close support context. It was not unknown for a single under-strength *Gruppe* of Bf 109Es to be provided as escort for two bomber and one Stuka *Geschwader*. One disastrous raid was carried out by III/KG 27 "*Boelke*" without any fighter cover, and the limited range of the Bf 109 cannot be held responsible in this instance. Following the announcement that R.A.F. Fighter Command had for all practical purposes ceased to exist, the *Gruppe* was sent on a mission over several English south coast towns. Only 14 Heinkels returned, all severely damaged.

When the night assault on English cities began, He 111 crews were granted a brief respite from losses of this order. However, by the early months of 1941 R.A.F. night-fighter defences had been strengthened to provide a very real threat to raiders and the morale of *Luftwaffe* bomber crews suffered accordingly. Wireless interference sent many bombers astray, especially on flights to Midland targets when their route crossed the Bristol Channel. This estuary was a constant source of confusion to *Luftwaffe* pilots and navigators.

Probably because of their greater experience in accurate navigation under difficult conditions (they

The Heinkel He 111H-O.

The H 111H-1 in flight.

provided the path-finder element in the great Coventry raid), the crews of *Kampfgruppe* (later *Kampfgeschwader*) 100 were withdrawn from night operations over the British Isles in mid-May of 1941. The battle-cruiser *Bismarck* was approaching the violent end of her career in the Atlantic, and urgently required air support. The Heinkels never located her; by the time they reached the great ship's last known position she had already been sunk, and KGr. 100 was unable to find "Force H".

Many units involved in these operations flew the Heinkel 111H-3. Popular with crews for its good handling and control qualities and first-class stability, this variant normally carried 760 Imp. gallons of fuel in its wing cells. The H-4 (Junkers Jumo 211F-2 engines) was fitted with an additional fuselage tank of 184 Imp. gallon capacity in the bomb-bay, the warload being carried externally under a specially strengthened centre section. The He 111H-5 carried an increased external bomb-load of 5,510 lbs.

THE VERSATILE H-6

One of the most widely used versions of the He 111H was the H-6 variant. Appearing in all theatres of operation in a variety of rôles, the H-6 first proved its worth as a torpedo-bomber with I/KG 26 of the famous "*Löwen Geschwader*". Powered by Jumo

211F-2 engines of 1,340 h.p. the Heinkel He 111H-6 could carry two torpedoes externally. In April of 1942 the advance party of I/KG 26 arrived at the new airfields of Banak and Bardufoss on the north-west coast of Norway. In the period June–September 1942, the Heinkels carried out intensive operations against Anglo-American convoys on the "Kola run", the vital series of supply shipments to Murmansk and other North Russian ports. Considerable success was achieved, including profitable sorties against the ill-fated PQ 17, and the He 111H-6 proved itself highly suitable for the maritime attack rôle.

DESERT OPERATIONS

The North African campaign was not remarkable for the scope it offered either the Allies or the Axis for multi-engined bomber operations on a large scale. The rapidly fluctuating front lines and the absence of densely populated areas rendered such operations both wasteful and unwise. Nevertheless, at one time elements of at least three Heinkel-equipped *Geschwader* were active in this theatre.

The desert campaigns did produce at least two Heinkel operations of interest. In January 1941, II/KG 26 was transferred from its base in Norway to Sicily, and at least one *Staffel* flew on to Benghazi. This formation mounted a small-scale raid on the Suez

A Staffel of He 111Hs over the English Channel; February 1941.

(Photo: Imperial War Museum)

Many He 111H variants carried external bomb-loads on strengthened underwing centre-sections, as on this aircraft displayed in London after the war.

discovered and mapped in 1935. One He 111H, piloted by Leutnant Bohnsack, took off from Campo Uno at 08.00 hrs. on 21st January 1942 with 1,000 gallons of fuel on board. The crew included Blaich (who almost exactly a year previously had been involved in the transport of German agents in He 111Hs of KG 26) and Major Count Vimercati, the Italian Army's desert expert. At 14.30 hrs. the Heinkel made its run-in over the perimeter of Fort Lamy, and destroyed 80,000 gallons of fuel and ten parked aircraft in the face of light and disorganised opposition.

Four hours' northward flight expended the He 111Hs fuel and the aircraft was successfully landed in the desert. After nearly a week the party was located and the Heinkel refuelled by a Junkers Ju 52/3 m of the *Wüstennotstaffel* (Desert Rescue Flight).

THE H-10 TO H-18 VARIANTS

The He 111H-10 began its service in 1943. The bomb-load was carried internally and various modifications were made in defensive armament. Nose armament was standardised at one MG FF cannon and a slightly altered dorsal position with increased armour-glass protection mounted either one 13 mm. MG 131 machine gun or twin 7·9 mm. weapons in the MG 81 *Zwilling* combination. Few machines of the He 111H-11 sub-type reached the front; this version was an H-6 with fuselage fuel tankage and external racks for five 550 lb. bombs. Special mountings were substituted on the He 111H-12 for the launching of the Hs 293 "semi-guided" bomb, and the H-14 was a variant of the H-10 with improved radio aids for anti-shipping operations. This type served in 1944 on the much-diversified strength of *Kampfgeschwader* 40 under the control of the *Fliegerführer Atlantik*.

All the above-mentioned He 111 variants were powered by Jumo 211F-2 engines, as was the next production model to appear, the He 111H-16. Cockpit layout was improved and the nose was more extensively glazed to improve visibility. Both internal and external bomb-loads were carried at various times, and two additions to the defensive fire-power first tested in the H-6 were re-introduced on some machines. These comprised a forward-firing MG FF cannon in the ventral gondola and a remote control 7·9 mm. machine gun in the extreme rear of the fuselage. The He 111H-18, a sub-type intended for night operations, was basically an H-10 with improved exhaust flame-dampers.

Canal, presumably with the object of mining the narrow channel. On the return flight, all but one of the Heinkels crash-landed in the desert, and several crews were never found. This raid is more significant for its audacity than for its chances of success. In January 1941 the front line lay between Tobruk and Derna, an intermediate landing for fuel was thus impracticable, and the He 111s faced a 1,200 mile round trip. This was near the upper limit of their range potential even with reduced bomb-loads, and navigational errors may well have proved disastrous.

Another imaginative mission was carried out by a Heinkel (probably seconded from KG 4 "General Wever") against the French stronghold of Fort Lamy, 1,200 miles south of the *Luftwaffe's* coastal airfields. The mixed German/Italian force which carried out the operation, *Sonderkommando Blaich*, was led by pre-war explorer Theo Blaich, who by Christmas of 1941 was a Hauptmann (Captain) in the *Luftwaffe*. The raid was mounted from Campo Uno, a natural firm-sand airstrip far out in the Libyan Sahara which had been

The He 111H-8 was simply an H-3 or H-5 variant with the 550 lb. balloon-cable fender/cutter installed. Note the temporary night-camouflage applied to this aircraft.   (Photo: Imperial War Museum)

An He 111H-6 at the moment of take-off.

RUSSIAN SERVICE

Various models of the He 111H were used in Russia by the *Luftwaffe* and the satellite air forces of Hungary, Rumania and Slovakia. *Luftwaffe* bomber operations in the Soviet Union were dictated rather by local necessity than by any all-embracing strategy. After their initial victories in the western provinces, during which period they to some extent repeated the triumphs of the European *blitzkrieg*, the unfavourable conditions and stiffening resistance from the Soviet Air Force wore down the strength and effectiveness of the *Kampfgeschwader*. The most desirable targets, that is, the industrial centres of the Soviet armaments machine, had been evacuated beyond the range of the Heinkels, Dorniers and Ju 88s. Relegated to the more immediate

support of the German Army, the bomber units suffered increasingly at the hands of Russian fighters which were in their element at the low altitudes essential for effective ground support.

Many units sustained heavy losses attempting to fulfil Goering's boast that von Paulus' VIth Army could be supplied exclusively by air in the Stalingrad pocket. The entire strength of KG 55's He 111Hs was employed on transport flights in this area in the mid-winter 1942/43. During and after 1943 the central organisation of these units tended to break down, leaving operations largely in the hands of local commanders. *Gruppen* were decimated, recalled to Germany, brought up to *Gruppe* establishment and returned to the *Ostfront*, sometimes redesignated on

He 111H-6 of I/KG 26 "Lowen Geschwader" with practice torpedoes slung beneath the wing-roots.   (Photo: Real Photographs)

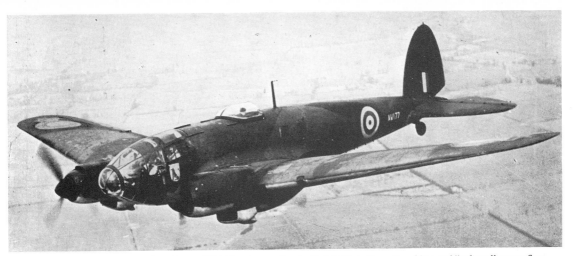

Above and Below: *a captured machine of KG 26 under test by the R.A.F. Note the unit emblem and "splinter" camouflage.*
(Photo: Imperial War Museum)

paper as complete *Geschwader*. Survivors were formed into composite units, and many formations lost their autonomous identity altogether.

One of the relatively few occasions on which successful strategic use was made of the *Kampfgeschwader* in the east was the Poltava raid on 22nd June 1944. Alarmed by the first "shuttle raid" between Italy and Russia carried out by Flying Fortresses and P-51s of the 15th U.S.A.A.F. early in the month as the overture to "Operation Frantic Joe", the *Luftwaffe* kept a close watch on the Soviet airfields set aside for American aircraft. On 21st June the operation was repeated by a force of B-17s and P-51s which branched off from a raid on Berlin. The formation was shadowed by an He 177 *Grief*, and in the early evening 200 bombers took off from Polish bases. Many He 111Hs of IVth Air Corps units such as KG 4, KG 27, KG 53 and KG 55 took part in the raid, which was executed in imitation of British "bomber stream" methods. There were no German losses, and the weather was

mild. Forty-three B-17s, 15 Mustangs and various Soviet machines were destroyed at Poltava, together with 300,000 gallons of fuel. The other "borrowed" airfields at Pirjatin and Migorod were raided the following day and their bomb and fuel dumps destroyed. The *Kampfgeschwader* never repeated this triumph; a new Red Army offensive on 23rd June sent them back to the aid of the ground troops.

FINAL VARIANTS

The delays in production and testing which kept the He 177 from appearing in any numbers with *Luftwaffe* front-line units until 1944, necessitated the introduction of improved He 111H variants in the meantime. The He 111H-20 displayed several innovations. Armament improvements included the replacement of the hood-type dorsal position with an electrically-operated EDL turret mounting a 13 mm. MG 131 machine-gun

(similar to the installation employed in the Dornier Do 217J). The nose and ventral positions also mounted MG 131s, and each beam position contained twin MG 81s. The gondola carried heavier armour than previously.

Both the He 111H-20 and H-21 sub-types (the latter differed only in having flame-dampers for night operations) were eventually powered by Junkers Jumo 213E-1 engines, affording a maximum speed of 295 m.p.h. and an operational ceiling of nearly 33,000 ft. These powerplants were rated at 1,750 h.p. for take-off and 1,320 h.p. at 32,000 ft., as compared with the 1,776 h.p. take-off rating and 1,600 h.p. developed at 18,000 ft. by the Junkers Jumo 213A-1s which powered initial production models of the H-20 when quantity production commenced in 1944.

The He 111H-23 was the final production variant of this versatile aircraft. A paratroop transport powered by Jumo 213A-1s, the H-23 carried eight *Fallschirm-jäger* who dropped from a hatch in the rear of the modified ventral gondola. This variant featured the nose-section of the H-16 and the EDL turret of the H-20 and H-21.

One of the last operational tasks undertaken by the He 111H before the close of hostilities in Europe was the air-launching of V-1 flying bombs. The late summer of 1944 saw III/KG 3 "*Blitz Geschwader*" engaged in launching operations from Gilze-Rijen in Holland, and in September crews drafted from several units were formed into a re-born KG 53 for training in N.W. Germany. Later in the month operations commenced from Venlo, the missiles being launched at night on a westerly course from positions over the North Sea. Tests at the Peenemünde experimental

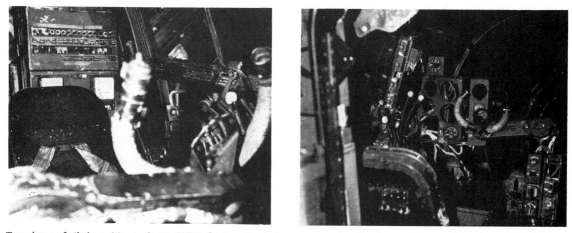

Two photos of pilot's position in the He 111H, **show**ing electrical systems panel and engine controls.   (Photos: J. L. E. Maskall)

Despite the quality of this wartime photograph, the Iraqi markings on this Heinkel are discernible. The aircraft, which was used in Syria, still displays its original Luftwaffe swastikas under a thin coat of paint.   (Photo: Imperial War Museum)

Royal Air Force officers inspect a wrecked He 111H of 7/KG 4 "General Wever" in Libya. This machine, 5J+ER, carried the last two letters of its identification code repeated in small white characters on the leading edge of the port wing, half way between nacelle and tip. Note the "sleeve" for the nose cannon, and the retractable windscreen for use when the pilot's seat was raised for a bad-visibility landing.

(Photo: Imperial War Museum)

establishment had proved that the most satisfactory method was to release the bomb from an underwing carrier between the fuselage and the starboard engine of the He 111H at an altitude of 1,500 ft. More than 800 V-1s were launched in this manner before the advance of Allied troops closed the programme in December 1944–January 1945. Losses through accidents and the action of R.A.F. night-fighters were appalling.

TWILIGHT OF THE HE 111

The characteristic silhouette of the He 111 did not entirely disappear from the skies of the world after the collapse of the Third Reich. Apart from two examples of the He 111H flown by the Czech Air Force well into the 1950s, the Spanish aircraft industry continued quantity production and regular overhaul of the He 111H-16 until very recently.

When hostilities ended in Spain and the *Legion*

Condor returned to Germany, 58 Heinkels of the earlier types remained in Franco's service as the equipment of the 14th and 15th Regiment of the Spanish Air Force at Logrono and Zaragoza. These "Pedros" were very popular with Spanish aircrew, and when the question of new equipment arose the choice fell on the latest model of the well-tried Heinkel design. The Spanish government opened negotiations with the Ernst Heinkel A.G. for the licence manufacture of a batch of He 111H-3s; but eventually it was the H-16 variant which entered production at a new plant at Tablada in Seville. The Construcciones Aeronauticas S.A. received an order for 200 aircraft, but it was not until 1945 that the first batch was ready to fly.

By this time it was apparent that no further supplies of Jumo 211F-2 engines would be forthcoming after existing stocks had been exhausted. Variants represented among the 130 examples of Jumo-powered machines delivered to the Spanish Air Force included the C.A.S.A. C2111-A, A1, A2 and A3 bombers; the C.2111-C, C1, C2 and C3 reconnaissance bombers; and the C.2111-F and F1 dual control trainers.

It was finally decided to adapt the C.2111 series for future production with the Rolls-Royce Merlin 500-20, and an order for 173 of these powerplants was placed in April 1956. Several Merlin-engined variants were delivered, including the C.2111-B bomber, the T8 transport (with gun positions removed and accommodation for nine passengers) and the C.2111-D and D1 reconnaissance bombers. At the time of writing, more than one unit equipped with aircraft of this series is still in service with the Spanish Air Force.

LUFTWAFFE UNITS AND MARKINGS

The basic *Luftwaffe* tactical unit was the *Geschwader*. The bomber *Geschwader* (*Kampfgeschwader* or KG) consisted of three, four, or five *Gruppen*, each of which was in its turn made up of three *Staffeln*. These sub-units were numbered independently; thus I/KG 2 (the first *Gruppe* of *Kampfgeschwader* 2) consisted of 1/KG 2 (the first *Staffel* of *Kampfgeschwader* 2), 2/KG 2 and 3/KG 2. Similarly, 7/KG 2, 8/KG 2, and 9/KG 2 made up the strength of III/KG 2.

The operational strengths of these formations

An He 111H-6 takes off with an external bomb-load.

(Photo: Imperial War Museum)

A Heinkel He 111H at Algiers airport, November 1942. Despite the commercial markings, the machine-gun in the nose is clearly visible. Such aircraft were used by the Franco-German Armistice Commission in North Africa.   (Photo: Imperial War Museum)

varied greatly, but an average *Staffel* mustered between ten and 16 aircraft, thus giving a *Geschwader* an establishment of some 110/150 machines.

    Kampfgeschwader, Stuka Geschwader, Nachtjagdgeschwader, Zerstörergeschwader, Transportgeschwader, Aufklärungsgruppen (Reconnaissance Squadrons) and miscellaneous units used a four-symbol code on the fuselage sides of aircraft for identification purposes. A numeral/letter code appeared on the left-hand side of the national marking, identifying the *Geschwader*; e.g., U5=KG 2. From 1943 onwards this combination either appeared in very small characters or was omitted altogether. Sometimes it was reproduced in small characters on the vertical tail surfaces of bombers, and often temporary camouflage finishes were applied in such a way as to obscure it.

    On the right of the national marking two letters appeared. The first, painted or outlined in the *Staffel* colour, or in green on staff aircraft, identified the individual aircraft. The second letter identified the *Staffel* within the *Geschwader*. Towards the end of the war, it increasingly became the practice for the individual marking only to be applied to the fuselage; and this was often repeated under the wingtips.

Units known to have operated the He 111H during their service include:—

KG 1 "Hindenburg" (V4); KG 4 "General Wever" (5J); KG 26 "Löwen Geschwader" (1H); KG 27 "Boelke" (1G); KG 40 (F8); KG 51 "Edelweiss-Geschwader" (9K); KG 53 "Legion Condor" (A1); KG 54 "Totenkopf Geschwader" (B3); KG 55 "Griefen Geschwader" (G1); KGr. (later KG) 100 (6N).

Specification

HEINKEL He 111H-6

Dimensions: Span 74 ft. 1½ in.; Length 54 ft. 5½ in.; Height 13 ft. 9 in.; Wing Area 942 sq. ft.

Weights: Normal loaded 25,000 lbs. Maximum 27,400 lbs.

Powerplant: Two Junkers Jumo 211F-2 twelve-cylinder inverted-Vee liquid-cooled engines of 1,340 h.p. (take-off rating) and 1,060 h.p. (17,000 ft.).

Armament: Bomb load capacity: 5,510 lbs. (mounted externally) or two torpedoes mounted externally on maritime variant. Defensive armament: One 7·9 mm. MG 15 machine-gun in nose position. One 7·9 mm. MG 15 in each of two beam positions. One forward-firing 20 mm. MG FF cannon in ventral gondola. One rearward-firing 7·9 mm. MG 15 in ventral gondola. One 7·9 mm. MG 15 in dorsal position. One fixed remote-control 7·9 mm. MG 17 in extreme rear of fuselage.

Performance: Maximum speed 258 m.p.h. at 16,400 ft.; Cruising speed 224 m.p.h. at 16,400 ft.; Service ceiling 25,500 ft.; Range with maximum bomb load 760 miles; Maximum range 1,740 miles.

C.A.S.A. C.2111-D

Dimensions: Span 74 ft. 3 in.; Length 54 ft. 6 in.; Height 13 ft. 9 in.; Wing Area 931 sq. ft.

Weights: Normal loaded 26,455 lbs. Maximum 30,865 lbs.

Powerplant: Two Rolls-Royce Merlin 500-29 twelve-cylinder Vee cooled engines of 1,610 h.p. (take-off rating) and 1,015 h.p. (15,500 ft.).

Armament: Bomb load capacity: 2,200 lbs. (carried internally). (The four starboard bomb cells are replaced by a universal camera mounting.) Defensive armament: One 12·7 mm. Breda-SAFAT machine-gun in nose position. One rearward-firing 7·92 mm. M-15 machine-gun in ventral gondola. One 7·92 mm. M-15 in dorsal position.

Performance: Maximum speed 260 m.p.h. at 14,760 ft.; Cruising speed 245 m.p.h. at 16,400 ft.; Service ceiling 27,890 ft.; Maximum range 1,550 miles.

Thus, U5+(red F) N was machine "F" of 5/KG 2.

Staff Aircraft Identification.

These letters took the place of the fourth, or *Staffel*, symbol.

Geschwader Staff = A		III Gr. = D
I Gruppe = B		IV Gr. = E
II Gr. = C		V Gr. = F

Staffel Identification

Staffel Colour			I Gruppe	II Gruppe	III Gruppe	IV Gruppe	V Gruppe
White...	...	...	1st Stfl. = H	4th Stfl. = M	7th Stfl. = R	10th Stfl. = U	13th Stfl. = X
Red	...	...	2nd Stfl. = K	5th Stfl. = N	8th Stfl. = S	11th Stfl. = V	14th Stfl. = Y
Yellow	...	...	3rd Stfl. = L	6th Stfl. = P	9th Stfl. = T	12th Stfl. = W	15th Stfl. = Z

The Fiat C.R.42

The Fiat CR.42

by Gianni Cattaneo

Standard C.R.42 fighters of the 9° GRUPPO, 4° STORMO. Note the horse motif on the fuselage and leg on the fin.

THE chair-borne pundit avers that the biplane fighter was obsolescent when pitted against the modern monoplane bomber of the late 1930s, yet it still served with the combatant air forces when World War II began in September 1939. Monoplane interceptors were leaving the production lines in ever increasing numbers, but until they could be integrated into the broad pattern of air power strategy, the second-line biplane was called upon to fill the gap.

When, in early 1939, the prototype Fiat C.R.42 Falco (Falcon) began its first flights the days of the biplane formula for fighters were already numbered. But, despite the built-in obsolescence, the new aeroplane was destined to participate in operations in World War II until the closing months of 1943; to fight bitterly on all fronts where the Italian *Regia Aeronautica* was present, and to be built in greater numbers than any fighter of the Italian aircraft industry.

The C.R.42 was an excellent machine in its class and was the last development of a formula dear to Ing. Celestino Rosatelli, Chief Engineer of the Fiat Company. The lineage was born in 1923 with the C.R.20 and 30 series and refined with the next experimental prototype C.R.33, 40 and 41.

The sparkling success gained by the C.R.32 in Spain was one of the main reasons for the persistent confidence of the Ministero dell' Aeronautica in the biplane configuration, with its agile manœuvrability in dog-fighting. And it was only one of the many negative aspects drawn from the victorious conclusion of the Ethiopian and Spanish campaigns.

These two wars, even if they enabled modern military equipment to be tested under genuine operational conditions, gave a completely false impression of Regia Aeronautica efficiency. The demand for, and attrition of, war materials was to some extent

Head-on view of the Falco prototype shows wing bracing and biplane arrangement.

(Photo: G. Apostolo)

Early production C.R.42. Metal covered front and fabric covered rear fuselage is evident in this view.

lacking, and above all the somewhat unorganised opposition created the illusion that war was easy for the belligerent nations.

In Spain the highly-trained Italian pilots, backed by an efficient ground service and high quality aeroplanes, permitted an ascendency over the opposing pilots, generally poorly-trained mercenaries with little "esprit de corps". It was only towards the end of the struggle that the younger, more aggressive pilot from the Russian schools appeared. However, no comparison was possible between the events of a civil war with those of the struggle-to-be among the big European powers.

The series production of the C.R.42 was ordered in late 1939, following the initiation of the well-known "R" plan, that provided for the realisation and production of 3,000 new aircraft such as the monoplane G.50 and MC.200 fighters. Of clean aerodynamic design and an immensely strong structure, the Falco was perhaps the best biplane in service anywhere, and it was well able to give a good account of itself against faster aircraft. Characterised by superlative manœuvrability it combined all the qualities dear to the heart of the Italian pilot.

Power plant installation on the C.R.42.

THE FALCO STRUCTURE

The biplane arrangement was of unequal span, for the two wings were braced by the rigid warren-truss, hall-mark of all the fighters designed by Rosatelli. The fuselage was a welded, steel-tube, triangulated framework of manganese-molybdenum, with light alloy formers, the resultant oval section covered with a metal skin forward and fabric aft of the cockpit. Careful attention was given to the NACA engine cowling fitted with regulable cooling flaps.

Basic structure of the wings was of light alloy and steel, with a metal-skinned leading edge and a fabric main covering. The top wing was in two sections joined at the centre and supported above the fuselage by an inverted "V" cabane. Lower wings were attached to the bottom fuselage longerons. Ailerons were fitted to the upper wing only. Tail unit was a cantilever monoplane with a duralumin framework covered with fabric. Undercarriage consisted of two independent legs with oleo-pneumatic shock absorbers attached to the upper ends of the lower wing stubs, and braced midway with light tubes to the fuselage centre-line. Legs and wheels were enclosed in streamlined fairings. The tailwheel, retractable on the prototype, was fixed on production aircraft.

Armament was one 7·7 mm. (0·3-in.) and one 12·7 mm. (0·5iin.) S.A.F.A.T. machine gun installed in the upper fuselage decking and firing through the airscrew. A rounds-counter, normal fixture on all Italian fighters, was installed on the instrument panel. The light machine gun was replaced by a second 12·7 in later production machines.

Engine was the reliable Fiat A74R.1C.38 of 840 h.p. driving a constant-speed Fiat 3D41 propeller, and in the engine bay a fire extinguisher was carried. Strangely enough, no radio aids or equipment was fitted.

The prototype C.R.42 displayed excellent flight qualities with a maximum level speed of 274 m.p.h. at 20,000 feet, a fast climb and a minimum speed of 80 m.p.h. The robust structure permitted every conceivable manœuvre and the ultimate load co-efficient

C.R.42s of the 162 Squadriglia over the Aegean Isles in 1940. Below: *a close-up view of the aeroplane in the foreground shows cat motif of the squadron.*
(Photos: via G. Cattaneo)

of the aircraft at 5,060 pounds maximum weight was in fact 14.

INTO SERVICE

First units to be issued with the new fighter began equipping in 1939, the same year of the prototype's first flight. Simple construction made for easy production, and the familar biplane configuration enabled the squadrons to work up to front-line efficiency in a short period. At the outbreak of war in September 1939, the C.R.42 equipped three STORMI*. This compared with the five STORMI, equipped with the C.R.32, one STORMO with the G.50 and one with the MC.200.

A total of 143 Falcos, 110 of which were in a state of front-line readiness, were based on the Italian homeland at the time of the entry of Italy into the war on 10th June 1940. The period between September 1939

*The Fighter STORMO was composed of two GRUPPI; every Fighter Group comprised three SQUADRIGLIE, with 12 aircraft to every squadron.

and 10th June, the so-called "phoney war", was a time of great activity for the Regia Aeronautica. Build-up of squadrons was being activated and while awaiting delivery of the G.50 and MC.200 a further contract

Falco left behind after the Axis retreat in North Africa. Aircraft is of the same STORMO as those in photograph on page 182.
(Photo: Imperial War Museum)

for the Falco was placed in order to continue this expansion. Newer designs in the form of the MC.202 and Re.2001 were on the drawing boards, but these were in the future and did not go into service until the late summer of 1941 and May 1942 respectively.

At the time of Italy's entry into the war C.R.42 squadron disposition was as follows:—Northern Italy (Nove Ligure and Caselle)3° and 53° STORMI; Southern Italy (Palermo) 1° STORMO. In the west sector of Libya at Castelbenito was 13° GRUPPO and at Benina in the Eastern Sector was 10° GRUPPO of 4° STORMO. In Africa Orientale Italiana (Italian East Africa) were two squadrons, 413 and 414 at Gura and Assab respectively. A grand total of 330 aircraft, 290 of which were available for service, were at a state of readiness, with 40 machines at depots or with the Fiat company.

OPERATIONAL DEBUT

The C.R.42 made its operational debut in the brief, 14-day campaign against Southern France. Two principal actions were carried out by the Italian Fighter Units; the Falcos of the 23° GRUPPO (3° STORMO) and 151° GRUPPO (53° STORMO) attacked the air bases at Fayence and Hyeres on 13th June, and also accompanied the bombing missions by

Fiat BR.20s on the harbour of Tolone. Two days later, in fine weather conditions, two complete STORMI (150° and 151° GRUPPI of 53° STORMO), 18° and 23° GRUPPI of 3° STORMO) strafed the air bases of Cuers Pierrefeu and Cannet de Maures. The French Air Force reacted immediately. Against the Luftwaffe in Northern France the Armée de l'Air was a beaten, dispirited force, but the Côte d'Azur and Southern Provence was in the heart of the training area of the French Fighter Arm, and opposition was determined. The C.R.42 faced the Dewoitine D.520 of Groupe de Chasse G.C.III/6 and the Bloch 152 of A.C.3, these fighters being among the best of the mixed French equipment.

Mutual victories and losses were claimed and inflated by both sides, but post-war figures reveal that the victory/loss ratio on both sides was small. On 13th June the C.R.42s destroyed a French fighter in the air, in addition to a number on the ground, without loss to themselves, and on 15th June the Italian machines destroyed eight French fighters (three Blochs and five Dewoitines) for the loss of five Falcos. During the days that followed the Italian Fighter Units performed escort missions only without opposition until the French capitulation on 24th June. Other C.R.42s of the 1° STORMO based in Sicily escorted SM.79

Upper and two lower views are of C.R.42s of the Corpo Aero Italiano based in Belgium during the Battle of Britain.

bombers on raids on a number of Tunisian aerodromes. During strafing runs after the main raid there was no opposition from enemy fighters.

The light losses sustained by the Italian fighters during the French campaign again persuaded the Regia Aeronautica that it was almost unbeatable, and in September 1940 it was decided for prestige and political reasons to send a contingent of the Air Force to collaborate with the Luftwaffe in the Battle of Britain. Thus was born the Corpo Aero Italiano (Italian Air Corp) composed of bomber, fighter and reconnaissance units. The fighters formed the 56° STORMO consisting of 18° GRUPPO (seconded from 3° STORMO) and equipped with 50 C.R.42s; the 20° GRUPPO (from 51; STORMO) with 48 G.50s. They moved to Ursel and Maldegen in Belgium and were accompanied by two STORMI of BR.20s and one squadron of CANT Z.1007Bis.

But all did not go well with the Italian contingent. The weather of Northern Europe was so different from that of the homeland, and the fast Bf 109 fighters of the German 2 Loftflotte found it difficult to keep formation with the slower biplane. The German aircraft, like their British opponents, were equipped with VHF radio and this equipment was lacking in the C.R.42.

However, it was decided to commit the Falco into battle against the Spitfires and Hurricanes and the Italian biplane first crossed the Channel on 11th November 1940 for a raid on Harwich. A second attempt was made on 23rd November when the C.R.42 took part in an offensive sweep against the towns of Margate and Folkestone.

The inevitable victory/loss claims were made by both sides with the Italians claiming nine probables for the first raid at the cost of three aircraft, and five victories and two losses on the second. Royal Air Force records show that these claims were, in fact, inaccurate.

Falco of the 95 Squadriglia of the Corpo Aero Italiana showing typical upper surface camouflage.

Heavy demand for the Falco in the Mediterranean Theatre, coupled with the obvious deficiencies against the R.A.F. speeded the return of the C.R.42 to Italy in January 1941. Two squadrons, 352 and 353 of 20° GRUPPO were left behind and did not leave Belgium until the following April.

THE MIDDLE EAST ACTIONS

The widest use of the C.R.42 was in North Africa, where it equipped the majority of the Italian Fighter Units during the initial stages of the desert campaigns, but as an interceptor and fighter it was no match for the Hurricanes and Tomahawks that appeared later, and it was relegated to the ground attack rôle. In Libya it served with the famous 10° GRUPPO, consisting of 84, 90 and 91 squadrons, of 4° STORMO and 9° GRUPPO, 73, 96 and 87 Squadrons of the same STORMO.

The Falco was particularly active during the first cycle of operations which lasted from June 1940 to

Night fighter version of the Falco was the C.R.42 CN (Caccia Noturna). Aircraft belongs to the 300A Squadriglia.

C.R.42 of the 1/4 Fighter Squadron, Hungarian Air Force.

(Photo: via G. Cattaneo)

February 1941, and it was in the forefront of the Italian offensive which culminated in the conquest of Sidi Barrani. It went over to the defensive when the British counter-offensive swept the Italian Forces out of Cyrenaica. This campaign is significant for it was the first time that the fighter and fighter-bomber took a major part in a land battle, and it set the pattern for all future desert fighting.

Until December 1940 the C.R.42s of 4° STORMO, with the C.R.32s of 151° GRUPPO (53° STORMO) had to contend only with the Gloster Gladiator biplane and the Italian aircraft displayed a marked advantage over the British machine. But when the Hurricanes began to appear it was the C.R.42 that was the inferior aircraft.

By January 1941 many of the new units serving in Africa were equipped with the G.50, but demand for the Falco was still insatiable and as a consequence 18° GRUPPO with its C.R.42s were transported from Belgium to the Middle East. From June 1940 until February 1941 Italian Fighter Units equipped with the Falco flew a total of 11,286 hours on offensive sorties. An average of 36 aircraft per day was engaged—

157 victories and 41 losses was the price paid for this activity. During this time also Falcos of 17° GRUPPO, 157° and 23° GRUPPI based in Sicily took part in the first air strikes against Malta, and acted as escorts to the bombers and torpedo aircraft attacking Allied convoys in the Mediterranean.

THE GREEK CAMPAIGN

At the end of October 1940, when the war against Greece began, Italian fighter units consisted of one GRUPPO of C.R.32, two GRUPPI (24° and 154°) of G.50s and one GRUPPO (363, 346 and 365 squadrons) with the C.R.42. The Greek fighter force composed 44 aircraft: 30 PZL P.XXLVs, two Gloster Gladiators, 7 Avia B.534s and five Bloch 151s, a curious mixture which was soon reinforced by British aircraft.

In the air fighting that followed, the Italian pilots displayed a marked superiority over Greek pilots who struggled bravely, but were soon defeated. And, even against the British fighters, well trained and pugnacious the Italian aircraft showed up well. The robustness and reliability of the C.R.42 was to stand it in good stead in the difficult terrain and weather

A J.11 (C.R.42) of the F9 Wing, 1st Air Division, Swedish Air Force.

(Photo: Bo Widfeldt)

J.11, serial 2528, of the 2nd Air Division. (Photo: Bo Widfeldt)

conditions prevailing in Greece, and of the 156 days of the campaign only 64 were good enough for flying. The average number of fighters despatched per day was 125 and the victory/loss ratio in favour of the Italians was 160 to 29.

In May 1941 the Falco fighter units in the Aegean Isles co-operated effectively with German forces for the conquest of Crete. Number 162 Squadron based at Scarpanto and 163 Squadron at Godurra carried out escort missions with Ju 87 dive bombers, strafing Heraklion Air Base, embarkation harbours and land forces. In June 1941 the 161° GRUPPO was formed in the Aegean and it joined 162, 163 and 164 Squadrons with the C.R.42 as main equipment. The biplane remained in service with these units until November that year, when the Fiat G.50 entered service.

THE END IN ETHIOPIA

Following the easy victory in Ethiopia, now called Italian East Africa by the occupying forces, the efficiency of the Regia Aeronautica began to suffer through lack of supplies and reinforcement. Before joining in the main struggle with Germany against the Allies, the Italians found it fairly easy to get supplies to their forces by shipping them across the Mediterranean. But at the outbreak of hostilities the Royal Navy stopped this traffic and the Italians were forced to transport all war materials by air.

During the period immediately before June 1940 it had been possible to send to A.O.I. 36 of the new C.R.42s, enough to equip two Squadrons, 412 and 413. To offset losses and maintain a limited operational efficiency a series of long-distance, non-stop flights over the hostile territory of Egypt and the Sudan was initiated, the prime carrier being the three-engined SM.82 transport. Complete aircraft, dismantled, and spares were flown in, and from August 1940 until the Spring of 1941 a total of 51 Falcos were delivered in this manner, adding much needed strength to the Italian Fighter Forces.

But from June 1941 onwards the impossibility of continuing these flights became evident. They were made without the aid of radio facilities, in the rainy season and with the added risk of enemy interception.

In addition, the task of finding the base after a flight of 2,500 miles was difficult. The Sm.82s lifted a total load of 795,000 lb. and evacuated 1,500 Italians during 330 return trips. In November 1941 the two remaining C.R.42s were destroyed, one on the ground, the other during a sortie during which the last ammunition was expended. The following day an aircraft of the South African Air Force dropped a message on the Italian base that read "Homage to the pilot of the Fiat—he was a valiant fighter SAAF". The Italian Air Force was no longer a force to be reckoned with in Ethiopia.

Following the reconquest of Cyrenaica by Axis Forces in May 1941, the Italian fighter units equipped with C.R.42 and G.50s were joined by 374 Squadron with MC.200s and for the first time the Falcos appeared as a fighter-bomber with 236 F.B. Squadron, carrying two 200 pound bombs on underwing racks. The obsolescent biplane found an immediate success in its new rôle, and it was responsible for the destruction of many armoured vehicles. As the result of experiments with the C.R.42 fighter-bomber the 5° STORMO ASSALTO (Attack), the 50° STORMO A (158° and 159° GRUPPI) and 15° STORMO A were equipped with the Falco. It was constantly in action during the alternate phases of advance and retreat on the North African front from Spring 1941 until November 1942, when the final Allied advance began at El Alamein.

Particularly active were Falco fighter-bombers in the Tobruk area, and even at night they were constantly strafing columns, camps, vehicles and air bases. Similar raids dotted the advance by Axis troops towards Alexandria, and in particular the Mersa Matruh area. In September 1942, when the Axis advance ground to a halt through lack of supplies, the C.R.42 equipped 50° STORMO A at Abu Nimeir (40 a/c), the 160° GRUPPO at Sorman, and the 101° GRUPPO A. The 15° STORMO A arrived from Italy to join these units and was thrown into hurried action during the Axis retreat that ended in Tripoli.

From 7th January to 19th the surviving 82 Falcos were repatriated to the homeland leaving behind them 3° STORMO (MC.202s) and 13° GRUPPO (MC.200s and 202s). On return to Italy the C.R.42s were then

Rare photograph of a two-seat trainer conversion of the C.R.42. Post-war codes Z-1 6 refer to First "Zona Territoriale"—Milan Area.
(Photo: Richard Ward)

used for attacks on the Allied convoys between Gibraltar and Malta, but the small bombs they carried were ineffective against the larger ships.

The C.R.42 was gradually superseded in day fighter units by more modern types, but it found a new lease of life as a night fighter. In this rôle it was equipped with radio, and with two searchlights installed in streamlined fairings under the lower wings. They were driven by a wind generator installed on the upper centre section. The first night fighter unit was formed in Sicily in October 1941 when 171° GRUPPO C.N. (Night-Fighters) came into being with two squadrons. The unit, however, did not see much action and was soon disbanded, but it did achieve a certain amount of success against the R.A.F. bombers attacking the industrial areas of Northern Italy in 1942/43. The C.R.42 Cassia Nocturnas were supplanted by Re. 2001s and a small number of Me. 110s and Do. 217Js received from Germany. One mixed unit was 60° GRUPPO, based at Lonate Pozzol (Milan area) and Casselle (Turin), and had on strength 2 Me. 110s, 10 Re.2001s, 7 Do. 217Js and 6 C.R.42s.

EXPERIMENTAL VERSIONS

The C.R.42 configuration did not alter much during its career, and only two other versions appeared. One was the C.R.42bis with two additional 12·7 machine guns in underwing fairings and the fighter-bomber version. The C.R.42ter designation was incorrect and never adopted. Aircraft used in North Africa carried the suffix A.S. (Africa Settentrionale-North Africa) after the military serial to denote the introduction of a special oil and air sand filter and other modifications to permit use in the desert.

A small number of C.R.42s were fitted with two underwing 20 mm. cannon in panniers.

In 1940 the CMASA company, a subsidiary of Fiat with factories at Marina di Pisa, constructed the prototype IC.R.42, a twin, float-plane version of the land fighter. Empty weight was 4,070 pounds and loaded weight 5,335 pounds, 273 pounds heavier than the land plane. Speed was decreased by only

5 m.p.h., but the marine version remained an experiment.

Another experimental Falco was fitted with a Daimler Benz DB601 in-line engine and had a designed speed of 323 m.p.h. The sole prototype was designated the C.R.42B. The installation of a retractable undercarriage was also considered, but it was clear that the Falco's basic design was unsuitable for such a modification.

A grand total of 1,781 C.R.42s had been constructed when production ceased late in 1942, and at the time of the Italian Armistice on 7th September 1943 only 113 remained. Sixty-four aircraft were serviceable and were distributed as follows:

I Squadra Aerea: 59 Gruppo Aut. Interc. 2 a/c; 60 Gruppo Aut. Interc. 2 a/c 2 Gruppo Aut. Interc. II a/c.
II Squadra Aerea: none.
III Squadra Aerea: 15 Stormo 46-47 Gruppo 6 a/c;
Aeronautica della Sardegna: Sez. 160 Gruppo 2 a/c.
Aeronautica dell'Egeo: Sezione Interc. 3 a/c.
Aeronautica Albania: 392 Squadriglia Aut. 9 a/c.
Aeronautica Grecia: Sezione Interc. 3 a/c.
Avaizione Slovenia Dalmazia: 383 Squadriglia Aut. Ass. 13 a/c.
Aviazone Ausiliaria per la Marina: 1 Squadriglia FF.NN. 2 a/c.
Total 53 Machines (11 unaccounted for).

At the time of the surrender four C.R.42s were flown to Allied lines to join the Co-Belligerent Force in Southern Italy, while the remainder served with the Repubblica Sociale Italiana in the North. The C.B. a/c served as trainers and some, modified as two-seaters, survived the war and were still in service in 1950.

FOREIGN FALCOS

Late in 1940 fifty C.R.42 were exported to Hungary and took part in the German-Russian campaign. It equipped the 2/11 Fighter Group of two squadrons and these, plus the 1/3 Fighter Squadron accompanied the Hungarian Army's Fast Corp from July to December 1941, being used mainly in the ground attack rôle.

Thirty-four Falcos were ordered by Belgium in September 1939, the first of which were delivered in March the following year. The C.R.42 equipped the 3eme Escadrille de Chasse and 13 of them were destroyed by Ju 87 dive bombers during the German

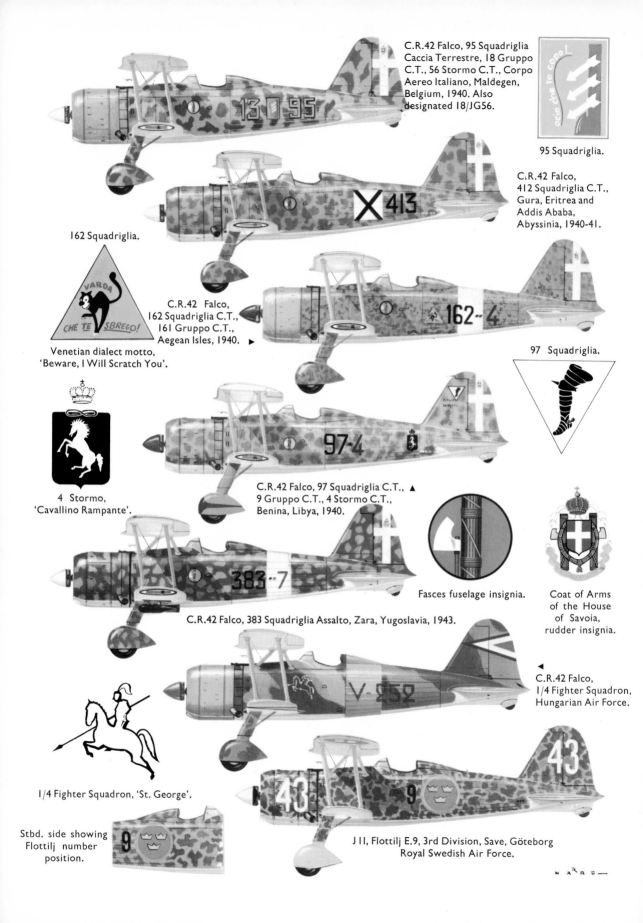

C.R.42 Falco, 95 Squadriglia Caccia Terrestre, 18 Gruppo C.T., 56 Stormo C.T., Corpo Aereo Italiano, Maldegen, Belgium, 1940. Also designated 18/JG56.

95 Squadriglia.

162 Squadriglia.

C.R.42 Falco, 412 Squadriglia C.T., Gura, Eritrea and Addis Ababa, Abyssinia, 1940-41.

C.R.42 Falco, 162 Squadriglia C.T., 161 Gruppo C.T., Aegean Isles, 1940. ▶

Venetian dialect motto, 'Beware, I Will Scratch You'.

97 Squadriglia.

4 Stormo, 'Cavallino Rampante'.

C.R.42 Falco, 97 Squadriglia C.T., ▲ 9 Gruppo C.T., 4 Stormo C.T., Benina, Libya, 1940.

Fasces fuselage insignia.

Coat of Arms of the House of Savoia, rudder insignia.

C.R.42 Falco, 383 Squadriglia Assalto, Zara, Yugoslavia, 1943.

C.R.42 Falco, 1/4 Fighter Squadron, Hungarian Air Force.

1/4 Fighter Squadron, 'St. George'.

Stbd. side showing Flottilj number position.

J 11, Flottilj E.9, 3rd Division, Save, Göteborg Royal Swedish Air Force.

WARD

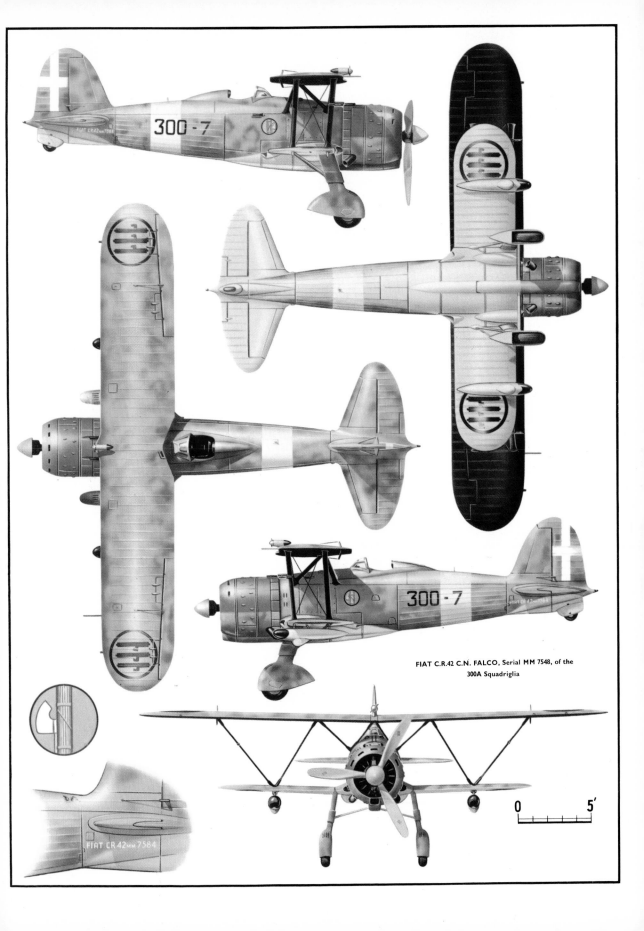

FIAT C.R.42 C.N. FALCO, Serial MM 7548, of the
300A Squadriglia

0   5'

Wheel spats have been removed from this C.R.42, pictured near Milan in the early post-war years. (Photo: Richard Ward)

invasion, the survivors taking little or no part in the air fighting over Belgium.

The largest export order for the C.R.42 was placed by Sweden and was for 72 a/c delivered between February 1940 and September 1941, bearing the serials 2501–2572. They were powered by Fiat A74R.1C.38 engines providing a maximum 870 h.p. The first dozen machines were flown to Sweden, but the remainder were crated and delivered to CVM (Centrala Fly Malm) and reassembled. By November 1941 all the Falcos were in service and they bore the designation of J 11. Modifications included 20 mm. armour plate behind the pilot, radio equipment and skis for winter service.

The C.R.42 was declared obsolete in 1945 and the remaining a/c were purchased by AB Svensk Flytjanst and used for target towing duties. Swedish registrations of the C.R.42s (serials in brackets) ran as follows: SE-AOH (2503); SE-AON (2506); SE-AOR (2514); SE-AOI (2520); SE-AOL (2521); SE-AOM (2525); 2528, 2531, 2539, 2545 (SE-AOO, -AOS, -AOP, -AOW); SE-AOK (2548); SE-AOU (2563); SE-AOX (2569).

At the outbreak of war C.R.42 equipped the following units of the Italian Air Force.

The Publishers acknowledge with grateful thanks the information and assistance so freely given by Captain Cesare Milani in the preparation of this PROFILE.

Specification

(Data from Technical Manual C.A.446 of "Ministero dell" Aeronautica.)

Powerplant: One FIAT A.74R.IC.38, radial air cooled, fourteen cylinder, double row of 840 h.p. rated at 2,400 r.p.m./12,500 ft.–FIAT constant speed propeller, three blades, diameter 9·186 feet.

Dimension: Wing span (upper)· 31·824 ft.; Wing span (lower) 21·325 ft.; Length 27·067 ft.; Height 10·033 ft.; Wing area 241·111 sq. ft.

Weight (lb.): Empty 3,929. Useful load 1,130 of which: Pilot 176; Rounds 187 (400 each gun); Various 17; Fuel 672; Oil 77; Total loaded 5060.

Performance: (at 5,060 lb. and 2,520 r.p.m.). Maximum speed: sea level 213 m.p.h.; 10,000 ft. 248 m.p.h.; 20,000 ft. 274 m.p.h. Landing speed: 80 m.p.h. Climb to: 3,000 ft. 1 min. 25 sec.; 10,000 ft. 4 min. 15 sec.; 20,000 ft. 9 min. Combat ceiling: 33,500 ft.; Takeoff run: 690 ft.; Landing run: 1,120 ft.; Range (20,000 ft. and 235 m.p h.) 485 miles; Ultimate loading coefficient 14.

Armament: First series one 12·7 mm. (0·5″) cal. and one 7·7 mm. (0·303″) cal. machine-gun. Later two 12·7 mm. with 400 rounds each. Two additional 12·7 mm. machine-guns in underwing fairings on some. Racks for two 220 lb. bombs underwing.

Units of Regia Aeronautica with FIAT C.R.42 Fighter a/c.

(1) Usually the Italian "Stormo C.T." (C.T. stands for Caccia Terrestre—Land Fighters), was composed by two "Gruppi C.T."; each "Gruppo" by three "Squadriglie C.T.", with 12 a/c each Sq.

The total of 72 a/c was rarely if ever accomplished, especially on last stages of war. Often Gruppi and Squadriglie got autonomous status, independently of specific Stormo.

(2) At outbreak of war (10 June, 1940 for Italy), C.R.42 fighters equipped the following units.

Stormo	Gruppo	Squadriglie	Location
3°	18°	83°– 85°– 95°	Novi Ligure (Italy)
3°	23°		Cervere (Italy)
53°	150°	363°–364°–365°	Caselle (Italy)
53°	151°		Casabianca (Italy)
1°	17°		Palermo (Italy)
1°	157°		Trapani (Italy)
	13°		Castelbenito (Libya)
4°	10°	91°– 96°– 97°	Benina (Libya)
4°	9°	73°– 84°– 90°	Gorizia (Italy)
		411°–412°	A.O.I. (It. E. Africa)

Units identified after this date

363° Sq.–150° Gr.–53° St.–5 Nov., 1940–Tirana (Albania)			
364° Sq.–150° Gr.–53° St.–5 Nov., 1940–Valona (Albania)			
365° Sq.–150° Gr.–53° St.–5 Nov., 1940–Argirocastro			
162° Sq.–161° Gr.	–6 June, 1941–Aegean Isles		
163° Sq.–161° Gr.	–6 June, 1941–Aegean Isles		
164° Sq.–161° Gr.	–6 June, 1941–Aegean Isles		
392° Sq.	–7 Sept., 1943–Tirana (Albania)		
– 3° Gr.	–9 Dec., 1940–Monserrato (Sardinia)		

73° Sq.
84° Sq. ⎫ 9° Gr.–4° St.–1 July, 1940–Libya
90° Sq. ⎭

83° Sq.
85° Sq. ⎫ 18° Gr.–56° St.–10 Sept., 1940–Maldegen (Belgium)
95° Sq. ⎭

– 23° Gr.– 3° St.–12 Dec., 1940–Sorman (Libya)	
– 60° Gr.	–July 1942–Lonate P. (Italy)
– 97° Gr.	–July 1943–Crotone (Italy)
–151° Gr.–53° St.–April 1941–Libya	
–153° Gr.–54° St.–April 1941–Grottaglie (Italy)	
–154° Gr.	–July 1943–Rhodes (Aegean)
–156° Gr.	–Jan. 1941–Sicily (Italy)
–157° Gr.– 1° St.–Sept. 1941–Caselle (Italy)	
–160° Gr.	–April 1941–Tirana (Albania)
–160° Gr.	–Dec. 1941–Sorman (Libya)
–160° Gr.	–Sept. 1943–Ajaccio (Corsica)
300° Sq.–171° Gr.	–Oct. 1941–Sicily (Italy)–Night Fighter Unit

The C.R.42 was used by many "Assalto" (Attack) units, with underwing bombs. Examples:

15° St. A.–El Alamein Area–Summer 1942
383° Sq. A.–Zara (Yugoslavia)–July 1943
236° Sq. A.–Ara Fileni (Libya)–Jan. 1942
50° St. A.–158° and 159° Gr. A.–Bengasi (Libya)–Spring 1942
3° Gr. A.–Martuba (Libya)–Spring 1942
101° Gr. A.–El Alamein Area–Fall 1942
5° St. A.–101° Gr. A. El Nofilia (Libya)–Nov. 1942
15° St. A.–Sorman (Libya)–Nov. 1942

The Spad XIII C.1

SPAD XIII, Escadrille SPA 48, flown by Capitaine Armand de Turenne. Serial unknown.

SPA 48 Motto 'Chant et Combat'.

France.

SPAD XIII, No. 23 Squadron, Royal Flying Corps.

B3479

△N

RFC.

SPAD XIII, Aviation Militaire Belge.

XIII
Sp
39

Belgium.

SPAD XIII, flown by Major Francesco Barraca, Italian Air Force.

94th Aero Squadron.

'Cavallino Rampante'.
insignia of Maj. Francesco Barraca.

Italy. The colours were sometimes reversed.

SPAD XIII, 94th Aero Squadron, American Expeditionary Force, U.S. Air Service, flown by Captain E. V. Rickenbacker.

XIII
S 4523

1

AEF.

SPAD XIII, 17th Pursuit Squadron, U.S. Army Air Service, Selfridge Field, Michigan.

8

17th Pursuit Squadron.

USAAS.

SPAD XIII, Czechoslovakian Air Force.

Poland.

Czechoslovakia.

SPAD XIII, Polish Air Force.

5

Note: Czechoslovakia, both the flag and roundel insignia were used in six positions during the period of time the SPAD was in service.

WARD.

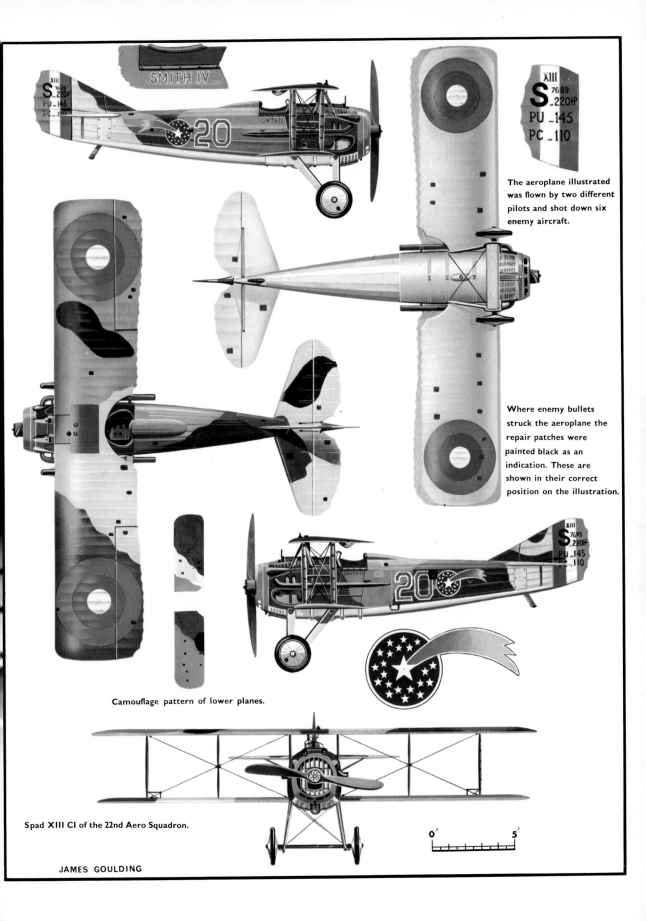

SMITH IV

XIII
S 7689 220HP
PU -145
PC -110

The aeroplane illustrated was flown by two different pilots and shot down six enemy aircraft.

Where enemy bullets struck the aeroplane the repair patches were painted black as an indication. These are shown in their correct position on the illustration.

XIII
S 76PS 220HP
PU -145
-110

Camouflage pattern of lower planes.

Spad XIII CI of the 22nd Aero Squadron.

0'   5'

JAMES GOULDING

The SPAD XIII C.1

by C. F. Andrews

SPAD XIII of the 22nd Aero Squadron, American Army, 1918. (Photo: P. R. Molt)

ONE of the most illustrious families of single-seat fighters of the Great War of 1914–1918 and one that has never received the acclaim accorded to others in the same class, is that represented by the initials SPAD. Much has been written about the S.E.5s, the Fokkers, the Sopwiths and the Nieuports, but no really comprehensive account of the technical merits of the SPAD, or of its service, has yet appeared in a single publication together with an appreciation of its remarkable engine—the Hispano-Suiza. This *Profile*, therefore, sets out to remedy the deficiency and deals with the final development in which the aeroplane went into service in World War I—the SPAD XIII C.1. The designation S.XIII has not been used in this narative as "S" was merely an abbreviation of SPAD, convenient for use on drawings, documents and on aircraft rudders. Similarly SPA identified a SPAD fighter *Escadrille*.

Considerable research has unearthed the probable reasons why the SPAD fighter has tended to be largely ignored by writers. The French method of recording aviation history, by glorifying their leading airmen has been, so it seems, at the expense of the aircraft they flew. The "Ace" system was introduced in the First World War with typical Gallic flair in recognising the great value, to combatant and national morale, of publicising the numbers of victories scored by the leading French fighter pilots. The Germans followed suit and only official British policy was against this practice.

Similarly the crack fighter squadrons of the air arm of the French Army (*L'Armeé de l'Air*—the French Air Force—came later) were also lionised at the expense of the rest of their flying comrades in arms. Hence the famous *Cigognes* Group consisted of five *Escadrilles* (squadrons) all wearing the *Cigogne* (stork) insignia on their aircraft in varying forms. They were indeed in French eyes the veritable aristocrats of the air war. All this hero worship had the effect of obscuring the merits of their mounts, the Moranes, Nieuports and SPADs, which served them so well.

A third reason is revealed by examination of French technical and aeronautical publications of the period, and also of published German technical reports on captured Allied aircraft. Security measures were much tighter in France than in Britain because the enemy was sitting on the doorstep, indeed, was in the house for most of the war. Consequently informed French journals such as *Aerophile* rarely published any tangible information on French military aircraft. For some unaccountable reason, there appears to have been no comparative analysis and dissection of the SPAD in German reports such as that presented and published on the S.E.5 reports that were subsequently republished in Allied journals.

True, in the middle months of 1916, a photograph arrived in England on an open postcard which disclosed the existence of a new French tractor biplane with racy lines and a fixed, water-cooled engine, as opposed to the rotary-engined types then much in vogue. Later it became public knowledge that this new fighter was the product of the successors to the former Deperdussin aviation enterprise of pre-war racing and high speed fame.

Founded in 1910, the *Société pour les Appareils Deperdussin* had been taken over in 1914 by the famous pioneer and aircraft constructor Louis Blériot, for Armand Deperdussin, founder of the company bearing his name, had run into serious financial difficulties. Blériot renamed the company the *Société pour Aviation et ses Dérivés*, so retaining the initials SPAD.

The Deperdussin designer, Louis Bechereau, was retained, for he had been responsible for the Deperdussin monoplanes which won the Gordon Bennett and Schneider Trophy contests of 1913.

Head-on view showing the narrow-chord propeller. Below: *Three-quarter rear view shows the aileron bell crank on the bottom of the outer rear strut.*
(Photos: Musée de L'Air)

THE SPADS ARE BORN

With this background of achievement, Bechereau turned his attention in 1915 to an evaluation of the new Hispano-Suiza engine, then undergoing initial trials at Bois-Colombes, the French works of a Spanish company formed in 1904 to produce high-grade motor cars.

The name Hispano-Suiza had already acquired the magic ring analogous to Rolls-Royce and Napier in the motor car world at that time. The early success of the enterprise has been achieved entirely through the genius of its founder and chief designer, Marc Birkigt, a Swiss engineer, born in 1878. He was a Senior Fellow of the College of Arts and Sciences of Geneva.

Bechereau realised that the rotary, air-cooled aero engine as exemplified by the French Gnome, Le Rhône and Clerget types, would rapidly reach its limit of development, largely because of centrifugal and gyroscopic forces becoming excessive in bigger and more powerful types. A fixed, water-cooled engine of indigenous French production

appealed to him as a basis on which to design a fighter; an engine providing at least 150 h.p. and more as development proceeded.

At around the same period German designers had also realised that however successful their Fokker monoplane had been with its rotary engine and fixed machine gun firing through its propeller with the aid of a synchronising gear, its days were numbered on performance alone. They, therefore, turned their attention to fixed engined fighters, for Germany was much more advanced than the Allies in the development of water-cooled engines, which consisted mainly of in-line, six cylinder arrangements. The appearance on the Western Front of the Albatros D.I with a 160-h.p. Mercedes or Benz in-line engine in August 1916, at once restored air supremacy to the Germans, which they had lost to the Allied fighters during the great battle of the Somme in July 1916.

This adverse turn of the tide against the Allies proved Bechereau's design concept to be right, and as the prototype SPAD VII had flown the previous

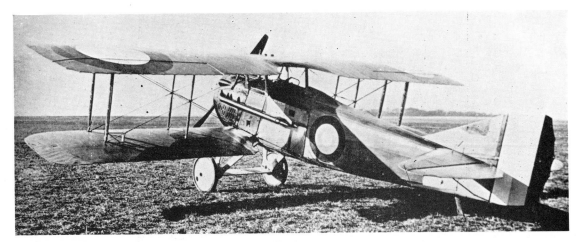

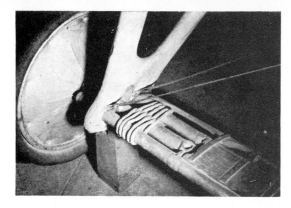

May in the hands of Bequet, the *Escadrilles* were able to begin re-equipping with SPADS in the Autumn of 1916, just in time to counter the Albatros threat. Britain, too, was turning to the fixed-engine formula, and had already evaluated the Hispano in a B.E.2d flying test bed in March and April 1916 at the Royal Aircraft Factory. The first S.E.5, designed around the new engine, was flown by Major Frank Gooden at Farnborough at the end of the year.

So, two new Allied fighters, the SPAD and the S.E.5, powered with the same type of liquid-cooled engine, entered the war and both survived to the end in developed variants—the SPAD XIII and the S.E.5a. Produced in large numbers by outside contractors, these fighters appeared in massive formation over the Western Front in 1918, assuming at once mastery of the skies. This superior air power did exert a decisive influence on the result of the war—victory for the Allies.

THE HISPANO ENGINE

Much of the credit for this reversal of fortunes must go to the inspiration of Marc Birkigt, designer of the Hispano engine, which was of advanced conception for its day. Its mechanical details differed little basically from today's high efficiency piston engines. The Hispano introduced monobloc aluminium cylinders with screwed-in steel liners, and the big ends and main bearings were lined with anti-friction metal. Overhead camshafts operated the large overhead valves, and the small ends of the machined connecting rods, carrying the gudgeon pins, were fed with a share of the forced lubrication generally incorporated in the design.

The Hispano was a broad "Vee" type of eight cylinders, with the two blocks set at 90-degrees, this providing ample space for the Claudel carburettor and induction system. Dual ignition was fitted; two magnetos were located at the rear of the engine (the camshaft driving-shafts being at the front), each cylinder having duplicated sparking plugs. The Hispano had a favourable weight/power ratio, which was a great improvement on the figures of water-cooled engines up to the time of its inception, and this figure improved as the power of the unit was increased by progressive development.

L. Bechereau and H. P. Folland (the latter was largely responsible for the S.E.5) proceeded with

Top of page: *Details of bungee undercarriage springing and cabane struts. The diagonal front strut was a production modification, added for strength.*

Left: *S.XIII receiving its final coats of dope and camouflage markings in the Levasseur factory.*
(Photo: Musée de L'Air

their individual designs around the Hispano according to the latest practice in the state of the art in their respective countries. The SPAD VII was, therefore, a typically French aeroplane while the S.E.5, which went into service in April 1917, some six months after the SPAD, was a design embodying straightforward engineering highly suitable for mass production by outside contractors. Both types made their impact felt in action, and their developments, the S.E.5a and SPAD XIII, followed up the initial success by consolidating their reputation during the latter part of 1917 and in 1918.

THE SPAD XIII

The SPAD XIII first flew in early August 1917 and was powered with the 220-h.p. Hispano-Suiza 8BA in its early versions and the 235-h.p. 8BEc in later production aircraft. Both were geared engines and the distinguishing feature of the Mark XIII was the opposite rotation of its propeller to that of the earlier Mark VII. Some trouble was encountered with the gearing in the Mark 8BA engine, a development of the direct drive 150-h.p. Hispano. The S.E.5a Hispano also suffered the same troubles and Wolseley Motors redesigned the engine into the 200-h.p. direct-drive Wolseley Viper, with high compression and higher revolutions to gain extra power. But Birkigt persevered with the geared version and success was evidently achieved for engine failure in the SPAD XIII was rare.

Following the SPAD XIII's first flight production mounted rapidly and the type soon replaced most of the earlier French fighters, including the SPAD VII as well as the Nieuport 28, in practically all the *Escadrilles*. The chief differences which distinguished the Mark XIII from its family predecessor

were the increased size of the aeroplane, its bulkier engine installation and cowling, the tapered chord ailerons and rounded tailplane tips. Twin Vickers machine-guns mounted on top of the front fuselage in front of the pilot replaced the single Vickers of the SPAD VII. The fin and rudder were also larger.

THE XIII DESCRIBED

Construction of both the SPAD VII and XIII was conventional, apart from the unique feature of interposing tie struts half-way along the wing span, to prevent the somewhat acutely-angled flying and landing brace wires from whipping and chafing in flight. This gave the SPAD the appearance of a two-bay biplane whereas, apart from the recognition aspect, it was in fact a single bay. The aspect ratio of the SPAD was greater than that of the S.E.5, and this was one aerodynamic factor which promoted the high rate of climb of the French aeroplane and the superior manoeuvrability of the British machine. Another was the high-lift wing section of the SPAD which, with ample undercamber, differed from the R.A.F. 15 section of the S.E.5, which had been developed as a high speed aerofoil, as air speeds were understood at that time.

Because of these differences in wing section the S.E.5 handled easily during aerobatics and was more stable in flight, two attributes which gave the aircraft an edge over its adversaries in the swirling dog fights. The SPAD climbed to fighting altitude faster than its British partner, and this characteristic enabled it to meet the German machines with power in hand. Evidence shows that these differences had little effect on the victory/loss ratio of both machines, and together they swept the German fighters from the skies. The SPAD was tricky to handle at low

Many and varied were the colour schemes of the famous "Hat in the Ring", 94th Aero Squadron, of the World War I period, as can be seen by these photographs. Top, *left to right: Black and white stripes; Lt. W. Palmer's aircraft in red and blue diamonds on white background.* Below, *left to right: Blue on white; Lt. J. M. Jeffers' red, white and blue S.XIII.*

Left to right: *Line-up of 94th Squadron's S.XIIIs; Lt. S. Kaye's SPAD. White wings, blue fuselage and fin covered overall with red and blue spots.* Below, left to right: *White S.XIII with green shamrocks and stripes; Lt. Outcault's SPAD.*

speeds and had to be flown on to the ground during landing with the engine power on, unlike the S.E.5 which could be "floated" on.

Another quality of the SPAD was its ability to dive at a higher rate than most, if not all, of its contemporaries, Allied or German. There was no fear of wings falling off or wing covering stripping, as happened to other types. The SPAD design of Bechereau was notable for its robust construction, a desirable attribute of a combat aeroplane, particularly a fighter which in those days of massive dog fights was thrown all over the sky, performing gyrations quite unknown in the Second World War.

The SPAD XIII construction followed general prevailing practice, that is, a wire-braced biplane with a box-section fuselage carrying the engine at the front and a tail at the rear in a structure of wooden members with metal joint fittings. The fuselage comprised four spruce longerons with spruce struts and cross-members, of square section and braced with heavy gauge piano wire, pulled tight and wrapped around thimbles at each end where they were attached to the wiring plates at the joints. This method had been discarded by British manufacturers, who used swaged steel tie rods with screwed ends attached to the wiring plates by machined fork ends and pins.

Similarly, the flying and landing wires of the SPAD were of wire cable, while British aeroplanes utilised rolled, streamlined section "Rafwires"* as typified by the S.E.5. The engine bearers of the SPAD were also quite unlike those of the S.E.5, the latter having spindled ash beams supported by thick plywood transverse bulkheads, the former featuring comparatively thin walnut panels standing vertically on their edges at the width of the engine, to which they were attached through steel angle brackets screwed to the bearers and bolted

through the crankcase bearer feet. The engine bearers also continued into the cockpit to support the pilot's seat.

The transverse bulkheads were of heavy gauge sheet steel punctured with lightening holes, two forward and a third aft at the junction of the front of the fuselage longerons. The rear bulkhead was in three sections, as the front centre wing struts were also located at this point in addition to, at the bottom, the top of the front undercarriage struts.

Made as a one-piece structure (as in the Sopwith Camel) the upper wing had hollow box-section spars made in short sections united by scarf-joints bandaged with linen strip and doped, presumably because long runs of spruce were unobtainable in France. The wing ribs had webs of plywood with spruce capping strips, and the internal bracing was piano wire.

Lower wings were attached to the bottom of the fuselage by the spar ends, which mated into duralumin sockets set in the lower longerons, thickened locally in cross-section. The leading edges of all surfaces were spruce members and the trailing edges were of wire. The latter method was characteristic of the SPAD and other French aircraft of the time, and when the surfaces were covered with fabric and dope tautened a scalloped effect was produced along the trailing edges.

The trapezium-shaped stabiliser was attached to the rear fuselage by four bolts, but not provision was made for tailplane incidence trimming in flight. The rudder and elevators were hinged with eyebolts and steel rods. Undercarriage legs were carved in one piece from laminated poplar sheets glued together under pressure and the axle was articulated at the centre, the wheels being sprung by the conventional "bungee" elastic cord, as was the steel-shoed wooden tailskid.

A car type nose radiator of an approximate circular shape with vertical "venetian" blind type

* *Devised by the Royal Aircraft Factory, hence the designation.*

shutters for temperature control, dictated the cross-section of the fuselage. This merged gradually into the vertical knife edge at the sternpost, a geometry followed with the aid of light fairings on the main box structure sides. Fuel was carried in under-belly tanks in the front fuselage, and was lifted to the service tank in the centre of the upper wing by an engine-driven pump. Engine-driven pumps also supplied oil under pressure to the engine and circulated water to the radiator from a header tank, also located in the upper wing.

On the SPAD XIII the main interplane struts were of duralumin tube faired to a streamline section with spruce mouldings. Ailerons were fitted to the upper wing and were operated through a system of tubular push rods via the thickened longerons at the bottom rear spar junctions, and thence through the lower wings to the vertical push rods behind the rear outboard struts to levers on the aileron front spars. The curious tubular bell cranks at the bottoms of the rear struts were the moving links between the enclosed horizontal push rods in the lower wings and the exposed vertical push rods.

Emblem of the 13th Aero Squadron.

Above: *S.XIII of the 91st Aero Squadron, motif, knight chasing a devil.* Below: *S.XIII of the 213th Aero Squadron.*

Capt. R. Soubiran, C.O. of the 103rd Aero Squadron, with his S.XIII. Below: *S.XIIIs of the 95th Aero Squadron.*

THE SPAD IN ACTION

The story of the war in the air as waged by the French fighters in 1914–1918 has been told through the deeds of the flying aces. Georges Guynemer was the first of these to achieve national fame, and he was the first French ace to fall while heading the table of victories. The SPAD XIII was only just entering service when he failed to return from an engagement over Poelcapelle in Flanders. He is known to have been flying one of the latest SPAD XIIIs. Although *Le Grand Chasseur* (the Great Fighter) had gone, other champions had arisen from the legion of French fighter pilots who flew SPADS.

Highest scoring ace of the Allies was René Fonck with a tally of 75 victories at the end of the war. He, like James McCudden the British ace, was a firm believer in markmanship and also took pains to perfect his aim by ground practice. But he could not have achieved his fantastic success in action had he not been mounted on such a steady gun platform as the SPAD. Included in his score were two sixes in one day, with numerous doubles and trebles.

On 9th May 1918, he was flying his SPAD XIII on morning patrol over the Somme sector of the Front when he encountered an enemy two-seat reconnaissance aircraft and two escorting Albatros fighters. Varying times have been quoted for his rapid despatch of all three, but it was certainly a matter of minutes, or even seconds, and their wreckage was found within 400 yards of each other. During evening patrol the same day, Fonck accounted

Striped S.XIII of the 138th Aero Squadron. Note stars on coloured fin, rudder, tailplane, elevators and cowling. Above: *S.XIII of the 213th Aero Squadron.*

Left and right: *Stork Emblem of the Escadrille SPA 3; personal emblem of Nungesser.*

for another two-seater and its two escorting Fokkers, presumably D.VIIs. All were flying in large formations of enemy fighters. Fonck was noted for his extreme economy of ammunition and on this occasion his expenditure averaged nine rounds for each victory. The second occasion he scored six in one day was on 26th September, when he shot down four Fokker D.VIIs, one Albatros D.V and a two-seater.

Third in the honours list of French aces was Charles Nungesser with 45 victories, mostly on SPADs. He was of the Albert Ball type with a complete disregard for danger and was in and out of hospital on numerous occasions. Many of his victories were obtained when flying SPAD VIIs or XIIs, and it speaks well for their sturdy structure that they hung together despite tremendous battle damage.

The fourth ace in the French ranking was Georges Madon with 41 victories. He combined the deadly marksmanship of Fonck with the persistence of Nungesser, pressing home his attacks just short of ramming his opponents. Madon's highest rate of scoring was when mounted on a SPAD XIII. One of the *Cigognes* who became a really skilled SPAD operator, both with the Mark VII and Mark XIII, was Albert Deullin whose 20 victories were scored in some of the hottest fighting of the whole war, notably in Flanders, on the Somme and over Soissons. In 1918 he was in command of a *Groupe de Chasse* flying SPAD XIIIs in the fierce and decisive battles of Château Thierry and St. Mihiel. Others who gained more than usual distinction of the SPAD XIII were Maurice Boyeau (35 victories), Michel Coiffard (34), and Armand Pinsard (27).

FOREIGN SPADS

Although the air service of the American Expeditionary Force saw action in World War I for seven months only, it made an impact on the air fighting and in so doing laid the foundations of the American Air Force. A number of Americans had indeed flown with the Allied Forces before the U.S. entered the conflict, notably with the *Escadrille Lafayette.* Most of the A.E.F. aircraft were obtained from Britain or France as their own were not up to battle standard at that time. Nearly all the fighters were in fact SPAD XIIIs, for the Nieuport 28 was discarded after a short while and replaced by the SPAD. Of the 893 SPAD XIIIs acquired by the A.E.F. after February 1918, 435 were shipped to the U.S.A. after the Armistice and most were re-engined with the American-built 220 h.p. Wright-Hispano. With this engine, however, the performance of the SPAD fell away, as shown in the specification on page 204. The leading American fighter aces who used SPAD XIIIs for most of their service flying were Edward Rickenbacker, Raoul Lufbery and Frank Luke.

In the Italian air services, 11 *Squadriglie* (squadrons) were equipped with SPAD XIIIs, although the Italian pilots seemed to prefer the French Hanriot HD.1, a much less powerful but more manoeuvrable aeroplane which probably suited their style of fighting in the mountainous flying terrain. The leading Italian ace, Francesco Barracca, with 34 victories, scored most of these with his SPAD VII and SPAD XIII. One Belgian *Escadrille* only, the 10th, used the SPAD XIII and one Belgian ace, Edmond Thieffry, won fame on the type. R.F.C. Squadrons Nos. 19 and 35 were equipped with the SPAD VII but no use appears to have been made

S.XIII of the Escadrille SPA 48.

59

SPAD XIII in Czechoslovakian national insignia.

(Photo: Pavel Vancura)

of the Mark XIII, although a footnote in the British official history of the War in the Air seems to indicate that 19 Squadron may have had them for a short while, pending delivery of British types.

CAMOUFLAGE SCHEMES

The variations of French camouflage patterns during 1917 and 1918 have been somewhat obscure. When colour protection was adopted early in the war as protection against air observation a comparatively simple scheme of large irregular patches of green and brown was adopted, with grey nose and undercarriage, under-surfaces being left natural dope and varnish finish. This form persisted until 1917 was well advanced, when a multi-colour scheme of irregular patches, usually five colours, was introduced, thus copying the German example of multi-colour but not the pattern.

The SPAD XIII shown in the five-view drawing is one supplied to the Americans finished in a 1918 colour scheme and it went to the 22nd Pursuit Squadron. It won six victories, hence the bullet hole black patches! It is now in the National Air Museum in Washington, D.C. The SPAD XIII in *Le Musée de L'Air* at Chalais-Meudon near Paris is painted in a bizarre colour scheme which was either an interim scheme or perhaps the creation of a painter-rigger in the field! It is certainly the original scheme as it was faithfully copied when the aircraft was restored and repainted some while ago, according to the Musée authorities, to whom thanks are due for valued assistance in the compiling of this *Profile*.

The SPAD XIII remained in service in the French forces until 1923, 37 were delivered to Belgium after the Armistice of November 1918, and the 435 airframes which went to the United States Army Air Corps were fitted with Wright engines. Other countries including Japan bought SPAD XIIIs in small numbers for their emergent air forces after the war.

Above: *S.XIII of the Italian Air Force.* Below: *Japanese S.XIII.*

Specification

Span : 26 ft. 3¾ in. (both wings in later production).
Length : 20 ft. 4 in. Height 7 ft. 6½ in.
Wing Details : Chord (upper) 4 ft. 7⅛ in. (lower) 4 ft. 5 in.
Gap 3 ft. 10½ in. Stagger 1½ degrees. Incidence (upper) 1¼ degrees (lower) 1 degree. Sweepback nil. Dihedral nil. Area 227 sq. ft. Loading 8 lb./sq. ft.
Power Unit : 220 h.p. Hispano-Suiza 8BA (1917). 235 h.p. Hispano-Suiza 8BEc (1918).
Power Loading : 8·2 lb./h.p.
Fuel Capacity : 30 gall. petrol. Oil Capacity 4½ gall.
Armament : 2 Vickers ·303 fixed machine guns.
Weights : (official French figures). Empty 1,245 lb. Petrol, oil, water 242 lb. Military load (incl. pilot) 320 lb. Total 1,807 lb.
Performance (Report No. 5)
Aeronautique Militaire, Ministre de la Guerre, 1917

		Climb	Speed	
Metres	Feet	(mins.)	km.hr.	m.p.h.
500	1,640	0·55	—	—
1,000	3,281	1·55	—	—
2,000	6,562	4·40	215	133·5
3,000	9,843	7·50	214	132·8
4,000	13,124	12·10	209	129·8
5,000	16,405	18·30	203	126·1

(Note: With 8BA engine—with 8BEc highest speed 138 m.p.h.)
Duration : 2 hours. Range 200–250 miles according to operational sortie.
Performance of American Air Corps SPAD XIII with 220 h.p. Wright-Hispano at A.U.W. of 2,036 lb. Speed at sea level 131·5 m.p.h. Speed at 6,500 ft. 128·0 m.p.h. Climb to 6,500 ft. 6·5 mins.
Production : SPAD 1,141, Blériot Aero. 2,300, Bernard 1,750, Kellner 1,280, Nieuport 700, Borel 300, Levasseur 340, Soc. Constr. A.P. 300, A.C.M. de Colombes 361. Total 8,472.

The Hawker Fury I

The Hawker Fury

by Francis K. Mason

Squadron Commander's Aircraft, No. 1 Squadron.

FAME attaches to an aircraft for any of a number of logical reasons: great achievements by its crews, significant technical advances portrayed or great responsibilities vested in large numbers built. The Hawker Fury I of the nineteen-thirties, while certainly heralding a considerable technical step forward, won fame and sentimental admiration for the purity of aerodynamic design according to contemporary standards. As the biplane disappeared from the scene, the Fury remained in mind as the epitome of classic design with in-line engine.

Nub of the Fury's concept lay, as with so many great aircraft, in radical powerplant development. Sydney Camm had, since the mid nineteen-twenties, striven to lead the development of the interceptor through the mediocrity of traditional air-cooled radial and overweight liquid-cooled in-line engines. The Hornbill of 1926, for whose later development he had been responsible, came near to achieving the magic 200 m.p.h. with the unsuitable Rolls-Royce Condor, but nevertheless proved the lie in the belief that fighter speeds could not increase without major aerodynamic advance.

With the advent in 1927 of the Rolls-Royce F.XI, which promised hitherto unapproached power/weight ratios possible with cylinder banks cast in one—replacing separate cylinder castings—Camm embarked on the Hart bomber and a lighter, but related, interceptor. These two designs, together with the Tomtit elementary trainer, represented in the Hawker family a co-ordinated airframe advance incorporating the new fabricated steel and aluminium tubular structure in the fuselage and the dumb-bell wing spars

that were to remain features of all Hawker aircraft until well into World War II.

After Camm's Hawfinch failed in its competition with the Bristol Bulldog (see pages 61-62), Hawkers went ahead with the independent development of an interceptor, using the F.20/27 specification as a guide to Air Staff fighter concepts. The un-named Hawker F.20/27 Mercury-powered interceptor prototype served to illustrate conclusively the inadequacy of current air-cooled radials, but into this design had been incorporated the ability to replace the radial with the F.XIA engine with little alteration to the basic "shape" of the fuselage; thus with the appearance of the in-line prototype, a fairly accurate comparison of speeds could be derived.

This aircraft—the Hawker Hornet—together with the Hart and Tomtit were the sensation of the 1929 Olympia Aero Show, their first public appearance. The Hornet, so named by Hawkers, was first flown by Flt. Lt. P. W. S. ("George") Bulman at Brooklands in March 1929, and although for initial trials the 420-h.p. F.XIA engine was used, when the prototype (registered *J9682*) was delivered for Service evaluation at Martlesham Heath it had been fitted with a 480-h.p. F.XIS.

Despite the fact that the Hornet's concept was entirely unsponsored by Air Ministry Specification or contract, it appearance at Martlesham was regarded by many senior Air Force staff officers as something of a face-saver. The 174-m.p.h. Bulldog fighter had just been adopted and ordered into extensive production, yet the appearance of the 184-m.p.h. Hart bomber brought about a disagreeable state of affairs—

amply demonstrated in the course of the 1930 Air Defence Exercises when the Harts went about their business virtually undisturbed by the fighter defence. But the appearance of the first Hart squadron in 1929 had already forced the Air Staff's hand; *J9682* was purchased for £6,500, placed on Air Ministry charge and the design re-named Fury I. Findings of the Martlesham trials spoke enthusiastically of the aeroplane's advanced features, drawing particular attention to the unexpected degree of accessibility to the finely cowled engine (now named the Kestrel IIS).

In the air the Fury set entirely new standards with its high rate of climb (reaching 10,000 feet in 4 minutes 25 seconds), fast rate of roll and lightness of control. It was also the first interceptor to serve with the R.A.F. capable of more than 200 m.p.h., its top speed being 207 m.p.h. at 14,000 feet. So impressed with the prototype were the Service pilots that Air Ministry Specification 13/20 was drafted about the design. This featured the standard steel and aluminium tubular structure built up on the Warren principle as a rectangular box section faired to oval by superimposed decking stringers. The unequal span, single-bay wings were mounted with considerable stagger and were built up on metal dumb-bell spars and spruce ribs, fabric-covered with ailerons on the top wings only. The undercarriage was of the cross-axle Vee type with oleo-rubber shock absorbers. The standard fighter armament of two synchronised Vickers 0·303-inch machine-guns was located in the nose top decking with ammunition supply of 600 rounds per gun.

The Kestrel IIS engine, supercharged to give 525 b.h.p. at 14,000 feet, drove a wooden two-blade fixed-pitch Watts propeller; its radiator was situated between the undercarriage legs and was equipped with controllable shutters.

FURIES IN SERVICE

Despite the opening remarks, the Fury I did *not* achieve widespread R.A.F. service. In view of the previous acceptance of the Bulldog, the relatively high cost (£3,900 per aircraft for early production examples, amortising to £3,700 for aircraft built during and after 1933) might well have prevented

Above: *The true Hawker Fury prototype was the Hornet, seen here before purchase by the Air Ministry and without registration J9682.* Left: *Side elevation of the Hornet.*

Side, front and rear views of the first production Hawker Fury I, K1926.

Furies from ever entering production—especially in view of the impending economic slump. The unquestioned superiority of the Fury I, however, prompted the Air Staff to regard the aircraft as the spearhead of Britain's air defence—the equipment of three Squadrons, Nos. 1, 25 and 43, the R.A.F.'s *corps d'elite*.

As a tentative beginning the Air Ministry placed a contract with the H. G. Hawker Engineering Company for 21 Fury I's (*K1926–K1946*) in August 1930, and returned *J9682* to commercial charge. Between then and the end of that year, the Hawker pilots, Bulman and P. E. G. ("Gerry") Sayer, took turns to demonstrate the prototype in Norway, Spain, Yugoslavia and Denmark, while at Kingston and Brooklands tooling got under way to commence Fury production.

Sayer flew the first production Fury from Brooklands on 25th March 1931, and all the 21 R.A.F. machines had taken the air by 15th April. The first squadron chosen to receive these was No. 43—"The Fighting Cocks"—based at Tangmere under the command of Sqdn. Ldr. L. H. Slatter (later Air Marshal Sir Leonard Slatter, K.B.E., C.B., D.S.O., D.F.C.) and 16 aircraft were delivered in May.

Straightway the Service learned of the Fury's aptitude for aerobatics, and no greater exponents in public display techniques lived than the pilots of No. 43. That legendary pilot, Sayer, also flew successive variants of the Fury through scintillating aerobatic displays at the annual Whit Monday Motor Races at Brooklands.

From an operational standpoint, The Fighting Cocks demonstrated in the 1931 Air Defence Exercises their ascendancy over all other defenders, the one Fury squadron achieving more successful interceptions than the entire remaining defences.

Further contracts under Specification 13/20 were placed with Hawker during 1931, the first—for 48 aircraft—being completed in the remarkably short period of eleven weeks. The two squadrons scheduled to receive these were Nos. 1 and 25, but those for the former squadron were delivered to the Air Storage Unit at Cardington for fitting of night flying equipment, with the result that No. 25 (Fighter) Squadron, based at Hawkinge under Sqdn. Ldr. W. E. Bryant, M.B.E., received its Furies before its traditional rival, No. 1.

Conscious that the public spotlight might fall upon his squadron, Bryant set about the systematic training of his pilots in complicated air drill and formation aerobatics, and one of his pilots recalls that it was the C.O.'s favourite pastime to drill the Officers on the parade ground—on bicycles! It has also been said that the official blind eye was invariably turned upon No. 25's ebullience, and countless Station Commanders made complaints to deaf ears after anonymous Furies had indulged in high spirits over—and not high over—their airfields. After all, the Secretary of State for Air, Sir Philip Sassoon, was an honorary member of No. 25.

By the turn of 1931, the famous No. 1 Squadron at Tangmere had completed re-equipment with Fury I's,

A late series Fury I serving with the Royal Air Force College at Cranwell.

and for the next four years an intense rivalry sprang up among the three Squadrons. Certainly therein lay many of the seeds of *esprit* so vitally mature in 1940. The R.A.F. Display at Hendon in June 1933, however, featured the Furies of No. 25 Squadron performing formation aerobatics, the aircraft being linked together by elastic ropes with streamers attached—the entire performance carried out without breaking the ropes. A grim sequel to this fine display came two months later on 7th August when a Horsley of No. 504 (County of Nottingham) Squadron, in summer camp at Hawkinge, struck a disused shed while landing and fell upon a hangar housing No. 25's machines. Both buildings caught fire and, together with the Horsley, whose crew narrowly escaped by falling from their

aircraft to the ground, six Furies were destroyed. It was, however, No. 25 Squadron that won the Air Defence Challenge Trophy for air fighting tactics and gunnery in 1933.

No. 1 Squadron, as air fighting champions in 1934, was chosen in July that year to participate under the command of Wg. Cdr. G. C. Pirie in the Canadian Centennial celebrations at Toronto and, to judge from Press comment, certainly upheld the best traditions of that premier Squadron.

By 1936 Fury I's were being replaced in the newly constituted Fighter Command by Fury II's and most of the older aircraft were withdrawn to second-line duties. Some were delivered to Flying Training Schools, prominent among them being Nos. 3 and 7,

The second production Fury K1927.

and the overseas draft Training Unit, then stationed at Sealand. At least one (and possibly as many as three) late-series Fury I's equipped the Advanced Training Flight at the R.A.F. College, Cranwell.

FURY I'S ABROAD

Foreign interest in the Fury I dated back to the months immediately prior to the appearance of the first R.A.F. Fury I. During the course of demonstrations of the Hornet towards the end of 1930 on the European continent, Yugoslavia displayed active interest in the type and placed an initial order for six aircraft, and these were commenced in the Hawker shops at about the same time as those for the R.A.F. These Yugoslav Furies, temporarily registered *HF1* to *HF6*, were delivered during June 1931, the first having been flown by Bulman on 4th April. The following year Hawker received an order to equip five of the Yugoslav Furies with wheel spats (a feature not adopted by the R.A.F.

until 1936 on the Fury II), and in one such aircraft, Capt. Sintic of the Royal Yugoslav Air Force won the International Alpine Air Race at the Zurich Show, leading the field at an average speed of 201 m.p.h.

The sixth Yugoslav Fury was returned to Brooklands before the end of 1931 for conversion to take the Hispano-Suiza 12 N.B., being flown by Sayer on 27th August. The engine proved unsuitable in the Fury, due to the lower thrust line, and the aircraft was returned to standard in 1933.

Norway, early in 1932, ordered a single Fury for evaluation, powered by an Armstrong-Siddeley Panther IIIA air-cooled radial engine. Registered *401* and first flown by Sayer on 9th September 1932, this one-off example was extensively evaluated at Martlesham Heath on behalf of the Norwegian Government, and although first trials seemed promising, the subsequent verdict of the R.No.A.F. showed the installation to be unsuitable. It appears that *401* displayed a tendency to nose-over while taxiing, the c.g. of the big Panther engine being 9 inches forward

Below: *Persian Fury with Pratt & Whitney Hornet engine and Hamilton 3-blade propeller.* ("*Aeroplane*" photo). Top of page, left: *The first Persian Hornet Fury with the standard Watts wooden propeller.* Right: *Head-on view of the Persian Fury with Hamilton 3-blade propeller.*

An early photograph of the Intermediate Fury, G-ABSE.

The High Speed Fury with Kestrel VI S engine, tapered wing and Vee interplane struts. ("*Flight*" photo)

of that of the Kestrel. At one time *401* was also flown in Norway on a ski undercarriage.

Perhaps the most interesting variant of the Fury I was that ordered by the Persian Government in January 1933. This country had acquired an extensive agreement with Pratt & Whitney for the purchase and servicing of the big Hornet radial engine. The initial order was for sixteen Hornet Furies to be equipped with the variable-pitch three-blade Hamilton propeller; for purposes of initial evaluation, however, and during most of the initial trials at Brooklands, large coarse-pitch wooden Watts propellers were used. Once again nose-heaviness resulted in taxiing difficulties but, after a taxiing accident at Martlesham, tail ballasting proved an adequate remedy—without significant performance penalty.

Despite fast accumulated experience with the Hornet engine in the Persian Furies, the complicated cooling shutter arrangement in front of the cylinders was found to be unreliable and was discarded, with the result that the engine life in the tropics was considerably reduced. Thus by 1934 the need for further Furies in Persia had arisen and a provisional order for about thirty Furies was placed with Hawker Aircraft Ltd. In the meantime, however, the Bristol Mercury had emerged as a reliable engine and already an alternative installation had been evolved at Kingston. The follow-up order by the Persian Government was, therefore, reduced and almost all the original Hornet Furies returned for conversion to the British radial.

Powered now by the Mercury, the new and refurbished Persian Furies were undoubtedly attractive little fighters, and on return to their parent Air Force embarked on a long and interesting career. Persian Mercury Furies visited almost every country in the Middle East and North Africa between 1935 and 1938, and later came to be flown by pilots of the *Regia Aeronautica*. As late as 1942, one squadron of about

The sole Norwegian Panther Fury.

ten aircraft was based at Meherabad in the remote province of Ustan Cheharum—poised to repel any infiltration by the German forces through the Caucasus to the Persian oil fields. During their spell of duty, they were joined by No. 74 (Fighter) Squadron of the R.A.F., and at least one of the Mercury Furies was equipped with a replacement Hurricane tailwheel!

The last known existence of a Persian Fury was at

Furies of No. 1 (Fighter) Squadron formate in characteristic fashion. ("*Flight*" photo)

Habbaniyah in 1948 where, minus engine, it was used to exercise the station fire crews.

Having recently acquired licence rights for the manufacture of Hispano-Suiza engines, and in anticipation of putting into effect these rights, the Yugoslav Government persisted in its efforts to match its Furies with various Hispano engines and there were reports that increased orders were to be placed with Hawker towards the end of 1933. The original Hispano Fury, *HF3* was returned to Brooklands once more and made ready for delivery of a new Hispano, but in the event the engine was delayed for another two years; in the meantime, as something of a privately-sponsored insurance against failure of the Hispano, Camm proposed a conversion to take the Lorraine Petrel 720-h.p. H frs twelve-cylinder in-line engine and this installation did in fact fly in 1934. Stressing problems prevented this from being accepted as standard.

One other country purchased Fury I's from the parent company. In November 1933 the Portuguese Government ordered three Fury I's with Kestrel IIS engines de-rated to give longer patrol endurance, and the first of these, *50*, was flown on 28th May 1934. The following month all three were delivered by air to the Portuguese Army Air Service and participated in the Lisbon Aero Shows of 1935 and 1936. The last surviving example is believed to have been shot down at sea during the Spanish Civil War late in 1937.

FURY I DEVELOPMENTS

Fury deliveries abroad continued almost up to the outbreak of World War II though after 1936 such variants as the Yugoslav and Spanish Hispano Fury should more accurately be classified as Mark II derivatives.

On the other hand the Fury I underwent active development between 1932 and 1935 in preparation for the R.A.F.'s Mark II and this development, carried out in standard or modified Mark I airframes is logically covered here.

It was the appearance of the Fury I on Air Ministry charge and the results of the Martlesham evaluation in 1930 that demonstrated the potential realism of the Air Staff Specification F.7/30. For some months previously some members of the Air Staff had sought a formula by which to break the bounds of the accepted interceptor limits containing a speed bracket between 160 and 200 m.p.h., the slavish adherence to an armament of two synchronised rifle-calibre machine guns and specialist day fighter capabilities. In its original draft form, without being too specific, F.7/30 sought to expand these limits. With the appearance of the Fury and the Kestrel IIS engine, the speed limit appeared to have been raised.

Camm, therefore, realised that should the early promise of increased power from the Kestrel materialise, only relatively limited attention to the airframe would enable the Fury to carry greater armament without sacrifice in performance. With this in mind, the manufacturers financed the construction of two airframes, the first to serve the dual purpose of company demonstrator and limited trial installation aircraft. Registered *G-ABSE*, the Intermediate Fury was flown by Sayer on 13th April, 1932 with a standard Kestrel IIS, and within a month was being used to flight test the wheel spats specified for the Yugoslav Fury.

As successive drafts of F.7/30 materialised, so did insistence on the use of the Rolls-Royce Goshawk steam-cooled engine. From the outset most British airframe designers were sceptical of the benefits of steam-cooling in a fighter, and Camm had already gained some experience with the vagaries of a steam-cooled Kestrel in a Hart test-bed. Nevertheless use of the Goshawk steadily became mandatory in the Specification and Hawker set about preparation for this engine in the Fury. By the end of 1932 *G-ABSE* had flown with a special Kestrel IVS to test the supercharger for the Goshawk, and in 1933 was fitted successively with Goshawk III, Kestrel VI and Kestrel VIS (Special). It is believed that *G-ABSE* soldiered on for many years from hack job to hack

Hispano-powered Fury.

The first Yugoslav Fury photographed early in 1931.

job, eventually finding its way on to Air Ministry Charge just prior to the Second World War.

While *G-ABSE* was clearly capable of only limited development work for F.7/30 (being only stressed for a maximum diving speed of 270 m.p.h.), the second P.V. prototype commenced by Hawker was stressed for terminal velocity dives of 360 m.p.h., with an increased proportion of steel primary structure in the fuselage. So expensive did this prototype threaten to become that its birth was only assured by part-purchase by the Air Ministry and when first flown on 3rd May 1933 it carried the registration *K3586*. Subsequent estimates of this aeroplane's development and manufacture showed it to have cost more than £12,000. As some justification for this high cost,

Furies of No. 25 Squadron.

("*Flight*" photo)

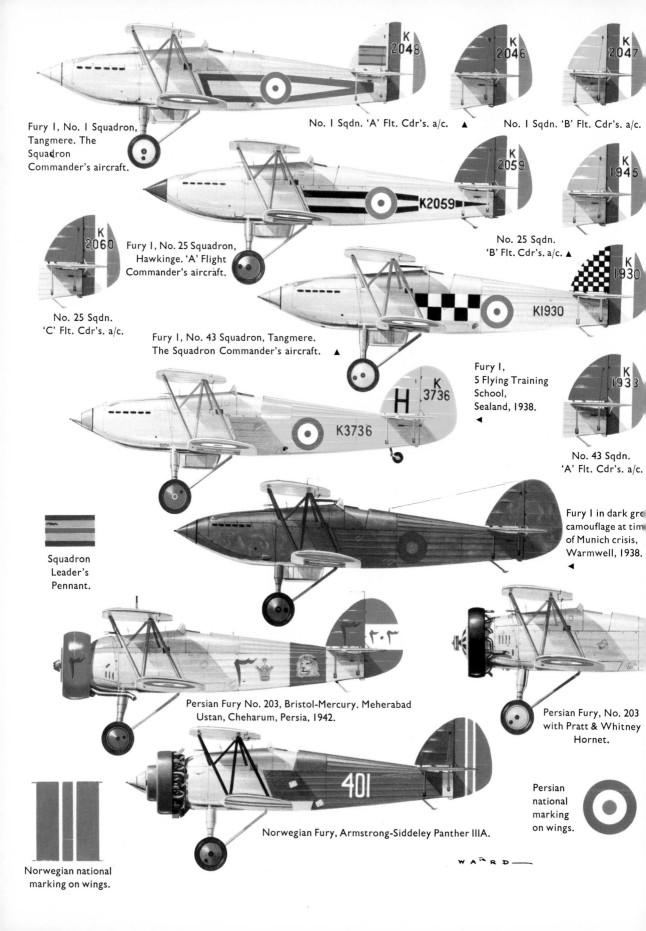

Fury I, No. 1 Squadron, Tangmere. The Squadron Commander's aircraft.

No. 1 Sqdn. 'A' Flt. Cdr's. a/c. ▲

No. 1 Sqdn. 'B' Flt. Cdr's. a/c.

Fury I, No. 25 Squadron, Hawkinge. 'A' Flight Commander's aircraft.

No. 25 Sqdn. 'B' Flt. Cdr's. a/c. ▲

No. 25 Sqdn. 'C' Flt. Cdr's. a/c.

Fury I, No. 43 Squadron, Tangmere. The Squadron Commander's aircraft. ▲

Fury I, 5 Flying Training School, Sealand, 1938. ◄

No. 43 Sqdn. 'A' Flt. Cdr's. a/c.

Squadron Leader's Pennant.

Fury I in dark green camouflage at time of Munich crisis, Warmwell, 1938. ◄

Persian Fury No. 203, Bristol-Mercury. Meherabad Ustan, Cheharum, Persia, 1942.

Persian Fury, No. 203 with Pratt & Whitney Hornet.

Persian national marking on wings.

Norwegian Fury, Armstrong-Siddeley Panther IIIA.

Norwegian national marking on wings.

WARD

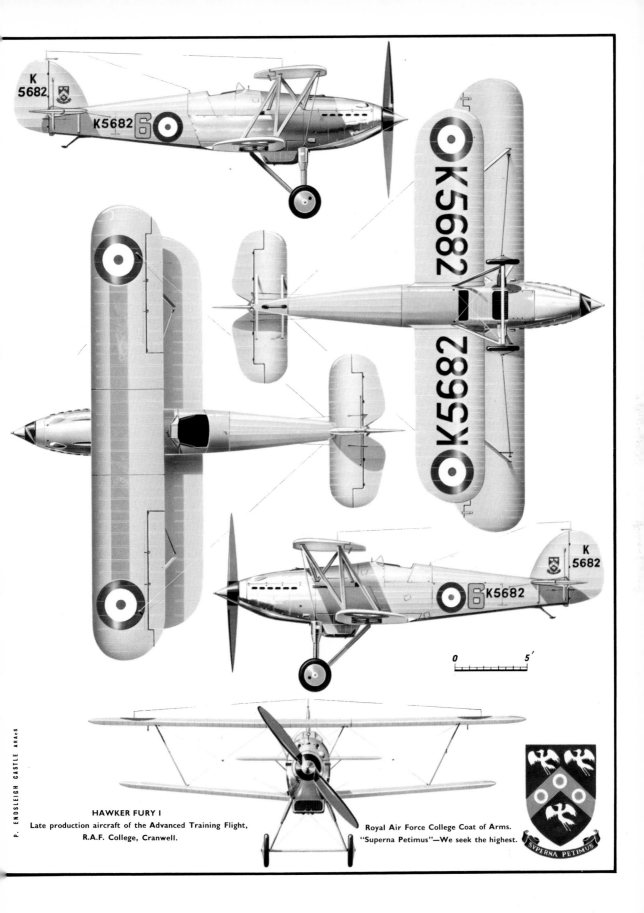

HAWKER FURY I
Late production aircraft of the Advanced Training Flight,
R.A.F. College, Cranwell.

Royal Air Force College Coat of Arms.
"Superna Petimus"—We seek the highest.

Fury I, No. 5 Flying Training School, Sealand, 1938.
(Ministry of Defence photo)

The Persian Fury re-engined with a Bristol Mercury engine.
("*Flight*" photo)

Specification F.14/32 had officially been written around it.

Throughout the period 1933-6 *K3586*, known variously as the Super Fury and, more correctly, the High-Speed Fury, amassed a total of over 800 hours test flying, being fitted in turn with a 525-h.p. Kestrel IIS, 600-h.p. Kestrel S, 525-h.p. Kestrel IIIS, 600-h.p. Kestrel VIS (with this engine it underwent handling trials with No. 43 (F) Squadron), 696-h.p. Goshawk III and Goshawk B.41. When fitted with evaporative-cooled engines, *K3586* featured a straight wing with built-in leading edge condensers, but for much of its life a swept-back tapered wing with Vee interplane struts was fitted. In this form *K3586* was credited by a Martlesham report with a top speed of 261 m.p.h. and was flown by Bulman in the S.B.A.C. Display of 1933.

Specification

Powerplant: Standard Mk. 1: 525-h.p. Rolls-Royce Kestrel IIS driving 2-blade Watts wooden propeller. Norwegian Fury: 530-h.p. Armstrong-Siddeley Panther IIIA driving 2-blade Watts propeller. Persian Fury: Either Pratt & Whitney Hornet S2BIG or Bristol Mercury VISP radial engines (Hornet driving 3-blade v.p. Hamilton and Mercury driving Watts 2-blade wooden propeller). Portuguese Fury: 515-h.p. Rolls-Royce Kestrel IIS(S) driving 2-blade Watts propeller. Yugoslav Fury: 525-h.p. Kestrel IIS, Hispano-Suiza 12 NB or Lorraine Petrel H Frs driving 2-blade Watts propeller.
Dimensions: Span (all versions) 30 ft. Length (Kestrel engine) 26 ft. 8 in. Height 10 ft. 2 in. Wing area (all versions) 252 sq. ft.
Weights: Empty (Kestrel engine) 2,623 lb. Loaded (Kestrel engine) 3,490 lb. (Persian Mercury VI), 3,490 lb. (Persian Hornet) 3,590 lb. (Norwegian) 3,575 lb.
Performance: Standard Mk. 1: Maximum speed, 207 m.p.h. at 14,000 ft. Climb, 4 min. 25 sec. to 10,000 ft. Range, 305 miles. Service ceiling, 28,000 feet.
Norwegian Fury: Maximum speed, 202 m.p.h. at 16,500 ft. Climb, 5 min. 40 sec. to 10,000 ft. Range, 310 miles. Service ceiling, 27,800 ft. Persian Hornet Fury: Max. speed, 178 m.p.h. at 6,500 ft. Climb, 4 min. 45 sec. to 10,000 ft. Range, 300 miles. Service ceiling, 26,000 ft. Persian Mercury Fury: Max. speed, 212·5 m.p.h. at 16,000 ft. Climb, 3 min. 55 sec. to 10,000 ft. Range, 310 miles. Service ceiling,

28,800 ft. Portuguese Fury: Max. speed, 169 m.p.h. at 10,000 ft. Climb, 5 min. 42 sec. to 10,000 ft. Range, 340 miles. Service ceiling, 26,500 ft.
Armament: Standard R.A.F. armament of two 0·303 in. Vickers guns with 600 rounds per gun. Foreign Furies were armed with 7·7 mm. Mauser, Colt or Spandau guns. Most aircraft had provision for light bomb racks to carry 25 lb. practice bombs or flares.
Other data: Fuel capacity on all versions was about 50 gallons. Wheel track was 5 ft. 9½ in. with 750 × 125 mm. Palmer wheels and Palmer hydraulic wheelbrakes.

Production

All Fury I's were built by the H. G. Hawker Engineering Co., Ltd. (or Hawker Aircraft Ltd., after July 1933), Kingston and Brooklands, Surrey.
One Hornet prototype, J9682, designed and built to the provisions of Specification F.20/27, under Contract 887063/28.
First Fury I production batch: 21 aircraft, *K1926-K1946.* Contract 40559/30.
Second production batch: 48 aircraft, *K2035-K2082.* Contract 102468/31, to Spec. 13/30.
Third production batch: 15 aircraft, *K2874-K2883, K2899-K2903.* Contract 184968/31, to Spec. 13/30.
Fourth production batch: 13 replacement aircraft, *K3730-K3742.* Contract 252331/33, to Spec. 13/32 with Vickers Mk. III guns.
Fifth production batch: 20 aircraft, *K5662-K5681,* Contract 409396/35, to Spec. 13/32.
Interim (Intermediate) Fury: 1 aircraft, *GABSE.*
Yugoslav Fury Series 1A: Six aircraft, *HF.1-HF.6* under Contract 289711/32.
Norwegian Fury (Panther IIIA) : *401.*
Persian Fury Series 1: 16 aircraft, *201-216,* under Contract 100118/33.
Portuguese Fury 1: Three aircraft, *50-52,* under Contract 331709/34.
Persian Mercury Fury Series II: Six additional aircraft, *217 et seq.* under Contract 366843/34 with Mercury VISP engines.
High-Speed Fury: One aircraft to Interim Spec. F.7/30, *K3586.*

Fury 1's in Service

Representative aircraft with R.A.F. units
No. 1 (F) Squadron, Tangmere: *K1943, K2046* (crashed 26/5/32), *K2881, K5668, K2048* (flown by Wg. Cdr. G. C. Pirie).
No. 25 (F) Squadron, Hawkinge: *K2060, K2877, K5677.*
No. 43 (F) Squadron, Tangmere: *K1935* (later used as Fury II prototype), *K2050, K2882, K3736, K5674.*
No. 3 F.T.S., Grantham: *K2058, K2880, K5680.*
Advanced Training Squadron, Cranwell: *K5682,* (aircraft '6').

Fury I's of No. 43 Squadron.   ("*Flight*" photo)

The Consolidated B-24 Liberator

B-24J Liberator, forming a/c 491st B.G., 8th A.F.

B-24J Liberator, forming a/c 491st B.G., 8th A.F.

B-24J Liberator, 98th B.G., 15th A.F.

B-24J Liberator, 451st B.G., 15th A.F.

B-24J Liberator, 5th A.F.

B-24M Liberator, All Weather Flying Centre

Liberator GR Mk.VI, 120 Sqdn. Coastal Command, R.A.F.

Liberator B Mk.VI, 356 Sqdn. S.E.A.C.

489th B.G.,
8th A.F.

492nd B.G.,
8th A.F.

449th B.G.,
15th A.F.

459th B.G.,
15th A.F.

460th B.G.,
15th A.F.

11th B.G.,
7th A.F.

90th B.G.,
7th A.F.

© WARRD

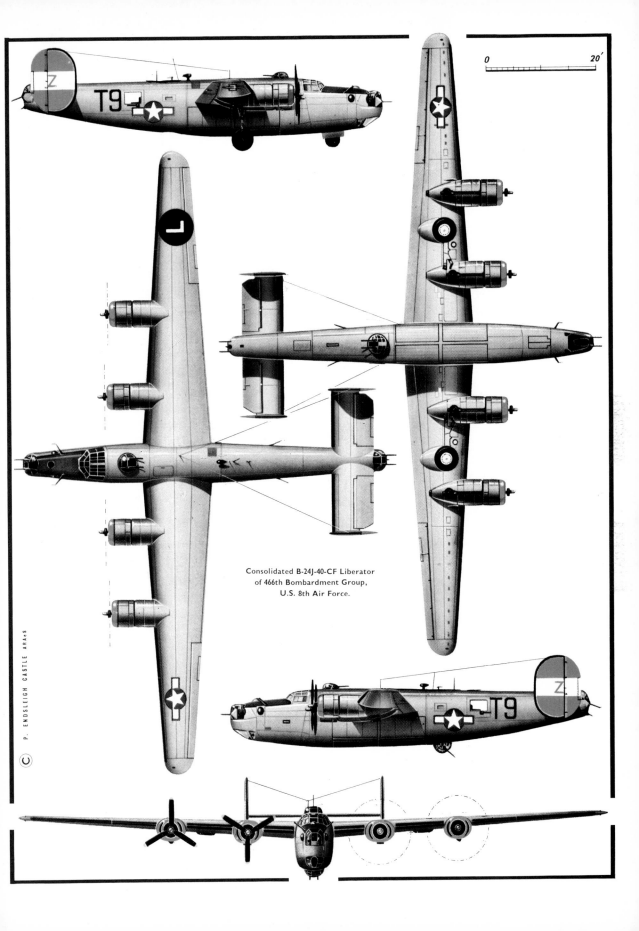

Consolidated B-24J-40-CF Liberator
of 466th Bombardment Group,
U.S. 8th Air Force.

P. ENDSLEIGH CASTLE ARAeS

Ⓒ

The Consolidated B-24J Liberator

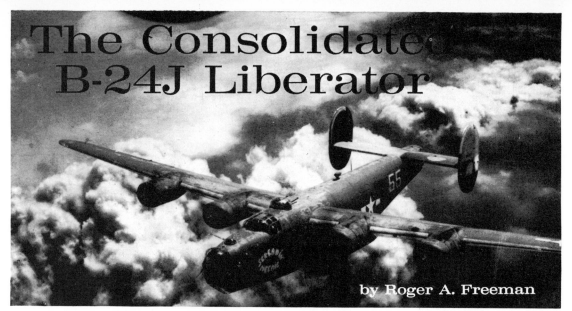

by Roger A. Freeman

B-24J of the 15th Air Force photographed during a raid on 15th July 1944, against Ploesti, Rumania.

THE B-24J was the major model of a bomber produced in greater quantity than any other American military aircraft of the Second World War. First flown in 1939, the Consolidated 32 was a design in keeping with the general American concept of a heavy bomber at that time—fast, multi-engined, multi-place, moderate bomb capacity, high altitude capability and good range.

Consolidated had previously been principally concerned with the design and manufacture of large flying-boats and this, their first large landplane, brought some novel design features to the realm of the heavy bomber. Tricycle undercarriage was one, heralding a future trend; and all the more impressive on the Model 32 because of the massive nature of the sideways retracting main wheels necessitated by the shoulder wing configuration. The nose wheel retracted forward and up, involving a rather complicated action by hinged members which were at first too delicate to withstand very heavy landings. Apart from better visibility afforded pilots in manoeuvring the bomber on the ground, the tricycle undercarriage in this instance also allowed the faster landing and take-off speeds demanded by the high wing loadings. The wing also was unusual, having high aspect ratio and low-drag aerofoil section. The bomb-bay doors were another departure from convention. They were basically dural sheet with fitments to a sliding track running round the underside of the fuselage up towards the wing root. When operated the doors flexed to follow the contours of the fuselage section.

Four neatly-cowled Pratt & Whitney Twin Wasp engines proved to be a prudent choice of power plant, their reliability and durability were to be universally accepted by airmen. In the late nineteen-thirties, tailplanes were often the identifying marks of designers and Consolidated chose to furnish their bomber with large twin fins and rudders of similar shape to those fitted to their PB2Y Navy flying-boat.

It was the general specification, regardless of the innovations, that attracted the attention of both U.S.A.A.C. and British military agencies, with the result that production on an unprecedented scale was ultimately undertaken. A manufacturing pool was officially established in February 1941 and in just over a year five major assembly plants were working on the bomber—U.S.A.A.F. designation B-24, and the name Liberator in that service and the Royal Air Force.

THE EARLY LIBERATORS

The initial production came from Consolidated's own factory at San Diego, California, and these aircraft went mostly to the R.A.F. where they were used for various duties. U.S. warplanes of the 1940–1941 period were generally lacking in many items which the British considered imperative to successful combat operations. Armour, armament, self-sealing fuel tanks and other equipment was, therefore, forthcoming in the first war standard model, the B-24D, which began to roll off the San Diego production lines at an increasing rate early in 1942. Fords commenced production of an equivalent model at their giant Willow Run factory near Detroit (built especially for the task) during that year, while other versions came from Douglas at Tulsa, Oklahoma, and the new Consolidated-Vultee plant at Fort Worth, Texas. (The Consolidated and Vultee aircraft companies merged in March 1943 and later adopted the abbreviated trade name Convair. The B-24, however, continued to be generally referred to as a Consolidated product.) North American also manufactured B-24s commencing in March 1943.

In war operations the B-24 showed great promise, its considerable range, in particular, made it highly valued for ocean patrol and anti-submarine work. As with most warplanes there was need of improvement to meet changes in tactical employment, and where the Liberator had come up against fighter

15th Air Force 24Js attack Theole-sur-Mer, near Cannes, on 12th July 1944. Note markings on upper tailplane surfaces.

opposition nose armament had been found wholly inadequate. The two hand-held 0·50 guns firing through apertures in the bomb aimer's "conservatory" had limited fields of fire which an interceptor could evade in frontal attack. Some local modifications did much to remedy this shortcoming but the Liberator was still considered vulnerable to frontal interception.

NOSE TURRETS MODS

A power-operated turret appeared the obvious solution, and in Australia, Fifth Air Force engineers successfully improvised the marrying of a salvaged hydraulically-operated Consolidated tail turret to the nose section of a B-24D. This, and similar experiments by the Seventh Air Force, led to a regular modification programme for a large pro-

portion of B-24s in the two South West Pacific air forces, the Hawaiian Air Depot installing turrets in the noses of over 200 Liberators during the spring and summer of 1943. Steps were also taken to introduce a nose turret on production machines, the Pacific theatre improvisations going some way to influence the layout of this feature. Alterations were frequently being made to the Liberator specification during the first part of 1943, culminating in new models best distinguished from their predecessors by production nose turrets, but also embodying improved engines, considerably increased ammunition stowage and many other internal changes.

The production turret was the electrically-powered Emerson design, introduced in June 1943 on the Ford production line with their 491st Liberator, and soon after on B-24s from Douglas and Fort Worth. Aircraft from all three plants were designated

Above: *B-24J-150-CO in natural metal finish.*   Below: *An Eighth Air Force B-24J-55-CO of the 93rd Bomber Group.*
(Photo: U.S.A.A.F.)

B-24J-95-COs, 448th Bomb Group, Eighth Air Force. (Photo: U.S.A.A.F.)

B-24H, whereas the introduction of the nose turret on North American's machines brought only a block number change and these Liberators continued to be designated B-24G, as were the first 25 from the factory.

THE 'J' IS IDENTIFIED

With the quickening pace of production it became apparent that the supply of Emerson turrets would be insufficient to meet the demands of all five plants, so San Diego planned to use a Consolidated-designed Motor Products manufactured turret which, like the tail turret, was hydraulically operated but drew its pressure from the main wheel brake accumulators. Distinctively shaped, it served as the chief recognition feature by which the San

Diego Liberators could be distinguished from those of the other factories. Designated B-24J and first appearing in August 1943, this model also differed from the G and H in the matter of nose wheel doors, for whereas those on the J opened inwards (like the B-24D-CO), those on the other models opened outwards. The B-24J also featured a new automatic pilot (C-1 model) and bombsight (M series), revised auxiliary fuel tank transfer system and electronic supercharger regulators.

Early in B-24D production three auxiliary fuel cells had been added in each wing aft of the outer engines to provide a further 450 U.S. gallons additional to the 2,343 gallons total fuel carried. The engines could not be fed directly from the auxiliary tanks, it being necessary to transfer the fuel to main tanks first. The original transfer system was

B-24J Liberator with badly-holed wing moments before it plunged to disaster. (Photo: Imp. War Museum)

Royal Air Force Liberator VI of Eastern Command. (Photo: Imp. War Museum)

such that a lapse on the part of the operator could jeopardise the safety of the aircraft. The revised transfer system in later models, further refined for the B-24J, lessened this danger.

The turbo-superchargers, essential power boosters, were operated via manual controls on the pilots' pedestal in earlier Liberators. With the B-24J electronic control was substituted, worked by a single dial to allow both simpler and smoother operation.

PRODUCTION QUICKENS

During the early months of 1944 the other four plants went over to the production of B-24Js, the change of model designation being accompanied by the fitting of the C-1 auto pilot and M series bombsight and supercharger refinements in the case of Ford, Douglas and North American, while at Fort Worth the Motor Products turret also accompanied the change. In the spring of 1944 both Convair factories went over to the Emerson nose turrets (by the 45th block at Fort Worth and the 190th at San Diego) which was considered superior, and at the same time adapted outward opening nose wheel doors.

With these changes all five factories were producing Liberators that were practically identical in external appearance. Construction methods differed and some components varied; enough to make aircrew and mechanics well aware of the source of a particular machine. Later in the year B-24J-210-COs were fitted with a new form of anti-icing equipment, known as Thermal Ice Preventive System, and utilising hot air piped from the engines to ducting inside the leading edges of wings and tail assembly. This proved superior to the electric/rubber de-icer boot that sometimes failed to prevent ice build-up. (All B-24J-NTs also had this system.)

Efforts to remedy operational shortcomings of the Liberator resulted in the G, H and, subsequently, J models had brought further weight increases to add to those introduced on late D and E models. Since delivery of the first production models for the R.A.F. the empty weight of the Liberator had increased by 8,000 lb. from approximately 30,000 lb. to 38,000 lb. But loaded for combat the bomber could now gross between 50,000 and 70,000 lb., figures at which the gross weight and centre of gravity limits intended by the designers

Coastal Command Liberator Mk. VI of No. 220 Squadron. (Photo: Imp. War Museum)

R.A.F. Liberator Mk. VI of No. 356 Squadron, Cocos Island.   (Photo: Imp. War Museum)

were approached and often exceeded. Performance suffered in these circumstances; there was little reserve power for take-off, and airspeed and rate of climb ranges were limited, and very high rates of fuel consumption were experienced. But, the most undesirable outcome of these weight increases was the alteration in flight characteristics rendering the aircraft less stable, particularly so at high altitude.

The mode of bombing attack practised by the U.S.A.A.F. in its daylight operations involved high altitudes (above 20,000 feet) and tight defensive formations of around twenty aircraft, an environment to which the Liberator had become less and less suited. In consequence the combat altitude of a B-24 formation was often lower than desirable, and collisions due to momentary loss of control were a reality prompting the prescription of less tight formations in adverse conditions.

Weight increase also aggravated the Liberator's chances of making a safe return when battle damaged, particularly if parts of the wing were severed or badly holed. B-24s were often susceptible to superficial wing damage and when this occurred loss of control would rarely see successful recovery. On the other hand, they could, and did, sustain very severe fuselage and tail damage and survive. On some occasions a complete half of the tail assembly was torn from the fuselage yet the aircraft flew on.

Control and stability was particularly poor when the retractable ventral "ball turret" (first introduced on the late D and E models) was in the lowered position, and with the idea of shedding weight U.S.A.A.F. commanders in the South West Pacific ordered its removal and replacement by two manually operated 0·50s firing through a floor hatch. From September 1943 B-24Js sent to that theatre of operations usually had the ball turret removed at modification centres in the U.S. prior to despatch. In Britain too, the ball turret was discarded during the spring of 1944 when sufficient long-range fighters became available for escort and the chances of interception from below were minimised. Subsequent models of the Liberator, the B-24L and M, were further attempts to improve handling qualities by reducing weight, this time by installing lighter rear turrets.

Men who had flown both the early D and J models usually considered the latter inferior from a pilotage viewpoint, the extra weight accentuating the heaviness of controls and sluggish response. There was a tendency for these characteristics to be exaggerated, for pilotage of the Liberator was inevitably judged by comparison to its Boeing counterpart, the B-17 Fortress, an aircraft with few vices and pleasant to fly. The G, H and J Liberators were also unpopular with crews due to the generally ill-fitting nature of the front turrets, and the resultant sub-zero draughts were anything but pleasant.

Making an emergency wheels-up landing in a B-24J could be accomplished quite successfully, although there was a tendency for the nose to dig

Late production B-24J in natural metal finish.   (Photo: R. Ward)

in and break. Ditching was far from easy and often disastrous. The rather flimsy nature of the bomb bay doors was the chief obstacle to success, for they took the first contact with the water and bursting under the pressure immediately swamped the interior of the aircraft. In the Pacific area, where long over-water flights were a regular occurrence, special strengthening formers, to be inserted into the bomb bay when ditching was imminent, were made and carried on many B-24s.

SPECIAL VARIANTS

While the B-24J may not have been the ideal vehicle for use in the U.S.A.A.F.'s high-altitude daylight precision bombing campaign, it was highly regarded elsewhere for its suitability to many forms of operational employment. The R.A.F. held the Liberator in some esteem and considered it by far the best American heavy bomber. The U.S. Navy found the aircraft well suited to the needs of long-range ocean patrol work and acquired 1,174 under the designation PB4Y-1. The majority had front turrets of Erco manufacture and embodied many of the refinements introduced on the B-24 models as production progressed. The U.S.A.A.F., too, had diverse uses for the B-24. A special version was produced for passenger and freight transport under the designation C-87. In both Europe and the East bomber Liberators were occasionally used as cargo transports, the large waist gun windows making handy loading apertures. Late in 1944 about fifty B-24J and L bombers were modified at depots as flying tankers to ferry motor spirit to advancing ground forces in Europe. These Liberators were stripped of armament and turrets, the nose and tail being neatly faired over, and fuel tanks fitted in the bomb bays. Many saw service during April and May 1945 with Troop Carrier Groups of IX T.C. Command.

In the U.K. the 492nd Bomb Group used B-24H and J models for agent and supply dropping missions at night over occupied Europe. Painted black overall these aircraft usually had the front turret removed and the nose faired over, interception directed at that quarter being highly unlikely during darkness. Similar B-24s were used by the 885th B.Sqdn. for the same type of operations in the Mediterranean theatre. The Eighth Air Force in England also had B-24J models in use for night leaflet delivery, radio counter-measures, and long range weather flights, all with special refinements dictated by the mission.

In the South West Pacific a special blind-bombing Liberator squadron was established in August 1943, with the object of seeking out and attacking enemy shipping at night. Fitted with SCR-717B and SCR-729 radars, plus other devices, these Liberators operated very successfully at low altitudes. The work was originally carried out by a provisional squadron (later the 868th B.Sqdn.) attached to the 5th B.G. in the Thirteenth Air Force, and also, later, by the 63rd B.Sqdn., 43rd B.G. of the Fifth Air Force further south-west.

Radar was also installed in PPF B-24Js of the Eighth and Fifteenth Air Forces in Europe and

Above: *"Well Developed", photo-recce variant of the B-24J.*
(Photo: E. Vagi)

Below: *"War Goddess", B-24J (Convair). Early a/c lacked nose wheel doors.*

used for bombing through cloud. This was H2X (the U.S. version of the R.A.F.'s H2S) installed in a retractable fixture in the position formerly occupied by the ball turret. An advanced form of radar that was tested experimentally on B-24J *42-73111*, amongst other types, was AN/APQ 7 "Eagle" with antenna in a 16 ft. wing-shaped housing just aft of the nose wheel.

A photographic reconnaissance version of the B-24 was developed during 1943 specifically to meet the long-range requirements of air forces combating the Japanese. Both H and J models were modified for this purpose. Of the Js, 86 with three nose and three bomb bay camera installations were designated F-7As, and 92 with all six cameras in the bomb bay were F-7Bs. These aircraft were employed operationally by the 6th Photo Recon Group in New Guinea and the Philippines and also by the 8th Photo Recon Group in India.

To meet operational needs in a particular theatre of war a good deal of improvisation was carried out locally on the B-24J, apart from the armament details already mentioned. U.S.A.A.F. bombing operations in the Pacific area, in contrast to those over Europe, frequently required smaller bombs. Seventh Air Force technicians, therefore, modified the bomb racks in their B-24s, doubling the number of stations from twenty to forty. Another modification peculiar to the S.W.P.A. was the removal of de-icing and engine winterisation equipment.

Some Fifteenth Air Force lead planes, carrying the lead bombardier and navigator, had alterations to the nose that allowed both occupants greatly enhanced visibility. The turret was removed and a perspex clad structure substituted that was not unlike the upper half of the nosepiece on the old

B-24D. A single hand-operated gun was incorporated for use by the navigator.

In Britain brightly painted "forming" or "assembly ships" were used as leaders in assembling bomber formations. A few of these were B-24J models with no armament and numerous identification lights set in the top of the fuselage.

SERVICE USE

First U.S.A.A.F. units to equip with production nose-turreted Liberators did so in August 1943, and the following month the first B-24H unit, the 392nd B.G., arrived in the U.K. B-24Js followed soon afterwards, chiefly as replacements to all theatres, including the remote C.B.I., where some joined the India based 7th B.G. in October. Later B-24Js were largely original equipment for seven bomb groups joining the Eighth Air Force, the last of these, the 493rd B.G., becoming operational on D-Day, 6th June 1944. The 494th B.G. assigned to the Seventh Air Force in the Pacific also had B-24Js as initial combat equipment, but did not commence missions against the Japanese until early November 1944.

Peak U.S.A.A.F. inventory of the B-24 was reached in September 1944 with a total of 6,043, about half of this number being in 177 bomber squadrons in combat areas. Highest B-24 unit strength, however, was in June 1944 when 46 bomber groups (184 sqdns.) and six special squadrons were overseas and twelve operational training bases were in being in the U.S.A. In July of that year the B-24 was withdrawn from some U.S.A.A.F. units in favour of other types; in England two groups commenced conversion to B-17s to be followed by three more in September; in November a group was sent home to convert to B-29 Superfortresses, and in April 1945 another from the U.K. and one from Italy were withdrawn for the same purpose. The end of hostilities saw a revision of plans and all E.T.O. B-24 groups were returned to the States, and although a few did survive to convert to B-29s, the majority were quickly disbanded. By December 1945 the Liberator was no longer an active bomber in U.S.A.A.F. squadron service.

R.A.F. LIBERATORS

The R.A.F. received over two thousand Liberators of various models, and many others on order were cancelled towards the end of the war. By far the greater number were J and L models, although

B-24J of the 577th Squadron, 392nd Bomb Group. Late production a/c with Emerson turret.   (Photo: J. E. Bode)

British mark numbers allocated did not necessarily have any connection with the U.S.A.A.F. model designations. Approximately 1,600 Liberators of the nose turret types were obtained between the spring of 1944 and August 1945, of which about 1,150 are believed to have been B-24Js. Most (believed 739) were from the Fort Worth factory and 411 from San Diego, all the latter and the first 500 B-24J-CF were given the British designation Liberator Mk. VI, while the remainder of the Fort Worth products became Mk.VIIIs, a designation that also applied to the following Ford built B-24Ls when B-24 production ceased at Forth Worth. The Mk.VI designation also embraced B-24G and H models that found their way to the R.A.F. Twelve Liberators taken over from the U.S.A.A.F. in Italy early in 1945 for special duties (i.e., agent dropping) over the Balkans, were half B-24Gs and half B-24H and J models yet all were identified as M.VIs in the R.A.F.

Both Mks.VI and VIII appeared in different forms to meet the needs of various commands and combat theatres. The bomber versions, the B.VI and B.VIII, were used in the Mediterranean and South East Asia, principally for night attacks. In Coastal Command GR.VIs and GR.VIIIs existed for long-range ocean patrol, many fitted with various sea-search radars and sprouting antenna from wings and fuselage, with the underwing Leigh light for anti-submarine operations at night. While a number of transport Liberators were procured in the U.S. as Mk.C.VII, some Mk.VI and VIII

Rare photograph of Indian Air Force Liberator.

B-24J of the 858th Bomb. Squadron, 8th Air Force. Special Operations a/c based at Harrington, U.K.

deliveries were given a transport configuration in the U.K. with faired noses, added tail cones and seating for 24 passengers.

Over forty R.A.F. squadrons flew Liberators at one time or another, and the Liberator endured longer in R.A.F. than U.S.A.A.F. service although all Marks except transport and GR.VIII were withdrawn by June 1946, and the last Coastal Command squadrons with the GR.VIII converted to Lancasters a year later. Some transports were taken over by B.O.A.C. and continued in use for a few years, taking part in the Berlin Airlift of 1948. Examples of the transport version also found their way to other nations during the immediate post-war years, and a few true bomber models were used by the Indian Air Force until quite recently. Although far more Js were built than any other B-24 model, none—as far as can be ascertained—are still in existence. The U.S.A.A.F. has preserved two Liberators, a B-24D and a B-24M.

While the B-24J Liberator was not the easiest of bombers to fly, it gave valiant service and was held dear by those who took it into battle. In addition to an outstanding record through use against the Japanese, the best piece of U.S.A.A.F. precision bombing against a single target over Europe was achieved with Liberators—mostly B-24Js.

U.S.A.A.F. Groups using the B-24J or equivalents.

Glossary		Group	Chief Area of Ops.
CBI	China, Burma, India		
CPA	Central Pacific Area	453 BG	ETO
ETO	European Theatre	454 BG	MTO
	of Operations	455 BG	MTO
MTO	Mediterranean	456 BG	MTO
	Theatre of Ops.	458 BG	ETO
NPA	North Pacific Area	459 BG	MTO
SWPA	South West Pacific	460 BG	MTO
	Area	461 BG	MTO
		464 BG	MTO
Group	Chief Area of Ops.	465 BG	MTO
		466 BG	ETO
5 BG	SWPA	467 BG	ETO
7 BG	CBI	484 BG	MTO
11 BG	CPA	485 BG	MTO
22 BG	SWPA	486 BG	ETO
28 BG	NPA	487 BG	ETO
30 BG	CPA	489 BG	ETO
34 BG	ETO	490 BG	ETO
43 BG	SWPA	491 BG	ETO
44 BG	ETO	492 BG	ETO
90 BG	SWPA	493 BG	ETO
93 BG	ETO	494 BG	CPA
98 BG	MTO		
307 BG	SWPA	Photo	Chief
308 BG	CBI	Recon Groups	Area of Ops.
376 BG	MTO	6 P.R.G.	SWPA
380 BG	SWPA	8 P.R.G.	CBI
389 BG	ETO	Special	Chief
392 BG	ETO	Squadrons	Area of Ops.
445 BG	ETO	36 BS (RCM)	ETO
446 BG	ETO	406 BS (Leaflets)	ETO
448 BG	ETO	652 BS (Weather)	ETO
449 BG	MTO	814 BS (Radar)	ETO
450 BG	MTO	885 BS (OSS, etc.)	MTO
451 BG	MTO	868 BS (Radar)	SWPA

Royal Air Force Squadrons using Liberator Mk. VI and Mk. VIII.

Sqdn.	A/c Mk.	Chief Area of Ops.
37	B.VIII.	MTO
40	B.VIII.	MTO
53	GR.VI, GR.VIII, C.VI, C.VIII.	UK—Iceland
59	GR.VI, GR.VIII, C.VI, C.VIII.	UK—Iceland
70	B.VI, B.VIII.	MTO
86	GR.VI, C.VI.	UK
99	B.VI, B.VIII.	FE
102	C.VI, C.VIII.	UK
103	C.VI, C.VIII.	UK
104	B.VI, B.VIII.	MTO
120	GR.VI.	UK
148	B.VI.	MTO
159	C.VI.	FE
160	GR.VI, GR.VIII.	FE
178	B.VI, B.VIII.	MTO
203	GR.VI, GR.VIII.	UK, FE
206	GR.VI, GR.VIII.	Azores.
214	B.VIII.	UK
215	C.VI.	FE
220	GR.VI, GR.VIII.	Azores.
223	B.VII, B.VIII.	UK
224	GR.VI, GR.VIII.	UK
232	C.VI, C.VIII.	FE
233	GR.VI.	UK, FE
243	C.VIII.	FE
246	C.VI, C.VIII.	UK
292	B.VI.	UK
301	B.VI.	UK
311	GR.VI, C.VI.	UK
321	GR.VI.	FE
354	B.VI.	FE
355	B.VI, B.VIII.	FE
356	B.VI, B.VIII.	FE
357	B.VI.	FE
358	B.VI.	FE
422	C.VI, C.VIII.	UK
423	C.VI, C.VIII.	UK
426	C.VI, C.VIII.	UK
502	GR.VI.	UK
547	GR.VI, GR.VIII.	UK
614	B.VI, B.VIII.	MTO

Small numbers of Liberators were also used by the following units: Conversion Units: 5 (HB)CU, 1330 (T)CU, 1332 (T)CU, 1584 (HB)CU, 1673 (HB)CU, 1674 (HB)CU, 1675 (H)CU; 1586 Special Delivery Flight; 111 OTU; 1425 Flight; 1 AGS; 1346 ASR; 1409 Met. Flight; and Coastal Command Flying Instructors School.

R.A.A.F. had four squadrons using Liberators of this type in the Far East, numbers 21, 23, 24 and 25.

Royal Air Force serial numbers allotted B-24J types.

BZ960—BZ999	Mk. VI	Believed all B-24J—CF—Boulton-Paul rear turrets.
EV812—EW249	Mk. VI	Believed all B-24J—CO.
EW250—EW322	Mk. VI	Believed all B-24J—CF.
KG821—KG999	Mk. VI & Mk. VIII	Mk. VIII by and after KG943.
KH100—KH124	Mk. VI	Believed all B-24J—CO.
KH125—KH420	Mk. VIII	Believed all B-24J—CF.
KK221—KK378	Mk. VIII	Believed all B-24J—CF.
TT336—TT343	Mk. B.VI	Ex-U.S.A.A.F.
TW758—TW769	Mk. B.VI	B-24G, H & J ex-U.S.A.A.F Italy.

Although the above serial batches were allocated to Liberator production no precise information is available on actual numbers and types delivered within these batches. While these details are believed to be correct they are unconfirmed.

With the exception of the TT and TW batch all Mk. VI Liberators appear to have had the Consolidated Motor Products nose turret, whereas the Mk. VIII appears to have been the Emerson-equipped model.

It is known that odd Mk. VIIIs were seen with serials outside the above ranges, and it is assumed that these were due to errors in application.

9th Air Force B-24J attacks Iwo Jima.

Specification

Wing span : 110 ft. *Total wing area :* 1,048 sq. ft. *Wing root chord :* 14 ft. *Fuselage length :* 67 ft. 2 in. *Overall height :* 18 ft. *Tail span (fin centre lines) :* 26 ft. *Wheel tread ;* 25 ft. 7½ in. *Wheel base (fore and aft) :* 16 ft. *Ground clearance fuselage :* 1 ft. 8 in. *Engines :* Four turbo-supercharged Pratt & Whitney R.1830-65*. *Propellers :* Hamilton Standard, 11 ft. 7 in. dia., three-blade fully feathering Hydromatic. *Engine rating :* 1,200 b.h.p. at take-off and at operating altitudes. *Max. Speed :* 300 m.p.h. at 30,000 ft., at 56,000 lb. take-off weight. *Usual combat operating speed range :* 180–215 m.p.h. between 10,000 and 25,000 ft. *Landing speed :* 95 m.p.h. light—125 m.p.h. loaded.

Rate of climb : 25 minutes to 20,000 ft. at 56,000 lb. take-off weight and Military power. *Service ceiling :* 28,000 ft. at 56,000 lb. take-off weight. *Take-off run :* 34,000 ft. to gain 50 ft. altitude. *Landing run :* 26,000 ft. from 50 ft. altitude. *Fuel capacity :* 2,364 US gls. main tanks. 450 gls. auxiliary wing tanks. 800 gls. in auxiliary bomb bay tanks if required. *Bomb capacity :* 5,000 lb. maximum internally was normal load. 12,800 lb. could be carried for short distances utilising wing racks. *Range :* 2,100 miles at 215 m.p.h. 25,000 ft., and 64,500 lb. loading including 2,814 US gls. fuel and 5,000 lb. bombs. *Empty weight :* 36,500 lb. *Loaded weight :* 56,000 lb. Combat loads were often around 65,000 lb. *Max. overload weight :* 71,200 lb. *Some R.A.F. a/c re-engined with R-1830-90.

U.S.A.A.F. serial numbers of B–24J Liberators.

San Diego production.
(Aug. 1943 to Aug. 1944)

B–24J–1–CO	42–72964	—42–73014
B–24J–5–CO	42–73015	—42–73064
B–24J–10–CO	42–73065	—42–73114
B–24J–15–CO	42–73115	—42–73164
B–24J–20–CO	42–73165	—42–73214
B–24J–25–CO	42–73215	—42–73264
B–24J–30–CO	42–73265	—42–73314
B–24J–35–CO	42–73315	—42–73364
B–24J–40–CO	42–73365	—42–73414
B–24J–45–CO	42–73415	—42–73464
B–24J–50–CO	42–73465	—42–73514
B–24J–55–CO	42–99936	—42–99985
B–24J–60–CO	42–99986	—42–100035
B–24J–65–CO	42–100036	—42–100085
B–24J–70–CO	42–100086	—42–100135
B–24J–75–CO	42–100136	—42–100185
B–24J–80–CO	42–100186	—42–100235
B–24J–85–CO	42–100236	—42–100285
B–24J–90–CO	42–100286	—42–100335
B–24J–95–CO	42–100336	—42–100385
B–24J–100–CO	42–100386	—42–100435
B–24J–105–CO	42–109789	—42–109838
B–24J–110–CO	42–109839	—42–109888
B–24J–115–CO	42–109889	—42–109938
B–24J–120–CO	42–109939	—42–109988
B–24J–125–CO	42–109989	—42–110038
B–24J–130–CO	42–110039	—42–110088
B–24J–135–CO	42–110089	—42–110138
B–24J–140–CO	42–110139	—42–110188
B–24J–145–CO	44–40049	—44–40148
B–24J–150–CO	44–40149	—44–40248
B–24J–155–CO	44–40249	—44–40348
B–24J–160–CO	44–40349	—44–40448
B–24J–165–CO	44–40449	—44–40548
B–24J–170–CO	44–40549	—44–40649
B–24J–175–CO	44–40649	—44–40748
B–24J–180–CO	44–40749	—44–40848
B–24J–185–CO	44–40849	—44–40948
B–24J–190–CO	44–40949	—44–41048
B–24J–195–CO	44–41049	—44–41148
B–24J–200–CO	44–41149	—44–41248
B–24J–205–CO	44–41249	—44–41348
B–24J–210–CO	44–41349	—44–41389

Total 2,792

Fort Worth production.
(Jan. 1944 to Nov. 1944)

B–24J–1–CF	42–64047	—4264141
B–24J–5–CF	42–64142	—42–64236
B–24J–10–CF	42–64237	—42–64328
B–24J–CF	42–64329	
B–24J–10–CF	42–64330	—42–64346
B–24J–15–CF	42–64347	—42–64394
B–24J–15–CF	42–99736	—42–99805
B–24J–20–CF	42–99806	—42–99871
B–24J–25–CF	42–99872	—42–99935
B–24J–30–CF	44–10253	—44–10302
B–24J–35–CF	44–10303	—44–10352
B–24J–40–CF	42–50452	—42–50508
B–24J–40–CF	44–10353	—44–10374
B–24J–45–CF	44–10375	—44–10402
B–24J–50–CF	44–10403	—44–10452
B–24J–55–CF	44–10453	—44–10502
B–24J–60–CF	44–10503	—44–10552
B–24J–65–CF	44–10553	—44–10602
B–24J–70–CF	44–10603	—44–10652
B–24J–75–CF	44–10653	—44–10702
B–24J–80–CF	44–10703	—44–10752
B–24J–85–CF	44–44049	—44–44148
B–24J–90–CF	44–44149	—44–44248
B–24J–95–CF	44–44249	—44–44348
B–24J–100–CF	44–44349	—44–44448
B–24J–105–CF	44–44449	—44–44501

Total 1,558

Ford production.
(April 1944 to Aug. 1944)

B–24J–1–FO	42–50509	—42–50759
B–24J–1–FO	42–95504	—42–95628
B–24J–5–FO	42–50760	—42–51076
B–24J–5–FO	42–51431	—42–51610
B–24J–10–FO	42–51611	—42–51825
B–24J–15–FO	42–51826	—42–52075
B–24J–20–FO	42–52076	
B–24J–20–FO	44–48754	—44–49001

Total 1,587

Douglas production.
(May 1944 to July 1944)

B–24J–1–DT	42–51226	—42–51292
B–24J–5–DT	42–51293	—42–51395
B–24J–DT	42–51396	—42–51430

Total 205

North American production.
(May 1944 to Nov. 1944)

B–24J–1–NT	42–78476	—42–78794
B–24J–2–NT	42–78475	
B–24J–5–NT	44–28061	—44–28276

Total 536

Block numbers other than the above were the result of modifications by air depots, etc.

The North American F-86A Sabre

The North American F-86A Sabre

by Edward Shacklady

Main armament of the F-86A Sabre was six ·50 machine guns grouped in the nose section, but various underwing loads could be carried as may be seen by the selection in this photograph.

FEW warplanes make history, but those that do are remembered long after their deeds are forgotten. Prime examples are Great Britain's Supermarine Spitfire and Hawker Hurricane; Germany's Messerschmitt Me 109 and Focke-Wulf Fw 190, and Japan's A6M1-3, better known by its wartime appellation of Zero. All these famous fighters had one thing in common—they were designed and built for a war that had been anticipated by the world's major powers for at least three years. And, when World War II finally exploded upon a waiting world in September 1939, this fighting quintet was in full production and awaiting testing in a bitter struggle that took nearly six years to decide.

One of the greatest warplanes of the years of uneasy peace that followed the end of World War II in 1945, was not specifically built for the conflict in which it played such a decisive part, but was, in fact, a development of a jet fighter ordered for the U.S. Navy.

In late autumn, 1944, the North American Aviation Company was engaged in the design of their first jet-propelled fighter, the NA-134, or XFJ-1, for the U.S. Navy. At about the same period the U.S. Air Force had issued a requirement for a medium-range day fighter, which could also be utilised as an escort fighter and, of all things, a dive bomber. A proposed variant of the XFJ-1 minus its naval equipment was offered to the Air Force, which on 18th May 1945, authorised construction of three aircraft under the designation XP-86. The XP-86, like its stablemate, had a straight, thin section wing set low on the fuselage, which was tubby and featured a straight through flow of air from nose intake to jet exhaust under a straight tailplane.

A mock-up of the aircraft was constructed and Air Force approval received in June. Salient details included a wing span of 38·2 feet, a length of 35·5 feet, and a height of 13·2 feet. At a gross weight of 11,500 lb. a maximum speed at sea level of 574 m.p.h. was estimated. But the specification had called for a speed of at least 600 m.p.h. for the Air Force already had nearing completion the Republic XP-84 Thunderjet possessing a speed of 587 m.p.h. It appeared that the XP-86 would remain just a drawing board design.

DESIGN CHANGES

At about this period, however, the North American P-86 design team, headed by L. P. Greene, became interested in captured German wind tunnel reports on the advantages of wing sweep-back. These reports were discovered amongst a mass of scientific data collected by the Allied armies swarming over a defeated Germany. The reports showed that whereas a straight-winged aeroplane was severely affected by compressibility as sonic speed was approached, a swept-wing delayed the effects of shock waves thus permitting control at higher speeds. One major defect, however, was the problem of low-speed stability.

Armed with this knowledge North American constructed a scale wind-tunnel model, subsequent tests revealing that the swept-wing raised the limiting Mach number to 0·875. A new design study for a swept-wing XP-86 was submitted to the Air Force, which swiftly approved the proposal. This

The prototype XP-86 on roll-out.

important decision was to have a decided effect on the outcome of the Korean War that began five years later in June 1950.

The sweeping changes to the design called for by the new wing resulted in a radically different aeroplane from that originally planned, and more than one thousand trials with the wing were undertaken by North American in their subsonic wind tunnel. A Messerschmitt Me 262A wing was studied in order to adopt the leading-edge slats for the XP-86 wing in an effort to overcome low-speed stability problems, but they proved unsuitable, and eventually a completely new automatic slat had to be developed.

The first of three prototypes serialled *45-59597* was completed on 8th August 1947, and it was powered by a Chevrolet-built General Electric J-35-C-3 engine developing 4,000 lb. static thrust. Taxiing trials took several weeks and on 1st October the XP-86 took to the air for its maiden flight with North American test pilot George Welch at the controls, just thirteen weeks before its would-be adversary, the Russian MiG-15, left the ground for its first flight. On 26th April 1948, the prototype exceeded Mach One for the first time in a shallow dive. Later production aircraft were limited for safety reasons to Mach 0·95, 669 m.p.h. The prototype was officially delivered to the Air Force on 30th November 1948, and was followed shortly afterwards by *598* and *599*.

PRODUCTION BEGINS

Like the majority of modern fighters production of the P-86A (or F-86A as it became later when the

The prototype, now bearing national insignia and serial numbers.

U.S.A.F. changed the P for Pursuit to F for Fighter) had been planned long before the prototype's first flight, a production contract for 33 aircraft having been approved during December 1946. Engineering drawings were released to the North American Los Angeles Division shops in June 1947, and the first production F-86A-1-NA, serial *47-605*, made its first flight on 20th May 1948. Production aircraft had the new General Electric J-47 engine and three 0·50 calibre machine-guns installed on either side of the pilot's cockpit. The first and second production aircraft *605* and *606* were officially accepted by the U.S.A.F. on 28th May, and by March the following year the final machine *47-637* had been delivered.

While the first production F-86s were under construction North American's design team was working on a U.S.A.F. requirement for larger tyres and had drawn up a scheme for a fuselage seven inches wider in order to accommodate them. The second production order of F-86s was for 188 of the modified aircraft and they were given the designation F-86B. Fortunately, higher pressure tyre design did away with the need for larger tyres, and the F-86B with the wider fuselage never went into production. The contract for 188 86Bs was transferred to the F-86A-5-NA at the suggestion of North American to the Air Force.

Deliveries of the A-5 with the new General Electric J-47 engine of 5,200 lb. thrust began in late March 1949 when *48-129* was accepted by the Air Force. The A-5 differed externally from the A-1 in having a V-shaped instead of rounded windscreen, and in place of the flush-fitted, automatic gun-muzzle doors of the earlier machines which opened and closed when the machine-guns

were fired, plastic plugs were installed. These were blasted clear with the first shots.

Performance-wise the F-86A-5 was far in advance of other jet fighters of the period, possessing a maximum sea-level speed of 679 m.p.h., a service ceiling of 48,000 feet, and an initial climb rate of 7,470 feet per minute. In common with contemporary American fighters it was armed with six 0·50 M-3 machine-guns with a rate of fire of approximately 1,100 rounds per minute. Ammunition supply was 267 rounds per gun.

The guns were aimed with the aid of a Mark 18 sight, a lead computing device that included both a gyro and fixed sighting system. When a target was identified the span selector lever was set to correspond with the aircraft's span, and when the target appeared within a circle of six diamond images on the reflector the range control was rotated until the circle diameter was identical in size to the target. With the target thus framed for one second the gun sight automatically completed the required lead and the guns were fired. A more advanced sight, the A-1CM, was coupled with an AN/APG-30 radar installed in the upper air intake lip of later production Sabres.

THE SABRE DESCRIBED

The F-86A Sabre was a low-wing cantilever monoplane featuring a modified N.A.C.A. 0012-64 (root,) 0011-64 (tip) wing section. Maximum thickness at 50 per cent chord and 35° sweep-back along 25 per cent chord line. Structurally the wing consisted of two spars with upper and lower skins, each of which was a sandwich of two sheets milled to tapering thickness separated by hat section

The prototype F-86A (XP-86) in the white overall finish applied for early trials.

F-86A Sabre of the 71st Squadron, First Group. Note Group emblem aft of squadron emblem.

extrusions. The whole formed a torsion-box structure. Split flaps were carried inboard of the ailerons. Wing area 287·9 sq. ft.

Fuselage was an oval section, all metal, flush riveted, stressed skin structure with lateral airbrakes on each side of the fuselage. Tail unit was a cantilever monoplane, all-metal structure with 35° sweep-back on all three surfaces. The "flying-tail" elevator and tailplane were geared together and moved differentially with movements of the control column to provide in-flight trim.

First U.S.A.F. combat organisation to receive the F-86 was the First Fighter Group at March Air Force Base, California. The 94th Squadron, the famed "Hat in the Ring" outfit of World War I fame, becoming the first F-86A tactical squadron, taking delivery of its aircraft in February and March 1949. The 27th and 71st Squadrons were equipped next and by the end of May the Group had accepted accepted delivery of 83 aircraft.

As yet the F-86 was unnamed and the First Fighter Group sponsored a contest in February for this purpose. Seventy-eight names were submitted, the best of these was deemed to be "Sabre", the name becoming official on 4th March 1949.

CANADA'S F-86A

Development of the Sabre had been watched with great interest by the Royal Canadian Air Force, and in early 1949 the Canadian Government decided to obtain a licence to manufacture the American fighter. In August of that year an order for 100 aircraft was placed with the Canadair Company under the designation of CL-13, Sabre Mk. 1.

It had been intended that the F-86A would be built by Canadair, and the first Sabre off the production was in fact an "A" bearing the serial number *191-010*. It flew for the first time on 9th August 1950, piloted by A. J. Lilly, just one year after the contract with North American Aviation had been signed, and one month before the fighter was to meet the MiG-15 in combat over Korea.

By August 1949, however, North American was

First squadron to receive F-86A-1s was the First Group's "Hat in the Ring" 94th Squadron of World War I fame.

Sabres of 27 Squadron, First Group.   (Photo: U.S.A.A.F.)

building the improved F-86E which had the "all-flying" tailplane, and Canadair introduced this major modification on the aircraft on their production line and built only one 86A. Almost 90 per cent of the 15,000 components were obtained from the United States for the Canadian aircraft industry lacked the facilities and technicians to produce them, but by 1956 almost 85 per cent of the Canadian Sabre was produced in the Dominion.

THE SABRE IN KOREA

As previously mentioned the Sabre was not designed from the outset for the Korean War, but it was, fortunately, in production when its appearance over the battlefield prevented the MiG-15 from sweeping the United Nations aircraft from the sky.

The division of Korea after the Japanese surrender in 1945 led to continuous friction between the Northern and Southern halves of the country, for one was dominated by the Communists in the shape of Russia and Red China, whilst the other half was strongly influenced by America. In 1948, as the result of elections, the Republic of Korea

was established. America aided the new Republic by organising and constructing an internal security force, and by July 1949 had withdrawn all its own forces with the exception of a small military group.

Just before dawn on the morning of 25th June 1950, the North Korean Army crossed the 38th Parallel, and just over 24 hours later they entered Seoul, capital city of South Korea. The United Nations Security Council adopted a resolution calling upon the North Koreans to cease their aggression and withdraw their forces to the 38th Parallel. But without avail for the North Koreans intensified their efforts.

On 27th June, on the instructions of President Truman, General MacArthur ordered the Far East Air Force into action against the invaders, the Americans flying Lockheed F-80 Shooting Star; F-51 Mustang and F-82 Twin-Mustang fighters, and Boeing B-29 bombers. Command of the air was soon established and as a fighting entity the North Korean Air Force was rendered completely ineffective.

With enemy air power neutralised the United Nations ground forces, now fighting alongside the South Koreans, fought to stem the North Korean army's advance down the peninsular. United Nations

F-86A-5 Sabre of the 116th Squadron.   (Photo: C. R. Elliot)

F-86A-5-NA, serial 48-205, of the 56th Fighter Group, O'Hare Air Force Base. It was named "Space Eater". (Photo: U.S.A.A.F.)

aircraft bombed and strafed the invading armies, and there is little doubt that without complete mastery of the air the whole of Korea would have come under the influence of Communism.

While the U.N. armies were being pushed back into a small area south of Naktong River, General MacArthur was planning an amphibious encirclement of the enemy. On the morning of September 15th, units of the U.S. X Corps went ashore at Inchon and the strengthened and reinforced Eighth Army broke out of the Pusan perimeter in an all-out drive to crush the enemy forces.

In just over fourteen days the whole of South Korea was clear of the invading armies and the counter invasion of North Korea began. Within a month the capital city Pyongyang fell and by the end of October the whole of the Korean peninsular

was in United Nations hands. It seemed that victory was complete until, quite suddenly, the armies of Red China were hurled into battle and once again United Nations forces began the retreat southwards.

SABRE v. MiG-15

It was during this period, November 1950, that the Russian-built Mig-15 swept-wing jet fighter appeared, flying from airfields situated in Manchuria, across the border in China. The F-80 and F-51 were no match for the Mig and the Americans decided to commit their new fighter the F-86A against the new menace.

On November 8th the 4th Fighter-Interceptor

F-86A-5-NA, serial 49-1216, of the Utah Air National Guard. Green trim on fin. (Photo: Roger Besecker)

91

F-86A-1-NA, 47-614, which took part in the Korean campaign. Named "Go for Broke" it is now on display at Chanute A.F.B.
(Photo: Roger Besecker)

F-86A-5-NA of the Delaware Air National Guard. Red-tipped fin.
(Photo: G. J. Letzer)

Wing was ordered to Korea and the unit's Sabres were flown from their home base at Wilmington, Delaware, to San Diego, California. There they were embarked aboard an aircraft carrier and shipped to Yokosaka, Japan.

FIRST SABRE SORTIES

The first Sabre missions against the Red Air Force were flown on December 17th, when an advance detachment of F-86A-5s based on Kimpo airfield in Korea took off for an armed reconnaissance of the Yalu River. Flying at 32,000 feet and at a speed of 472 m.p.h., they patrolled the area until four MiG-15s were sighted flying at 7,000 feet below the Sabres. The two 120-gallon drop tanks were jettisoned as the Americans made ready to take on the enemy fighters. The aircraft of 336 Squadron

led by Lt.-Col. B. H. Hinton closed rapidly on the MiGs, and in the matter of seconds one of them was diving earthwards, its entire rear section enveloped in flames. The other three MiGs got clear of the scrap by diving for the Manchurian border. It was first blood for the Americans and for the Sabre which, in its first air battle had emerged victorious.

Colonel Hinton led another four-plane flight from Kimpo on December 19th, and on approaching the Yalu they met six MiGs. The red jets made head-on passes through the American formation without firing a shot, and by the time the F-86s turned to give chase the enemy were diving for their home base. A further six MiGs appeared, but they did not enter the fight.

However, this situation was not to last for long as the American pilots were aware, and on December 22nd the MiGs stayed to fight. The day

Cocooned F-86As on a lighter at the beginning of the journey to Korea.

began with eight Sabres meeting MiGs at 40,000 feet, the enemy fighters attacking with cannons blazing. One of the Sabres fell in flames as the MiGs once again raced back across the border unscathed. Four hours later the Sabres returned to the scene to be met by 15 MiGs. Minutes later the exuberant Americans saw the enemy fleeing across the Yalu leaving six of their comrades diving in flames to their destruction. This high rate of loss deterred the enemy pilots and for the rest of December they studiously avoided the Americans as they patrolled the Yalu. By the end of the month the 4th Wing had flown 234 sorties, during which time the opposing sides had clashed 76 times, with eight victories to the Sabres for the loss of one.

But the situation on the ground had worsened. The Chinese armies had swept the U.N. forces from North Korea and on New Year's day 1951 had begun an invasion of South Korea. To escape the advancing Chinese the Sabres had to leave Kimpo and return to Johnson Air Force Base in Japan, this move putting them effectively out of range for the Korean fighting.

Before the end of the month, however, the Sabre was once again in the thick of it, operating from Taegu in the interceptor and ground attack rôle. Armament consisted of two 5-inch rockets in addition

Heavy battle damage sustained during the Korean air battles.

to the standard machine-guns, and since drop fuel tanks were needed to give the aircraft effective range, time over target was limited. Because of this lack of time over target the Sabres were not very successful in their new rôle.

The Chinese attack finally ground to a halt due to the problem of supplying front-line troops over

One of the original batch of 33 NA-151s, F-86A Sabres, now on display in America. Serial number is 47-614.

(Photo: Roger Besecker)

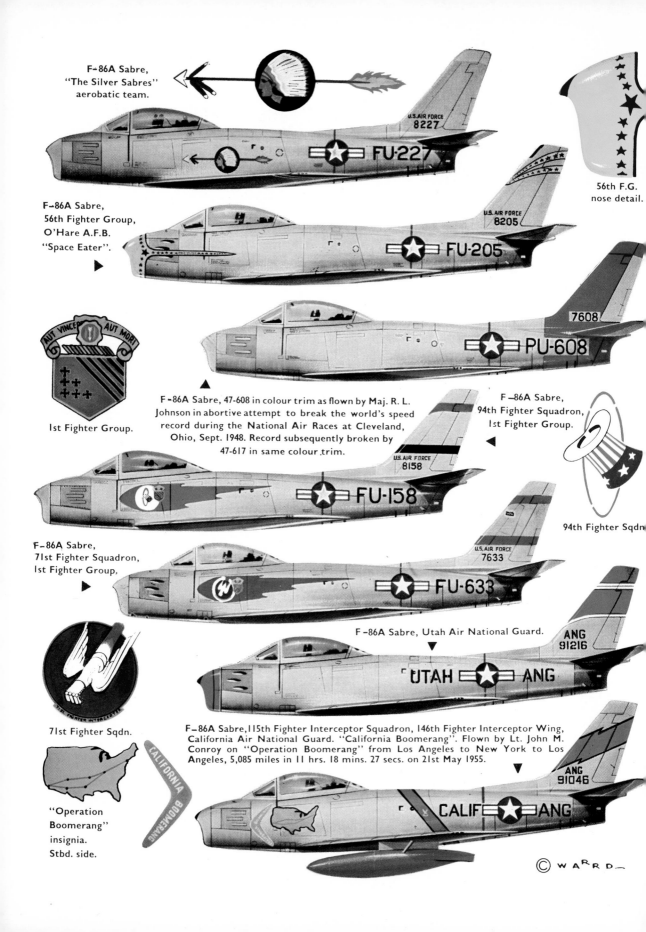

F-86A Sabre,
"The Silver Sabres"
aerobatic team.

U.S. AIR FORCE
8227

FU-227

56th F.G.
nose detail.

F-86A Sabre,
56th Fighter Group,
O'Hare A.F.B.
"Space Eater".
▶

U.S. AIR FORCE
8205

FU-205

7608

PU-608

AUT VINCERE AUT MORI

1st Fighter Group.

F-86A Sabre, 47-608 in colour trim as flown by Maj. R. L.
Johnson in abortive attempt to break the world's speed
record during the National Air Races at Cleveland,
Ohio, Sept. 1948. Record subsequently broken by
47-617 in same colour trim.

F-86A Sabre,
94th Fighter Squadron,
1st Fighter Group.
◀

U.S. AIR FORCE
8158

FU-158

94th Fighter Sqdn

F-86A Sabre,
71st Fighter Squadron,
1st Fighter Group,
▶

U.S. AIR FORCE
7633

FU-633

F-86A Sabre, Utah Air National Guard.
▼

ANG
91216

UTAH ANG

71st Fighter Sqdn.

F-86A Sabre, 115th Fighter Interceptor Squadron, 146th Fighter Interceptor Wing,
California Air National Guard. "California Boomerang". Flown by Lt. John M.
Conroy on "Operation Boomerang" from Los Angeles to New York to Los
Angeles, 5,085 miles in 11 hrs. 18 mins. 27 secs. on 21st May 1955.
▼

CALIFORNIA BOOMERANG

"Operation
Boomerang"
insignia.
Stbd. side.

ANG
91046

CALIF ANG

© WARD

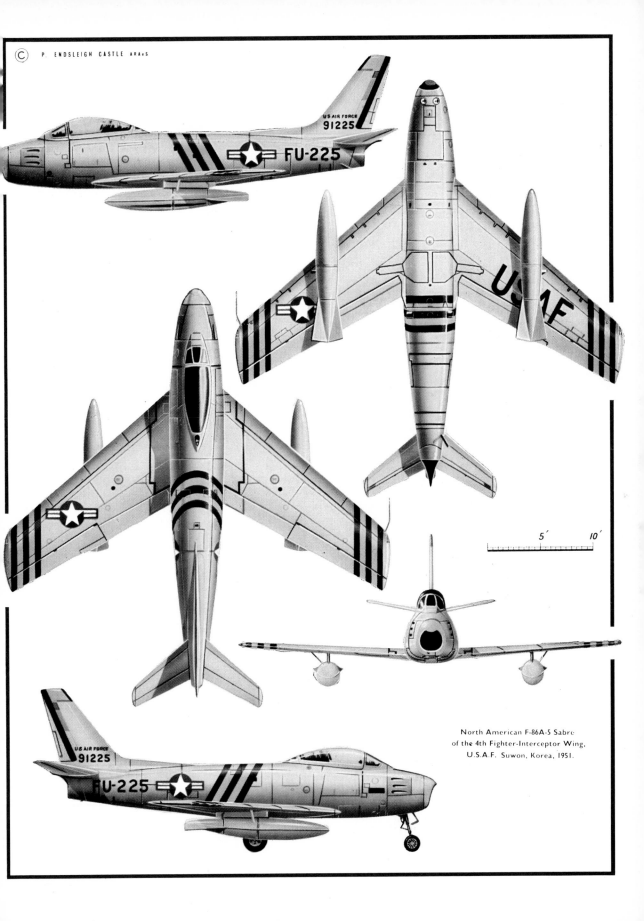

P. ENDSLEIGH CASTLE ARAeS

US AIR FORCE
91225
FU-225

USAF

5′   10′

North American F-86A-5 Sabre
of the 4th Fighter-Interceptor Wing,
U.S.A.F. Suwon, Korea, 1951.

US AIR FORCE
91225
FU-225

long supply lines that were constantly under attack by U.N. aircraft. After a lull in the fighting a new Chinese offensive started and it was heralded with an increase in aggressiveness by the MiG fighters. They were met determinedly by the Sabres of the 334th and 336th Squadrons of the 4th Wing. The pace quickened during April and more MiG-Sabre clashes took place, with the tactical advantage always to the former as they still fled across the border into China after making fast passes at the American 'planes from a superior height. The Americans, despite this handicap, still managed a loss/victory ratio of about 4 to 1 in their favour.

As the first year of the war drew to its close it was apparent that the Sabre had frustrated the MiG-15's bid for superiority, and without this superiority the efforts to rebuild the North Korean air bases came to nothing as the B-29s blasted them at regular intervals. With the start of the second year of war a programme was under way to increase Sabre strength in Korea. Continued development of the basic Sabre airframe had resulted in a new version designated the F-86E and in due course this improved fighter gradually replaced the tired 86As. The first 86E reached Korea during October 1951 and it was not until July the following year that the last "A" was returned home.

Wartime development of the Sabre produced a Mark that was basically an improvisation. For tactical reconnaissance the Lockheed RF-80A was used in Korea, but it proved too slow for the MiG-15 and had to be escorted. To provide a recce-fighter capable of operating without an escort six F-86A-5s were converted into RF-86As by installing two 2-inch K-24 and one 24-inch K-24 cameras in a compartment below the cockpit. Five were delivered to the 67th Wing, 15th Reconnaissance. Squadron. At least another five F-86As were converted to the reconnaissance rôle, and after the war a number were turned over to the R.O.K. Air Force. One was also used by the California National Air Guard.

Night gun firing tests. Note landing lamps under air intake.

Production Details

North American F–86A Sabre.

First production batch of 33 aircraft (NA–151), serialled *47–605* to *47–637* to Specification NA46–841A; Contract AC–16013. First flight of *47–605* took place on 20th May 1948. Deliveries commenced 28th May 1949 and ended in March 1949.

North American F–86A Sabre.

Second production batch of 188 aircraft (NA–151) serialled *48–129* to *48–316*. Deliveries commenced March 1949 and ended in September the same year.

North American F–86A–5 Sabre.

Third batch of 333 (NA–161) serialled *49–1007* to *49–1339* to Specification 48–506A; Contract AC–2167. Deliveries commenced October 1949 and ended in December 1950.

Wing and Squadron Allocation

1st Wing—Squadrons *27, 71, 94.*
4th Wing—Squadrons *334, 335, 336.*
33rd Wing—Squadrons *58, 59, 60.*
56th Wing—Squadrons *61, 62, 63.*
81st Wing—Squadrons *78, 91, 92.*
Air National Guard Squadrons—*115, 146, 195, 197, 198.*
Sabre F–86As lost due to enemy action in Korea, June 1951 to July 1952.
48–301, 49–1083, –1088, –1098, –1109, –1113, –1123, –1139, –1140, –1147, –1159, –1179, –1199, –1210, –1223, –1236, –1255, –1258, –1276, –1281, –1298, –1307, –1318, –1319, –1334, –1338.
Sabre F–86As converted to the RF–86A configuration.
48–183, –184, –185, –186, –187, –196, –217, –246, –257.

Specification and Leading Particulars

Dimensions: Span, 37·12 feet. Length, 37·54 feet. Height, 14·74 feet. Wheel track 8·3 feet.

Weights: Empty, 10,093 lb. Take-off weight, 14,108 lb. With two 120 gallon tanks, 15,876 lb. With two 1,000 lb. bombs, 16,223 lb.

Performance: Stalling speed, 121 m.p.h. Combat radius, 330 miles. Maximum speed, 679 m.p.h. at sea level, 601 m.p.h. at 35,000 feet. Cruising speed, 533 m.p.h. Maximum rate of climb, 7,470 feet per minute at sea level. Climb to 40,000 feet, 10·4 min. Service ceiling, 48,000 feet.

Powerplant: One General Electric J-47-GE-13 (GE-7 on F-86A-1) of 5,200 lb. thrust.

Nose radar detail. Note Indian head emblem under cockpit.

The Bristol Fighter

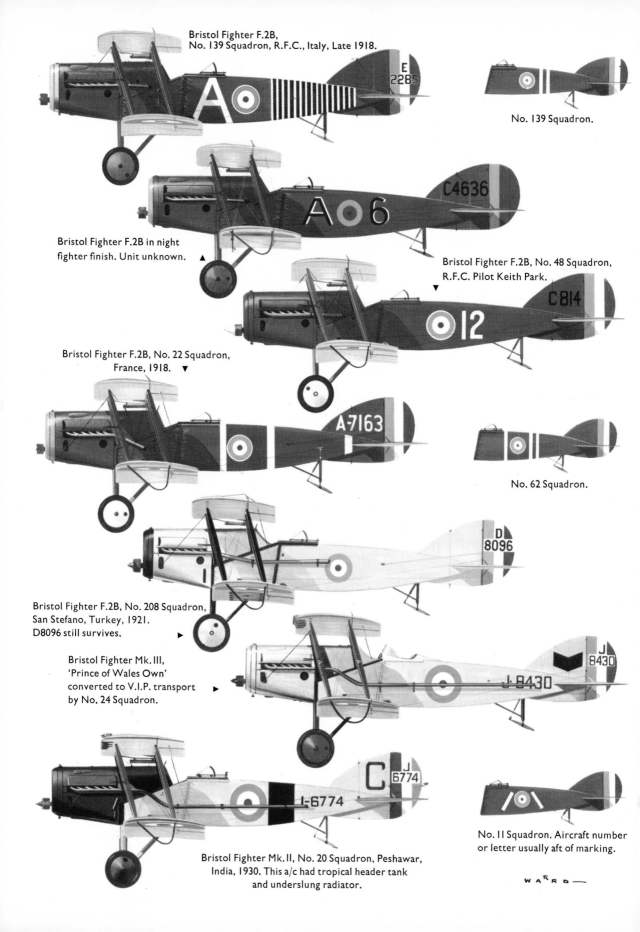

Bristol Fighter F.2B,
No. 139 Squadron, R.F.C., Italy, Late 1918.

No. 139 Squadron.

Bristol Fighter F.2B in night
fighter finish. Unit unknown. ▲

Bristol Fighter F.2B, No. 48 Squadron,
R.F.C. Pilot Keith Park.
▼

Bristol Fighter F.2B, No. 22 Squadron,
France, 1918. ▼

No. 62 Squadron.

Bristol Fighter F.2B, No. 208 Squadron,
San Stefano, Turkey, 1921.
D8096 still survives.
▶

Bristol Fighter Mk. III,
'Prince of Wales Own'
converted to V.I.P. transport
by No. 24 Squadron. ▶

No. 11 Squadron. Aircraft number
or letter usually aft of marking.

Bristol Fighter Mk. II, No. 20 Squadron, Peshawar,
India, 1930. This a/c had tropical header tank
and underslung radiator.

WARD

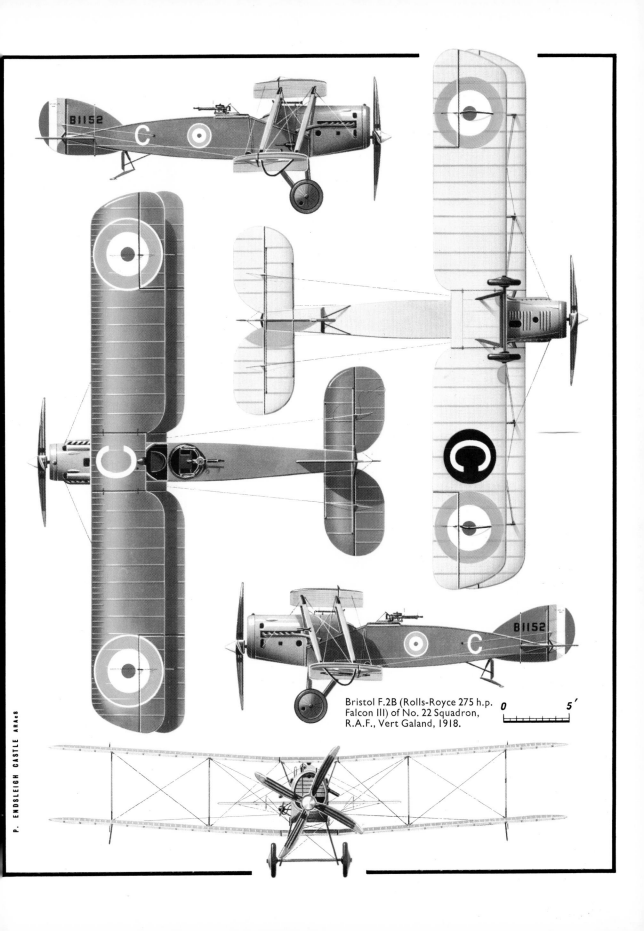

Bristol F.2B (Rolls-Royce 275 h.p. Falcon III) of No. 22 Squadron, R.A.F., Vert Galand, 1918.

B1152

0   5'

The Bristol Fighter
by J. M. Bruce

Extensively re-designed for greater loads H1420 was the prototype Bristol F.2B Mk. III, and is here seen at Filton in March 1926. An oleo tailskid was fitted; the message pick-up hook and trailing-aerial fairlead can be seen under the fuselage.
(Photo: Bristol Aeroplane Co., Ltd.)

ON 1st July 1916, when the Battle of the Somme began, the Royal Flying Corps had a total of 417 operational aircraft in France. Of these, 81 were single-seat scouts; of the 336 two-seaters 185 were B.E.2c's or B.E.2d's. The need for an effective replacement for the B.E. had been foreseen in the autumn of 1915, when R.F.C. Headquarters in France had sent home a specification for a corps-reconnaissance and artillery-spotting aeroplane. In it, particular emphasis was placed on the need for the aircraft to be capable of defending itself.

The Royal Aircraft Factory responded with the R.E.8 design, of which the preliminary layout was drawn in March 1916 and the first prototype was submitted for final inspection on 16th June 1916. The first production R.E.8 was completed by 13th September 1916, and thousands were built, unsatisfactory though the type was.

In March 1916, at the same time as the Royal Aircraft Factory design team were setting down their ideas for the R.E.8, Frank Barnwell at Filton was designing a replacement for the B.E. types. His first project, designated Bristol R.2A, was for an equal-span two-seat biplane powered by a 120-h.p. Beardmore. This was succeeded by a revised design for an

The first Bristol F.2A prototype, A3303, in its original form with twin flank radiators and end-plates on the lower wing roots. It is here seen at Central Flying School, Upavon, in September 1916. At this time the rear cockpit was simply a circular opening in the top of the fuselage; the observer's Lewis gun was carried in temporary fashion on the starboard upper longeron.

unequal-span biplane, the R.2B, with a 150-h.p. Hispano-Suiza. In both designs the fuselage was mounted in mid-gap, the crew were close together, the fuselage tapered to a horizontal knife-edge at the tail, the fin and rudder had a distinctive curved profile, and the pilot was armed with a fixed Lewis gun.

When the 190-h.p. Rolls-Royce Falcon became available, Barnwell drew up a third design that embodied in a completely revised airframe the features of the R.2A and R.2B mentioned in the preceding paragraph. The availability of a British machine-gun synchronising mechanism enabled Barnwell to install a fixed Vickers gun centrally immediately in front of the cockpit.

The new type was regarded primarily as a fighting aeroplane, a change of function that was reflected in its designation, Bristol F.2A. An order was placed for two prototypes, *A3303–A3304*, and fifty production aircraft numbered *A3305–3354*. The first prototype made its initial flight on 9th September 1916, at which time its Falcon engine had two tall side radiators in line with the front centre-section struts; the lower wings were attached to an open wing-anchorage frame and had end-plates at the roots. The second aircraft, which had been completed by 25th October, had a 150-h.p. Hispano-Suiza engine with a circular frontal radiator; its tail-skid was built into the base of the rudder.

At an early stage it became apparent that the radiators on *A3303* obscured part of the pilot's field of view. The nose was redesigned round a single frontal radiator of roughly circular shape in a deep nose cowling; no shutters were fitted at this stage. Soon afterwards, the end-plates were removed from the lower wing-roots and a shallow coaming was fitted about the cockpits; there was no gun mounting on the rear cockpit.

A3303 underwent official trials at Central Flying School, Upavon, on 16th and 18th October 1916,

The second F.2A prototype, A3304, with 150-h.p. Hispano-Suiza, in its original form.   (Photo: Bristol Aeroplane Co., Ltd.)

Production F.2A.   (Photo: Imp. War Museum)

The later Bristol F.2Bs of Home Defence squadrons had a Neame illuminated gun sight mounted on the centre section at an upward angle of 45°. The observer aligned his Lewis gun for and aft at this angle, the pilot used the special sight and gave the signal to fire. Experiments at Orfordness had shown that the trajectory of bullets fired at this angle from an aircraft flying at 100 m.p.h. remained straight for some 800 yards. Some of the proving flights were made by this F.2A, which was fitted with a mechanism that apparently enabled the pilot automatically to rotate the Scarff ring to the fore-and-aft position; this device was also tested with twin Lewis guns. In this case the pilot's sight was apparently an Aldis.

possibly in the form just described. It was tested with both a 4-blade airscrew of 9 ft. 2 in. diameter and a 2-blader of 9 ft. 8 in. diameter. By the time *A3303* reached the experimental armament station at Orfordness it had been fitted with a Scarff No. 2 Ring Mounting on the rear cockpit and an Aldis optical sight had been provided for the pilot's Vickers gun.

The fifty production F.2As were powered by the 190-h.p. Rolls Royce Falcon I. They were substantially similar to the final form of *A3303* but had blunt raked tips on the mainplanes in place of the B.E. planform of the prototypes, and there were detail differences in the engine cowling. The armour plate that had

been fitted to the pilot's seat on the prototypes was not perpetuated.

Deliveries of production aircraft began just before Christmas 1916. The first R.F.C. squadron to receive the F.2A was No. 48, its pilots having gained some experience of their new aircraft at Rendcombe, where a training squadron had been set up. No. 48 Squadron went to France on 8th March 1917, two days after No. 55 Squadron had taken its equally new and untried D.H.4s to the front. Preparations for the Battle of Arras were in hand, and Major-General Trenchard decided that, in order to achieve the maximum surprise, the use of these new types was to be restricted until the battle started.

Thus it was that Bristols of No. 48 Squadron did not cross the lines on their first offensive patrol until 5th April. Only two of the six F.2As returned, one of them badly damaged; the other four had been shot down by five Albatros D IIIs of *Jagdstaffel 11* led by Manfred von Richthofen. Other early disasters cast doubts upon the F.2A's effectiveness as a military aircraft. Fortunately, a few pilots chose to disregard the wholly baseless rumours that the Bristol lacked structural strength and flew their aircraft as if they were fighters, using the front gun as the primary weapon and leaving the observer to take care of attacks from the rear. This technique proved remarkably successful, and the Bristol never looked back.

Two hundred more Bristols, numbered *A7101–A7300*, had been ordered in November. On these aircraft the lower wing-anchorage frame was replaced by a fully covered centre section; and the upper longerons sloped downwards from the rear of the pilot's cockpit, allowing the upper fuselage ahead of the cockpit to be reshaped. The pilot's forward view was thus improved. New horizontal tail surfaces were fitted; these were of reduced chord and increased span. Most of these modifications were tried out on the second prototype F.2A, *A3304*, which was then fitted with a Scarff ring mounting on the rear cockpit and a revised radiator. The production aircraft were given the new designation Bristol F.2B, but to all who knew and flew the aircraft it was the Bristol Fighter.

The first 150 aircraft had the Falcon I engine; *A7251–A7300* had the 220-h.p. Falcon II. Radiator shutters were standardised on all Falcon-powered F.2Bs. On some of the F.2As the pilot's compass was built into the trailing edge of the upper centre section; this was standardised on the F.2B.

Further orders for Bristol F.2Bs quickly followed the initial 200. All subsequent aircraft built for fighter-reconnaissance duties had the 275-h.p. Rolls-Royce Falcon III; and it is with that engine that the Bristol is best remembered. The first installation of a Falcon III was made in *A7177*, and deliveries of the production Falcon III Fighter began with *B1101* on 18th July 1917.

The F.2Bs were issued to No. 48 Squadron to supplement and replace the F.2As of that unit, and were also allocated to R.F.C. Squadrons Nos. 11 (in May–June 1917), 20 (August), and 22 (August): Nos. 11 and 22 had had F.E.2b's, No. 20 F.E.2d's. The first Bristol pilot posted to No. 11 Squadron at the time of its re-equipment was a Canadian, Lt. A. E. McKeever. He and his regular observer, Sgt. (later Lt.) L. F. Powell were perhaps the finest exponents of the Bristol Fighter. After two combats on 20th and 21st June 1917, in both of which he bested his opponents, McKeever scored his first positive victory on 26th June, when he shot down an Albatros single-seater that crashed between Etaing and Dury.

An action typical of McKeever, Powell and the Bristol was fought on the morning of 30th November 1917. While on line patrol south of Cambrai they met two German two-seaters escorted by seven Albatros scouts. McKeever attacked and shot down one of the two-seaters from a range of fifteen yards; Powell shot down two Albatros; and McKeever destroyed another that had overshot the Bristol. Powell's gun jammed, and McKeever took the fight down to within 20 feet of the ground before breaking away from the five surviving enemy aircraft. By the end of 1917 McKeever's score stood at thirty, and Powell's ultimately totalled eight. McKeever returned to England on 25th January 1918 to serve as an instructor for the remainder of the war. When he was appointed

Captured F.2B, reported to have been used as a communications aircraft by Jagdstaffel 5. (Photo: Egon Krueger)

Another captured Bristol F.2B, believed to be A7231 of No. 11 Squadron, shot down on 17th October 1917 by Feldwebel Karl Bey of Jasta 5. *The crew of the Bristol were 2nd Lts. E. Scholtz and H. C. Wookey, who were tried by a German Court Martial on 1st December 1917 because their aircraft had been carrying propaganda leaflets; the British officers were sentenced to ten years' penal servitude (see* The War in the Air, *Vol. IV, pp. 219–226). The wording means "Good people, don't shoot".*

C.O. of No. 1 Squadron, Canadian Air Force, in 1918 he had as his personal aircraft the Bristol Fighter *F4336*. This Bristol was taken to Canada after the armistice and became *G-CYBC*.

In July 1917 the War Office decided to standardise the Bristol F.2B as the equipment of all fighter-reconnaissance squadrons and plans were made for a great increase in production. Eight hundred aircraft (*C751–C1050*, *C4601–C4800* and *D7801–D8100*) were ordered from the British & Colonial Aeroplane Co., under Contract No. A.S. 17573 dated 4th September 1917, but it was obvious that operational demands were greater than could be met from the Bristol company's output. Contracts totalling 800 aircraft were therefore placed with the Gloucestershire Aircraft Co. on 30th October 1917 (for *C9836–*

Above: *The final Arab installation, using a radiator of the shape designed for the 300-h.p. Hispano-Suiza, here seen on F4640.* (Photo: Imp. War Museum)

An early installation of a Sunbeam Arab engine was made in C906, seen here at Filton in April 1918. The twin radiator blocks and shutters were apparently of the same type as those used on the S.E.5a Arab and Viper installations. (Photo: Bristol Aeroplane Co., Ltd.)

Left: *Siddeley Puma engine in Bristol-built F.2B H1690.* (Photo: W. K. Kilsby); Right: *B1200 at Martlesham Heath with 200-h.p. Wolseley W.4A Viper, October 1918. The aircraft's serial number was painted under the lower wings.*

Left: *One of the R.A.E.'s experimental Bristols was A7260, here seen with a 200-h.p. R.A.F. 4d engine. It was used in 1918 in tests of the Calthrop A.1 parachute, and in comparative trials with other R.A.F. 4d F.2Bs that had single-bay and three-bay wings.* (Photo: P. L. Gray); Right: *This U.S.A. O-1 had twin radiators mounted in flank positions in line with the rear centre-section struts. At a later stage a single radiator was mounted on the centre section; it is believed an underslung radiator was tried.* (Photo: P. M. Bowers)

C9985), and with Marshall & Sons (*D2626–D2775*) and National Aircraft Factory No. 3 (*D2126–D2625*) on 22nd November 1917. On 22nd February 1918 further orders were given to the Standard Motor Co. (for *E5179–E5428*), Armstrong Whitworth & Co. (*E1901–E2150*), and Angus Sanderson & Co. (*E2651–E2900*); a second contract was given to the Gloucestershire company on 20th March (*E9507–E9656*); and on 21st May the Birmingham firm of shop fitters, Harris & Sheldon, were brought into Britain's aircraft industry with Contract No. 35A/1218/C.1158, which was for *F5074–F5173*. Last of the wartime contractors was the Austin Motor Co.

This expansion of production implied large demands for engines. Official indecision and delay had led to difficulties over Rolls-Royce engines, and by August 1917 the firm's output of new engines was seriously behind schedule. Alternatives had to be sought for the Bristol Fighter programme. One official document indicates that the 200-h.p. Sunbeam Arab was specified for all aircraft built by contractors other than the parent company, with the exception of those ordered from National Aircraft Factory No. 3, for which the 200-h.p. Hispano-Suiza was indicated. Apparently the

Arab was regarded as an acceptable alternative power unit for F.2Bs built by the parent company, but with few exceptions Bristol-built aircraft had the Falcon engine. The exceptions were those F.2Bs that had experimental installations of other engines and 171 aircraft made late in 1918 of which 153 had Arabs, the remainder Pumas. It seems that the Bristols of the Batch *C751–C1050* were meant to have Arab engines but in fact these aircraft were completed with Falcons and most of them saw operational use with the squadrons in France, Italy and on Home Defence; only two *C906* and *C1025*, are known to have had Arabs.

In point of time a Hispano-Suiza installation was the first to undergo official tests. In January 1918, *B1201*, fitted with the Brasier-made 200-h.p. Hispano-Suiza No. 16456/W.D.11334, was tested at Martlesham Heath; a frontal radiator of roughly circular shape was fitted. *B1204* with a Sunbeam Arab was similarly tested in March. Performance of both aircraft was poorer than that of the Falcon-powered F.2B.

At that time the supply of Hispano-Suiza engines had just passed crisis point, and Mayen-built engines were coming forward in sufficient numbers to enable S.E.5a production to develop. As it was obvious that

Left: *The first U.S. XB-1A, S.C.40125, with the semi-monocoque fuselage developed at McCook Field. This fuselage weighed only 165 lb.; that of the U.S.A. O-1 weighed 275 lb.* Right: *This XB-1A, A.S.64177 (P-205) had its lower wing faired into the fuselage.* (Photo: P. M. Bowers)

Left: *A few Falcon-powered Bristol F.2Bs had radiators of increased area that substantially altered the shape of the nose. This one was photographed at the Isle of Grain shortly after the Armistice; another was at Cranwell in August 1919.* Right: *In the early post-war years experiments were conducted with free-flying target gliders, one of which is seen here on a Bristol F.2B. A larger type of glider was launched from a Westland Walrus.*

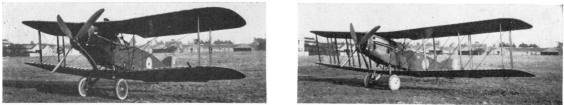

Left: *Single-bay wings of 30ft. 11½ in. span, 7 ft. chord and an aspect ratio of 4·69 were fitted first to A7860 (R.A.F. 4d engine). The Falcon-powered F.2B F4360 is here seen at the R.A.E., Farnborough, on 25th January 1923, fitted with similar wings.* (Photo: Crown copyright); Right: *Also photographed on 25th January 1923 was F4728, fitted with the experimental three-bay wings of aspect ratio 9·78.* (Photo: Crown copyright)

the supply of Hispano-Suiza engines would not suffice to meet the Bristol Fighter production programme the Sunbeam Arab was standardised for the type. In view of the reduced performance, it was decided to issue the Arab-powered F.2B to corps-reconnaissance squadrons as a replacement for the R.E.8; it was planned to start this re-equipment in April 1918. The Falcon-powered F.2B was to be reserved for the fighter-reconnaissance units. As the 200-h.p. Hispano-Suiza had been abandoned as a power unit for the Bristol, the aircraft built at the Cunard-managed National Aircraft Factory No. 3 were delivered with Falcon engines; the only known exception was *D2132*, which had an Arab.

Unfortunately, the Arab was a bad choice. On the recommendation of the internal combustion engine sub-committee of the Advisory Committee for Aeronautics, made under some pressure at the end of January 1917, the Arab had been ordered in large numbers from the Austin Motor Co. and from Willys-Overland of Canada Ltd., Toronto. At that time the engine's trials had not been completed, and by May 1917 serious weaknesses of cylinder and crank-chamber design had become apparent. So many modifications had to be made that the design of the Arab was not finally settled until the end of 1917. Willys-Overland production was further delayed owing to an extraordinary decision to convert all dimensions to inches from the metric units used on the original British drawings.

The substantial expansion programme for the Royal Flying Corps had envisaged an output of 1,800 Arab engines by the end of 1917: in reality only 81 were delivered by that date. Indeed, by the end of 1918 only 1,311 had been delivered, 116 of them made by Willys-Overland. Even after its lengthy development period the Arab was incurably unsatisfactory. It vibrated severely, a fault that, in the Bristol Fighter, led to the

Above: *Post-war use of the Bristol F.2B in India and the Middle East led to cooling problems that were investigated at Farnborough. One attempted solution was this liberally-louvred cowling, almost certainly on C4654, photographed on 29th April 1923.* (Photo: Crown copyright); Below: *The greatly enlarged upper fin and rudder fitted in 1920 to the Puma-powered Bristol Fighter C4655 were similar in outline to the original surfaces. At Farnborough a few years later C4776 was fitted with revised vertical surfaces incorporating a balanced rudder, foreshadowing the tail unit of the Bristol Fighter Mk. IV. This photograph is dated 23rd March 1925.*

(Photo: Crown copyright)

installation of more substantial engine bearers than were needed for the Falcon.

The Arab cooling system underwent several modifications. An early installation in *C906* used twin radiator blocks of the kind fitted to the Arab and Viper engines on S.E.5a's and had a generally similar appearance. In view of the vibration difficulties encountered with the Arab the possibility of using the new 300-h.p. direct Hispano-Suiza was examined, and the Arab installation, radiator and cowling were revised to accommodate either engine. This modified design was standardised, but at least one Arab-powered Bristol F.2B that was at Martlesham late in 1918 had a radiator "gable-end" shaped.

On 31st October 1918 the Royal Air Force had on charge 721 Arab-powered Bristol Fighters. Only 79 of these were in France, however; the only units known to have used the variant were the Long-Range Artillery Spotting Flights L, N, O and P.

Other alternative engines were tried in the Bristol Fighter. First of these was the 230-h.p. Siddeley Puma, a six-cylinder in-line engine that could only have been chosen because, like the Sunbeam Arab, it had been ordered into large-scale production in 1917. The earliest recorded trials of a Puma Bristol were conducted in February 1918, the subject aircraft being *B1206*. Performance was only marginally better than with the 200-h.p. Hispano-Suiza and Arab, and the Puma was difficult to install in the F.2B airframe. The installation, which had been designed at the R.A.E., resembled that of the D.H.9; a large, clumsy exhaust pipe was fitted on the port side and the radiator was underslung. The Puma engine had its own troubles, but later in 1918 a substantial number of production F.2Bs were fitted with it; in particular it seems likely that the aircraft ordered from the Austin Motor Co. were to have the Puma.

In September 1918 *C4654* was tested with the high-compression version of the Puma, which gave 290-h.p.

Above: *This Bristol Fighter was presented to King Albert of Belgium by Handley Page Ltd. on 14th May 1920. It returned to Cricklewood for modifications requested by its royal owner and was flown back to Brussels on 23rd July 1920. A second Bristol was presented to the Queen of Belgium.* Below: *The first Bristol Fighters to go to New Zealand, H1557 and H1558, retained their wartime khaki dope. The five aircraft subsequently delivered to the N.Z.P.A.F. were doped silver overall; this photograph is of 6857.* (Photo: D. P. Woodhall)

Dated 6th January 1930, this photograph depicts J6721, perhaps the most extensively modified Bristol F.2B of all. It had R.A.F. 34-section wings of steel construction embodying leading-edge condensers for the experimental evaporative cooling system fitted to the engine, which drove a Leitner-Watts adjustable-pitch airscrew. The wings had increased gap and were mounted at a large angle of incidence. (Photo: Crown copyright)

The extra power did not improve performance significantly and no development ensued. The Bristol *C4654* later had a Falcon engine installed and remained in use at the R.A.E., Farnborough, for some years as an experimental aircraft.

Directional control of the Puma Bristol was not good. The R.A.E. designed a greatly enlarged fin and rudder and fitted them to *C4655*. They were similar in shape to the standard surfaces, but their total area was 29·3 sq. ft., whereas that of the standard fin and rudder was 17·9 sq. ft. This improved the aircraft's response to the controls but made it heavier to handle. Squadron Leader R. M. Hill (the late Air Chief Marshal Sir Roderic Hill, K.C.B., M.C., A.F.C.) and Flight Lieutenant J. Noakes both suggested that a balanced rudder would be a more effective solution. The enlarged tail was not standardised, but later variants of the Bristol Fighter had balanced rudders.

A Wolseley Viper engine was tried in *B1200*; the radiator and cowling were generally similar to those that had enclosed the 200-h.p. Hispano-Suiza on *B1201*. When tested in October 1918 the Viper Bristol returned poor performance figures and no wartime development was undertaken.

Several Bristol F.2Bs were fitted with the 200-h.p. R.A.F. 4d engine at the R.A.E., Farnborough, but it seems unlikely that this air-cooled twelve-cylinder engine was ever seriously considered as a possible power unit for the aircraft. By 26th July 1918, *B1201* had acquired the R.A.F. 4d engine No. 30324/40 and had been fitted with three-bay wings of 44 ft. 1½ in. span and 4 ft. 9 in. chord. In this form it was flown in comparative trials with *A7260* and *A7860*, both of which also had the R.A.F. 4d; *A7260* had standard mainplanes, those of *A7860* had a chord of 7 ft., a span of 30 ft. 11½ in., and single-bay bracing. The Falcon-powered Bristols *F4360* and *F4728* were also fitted with the single-bay and three-bay wings respectively; they were at Farnborough in this form in January 1923, by which time *B1201* had reverted to standard two-bay wings while retaining its R.A.F. 4d engine.

The Bristol Fighter's fine reputation naturally commended it to the U.S.A., which had entered the war with nothing that could seriously be called a military aeroplane, either in being or under construction. On the personal recommendation of General Pershing, made on 1st August 1917, plans were initiated for the production of the Bristol F.2B in the U.S.A.; the power unit mentioned in the original proposal was the 200-h.p. Hispano-Suiza. A specimen F.2B, *A7207*, was sent to America and arrived at the Smithsonian Institution, Washington, on 5th September 1917.

Unfortunately, Colonel V. E. Clark of the Bolling Commission redesigned the aircraft to have the 400-h.p. Liberty 12, an engine that was quite unsuitable for the Bristol and was badly installed.

A contract for 1,000 aircraft was first placed with the Fisher Body Corporation but subsequently cancelled and re-allocated to the Curtiss Aeroplane & Motor Co. On 7th December 1917 the order was increased to 2,000. The first aircraft, which was given the designation U.S.A. O-1, was completed on 25th January 1918, despite the grave misgiving of Captain Barnwell, who foresaw serious difficulties. It did not fly until 5th March. Matters were not helped by the introduction of unnecessary modifications: the misdirected industry of Major E. J. Hall of the U.S. Signals Corps had, by the end of March 1918, rendered about 1,400 Curtiss production drawings obsolete. Output was held up, and crashes of O-1s on 7th May, 10th June and 15th July brought the design, quite unjustifiably, into disrepute: the first two accidents were caused by faulty workmanship, the third by pilot error.

By the end of June 1918, *A7207* (by then P-30 of McCook Field) had been fitted with the only existing specimen of the American-built 300-h.p. Hispano-Suiza. This combination seemed a better proposition to the U.S. Air Board, who suggested to Curtiss that work on the Liberty version should be abandoned in favour of the Hispano-Suiza. In spite of the company's protests the contracts for the U.S.A. O-1 were cancelled on 20th July after two prototypes and 25 production aircraft had been built.

A second British-built F.2B was sent to the U.S.A. in 1918 and, as P-37, was fitted with the 280-h.p. eight-cylinder Liberty 8. This aircraft crashed before trials could be conducted. The most sensible suggestion that emerged from the American Bristol Fighter débâcle was that put forward by W. C. Potter of the Bureau of Aircraft Production; namely, that the original Bristol Fighter be produced exactly as Frank Barnwell had designed it, but with either the Liberty 8 or the 300-h.p. Hispano-Suiza. Unfortunately, it was never taken up. The nearest approach to it was a proposal to fit four U.S.A. O-1 fuselages with the Hispano-Suiza and a further four with the Liberty 8, the aircraft to be designated U.S. B-1 and B-2 respectively. This scheme was abandoned, but work proceeded on two developments, using these engines but having semi-monocoque fuselages made by the McCook Field engineers, and the respective designations U.S. B-3 and B-4. These were subsequently changed to U.S. XB-1 and XB-2; the former was to have twin Marlin guns for the pilot, the latter two Brownings. The XB-2 was abandoned because the Liberty 8 was unsatisfactory; the XB-1 had to be rebuilt after storm damage and, with Browning guns in place of the intended Marlins, was re-designated U.S. XB-1A. It was tested at McCook Field on 3rd July 1919. Forty were built by the Dayton-Wright company, powered by the 300-h.p. Wright H; they were apparently intended for use as night observation aircraft. One was fitted experimentally with the 350-h.p. Packard 1A-1327 engine, another with the 400-h.p. Curtiss D-12. For all the effort that went into all the American variants none of them was any better

than the original Bristol F.2B.

The Bristol Fighter ended the war supreme in its class. It had fought with distinction with six fighter-reconnaissance squadrons in France; with the redoubtable crews of No. 1 Squadron, Australian Flying Corps, in Palestine; with No. 139 Squadron in Italy; and had equipped five Home Defence squadrons in England.

During the closing months of the war the operational use of radio telephony was pioneered by Bristol Fighter squadrons, of which the first to be equipped was No. 11. In No. 88 Squadron, which was using R/T in August 1918, only the flight commander's aircraft had a transmitter, all the other having receivers. The equipment relied on trailing aerials, which had to be wound in when combat was imminent, and its usefulness was therefore limited.

The Bristol was also used in early experiments at the R.A.E. with parachutes. Two Calthrop A.1 static-line parachutes were carried in the underside of the fuselage, the experiments starting in 1918 and continuing after the armistice. Bristol F.2Bs that were modified to accommodate the parachutes were *A7260* and *H1561*.

After the war the Royal Air Force adopted the Bristol as its standard army co-operation aircraft. In this capacity it equipped squadrons in England, India, Palestine, Egypt and Turkey, undergoing many modifications and acquiring much strange equipment. Production continued in 1919–20 with the Bristol Fighter Mk.II, which had a tropical radiator with more numerous shutters, and provision for desert equipment. The Mk.III, resdesigned to take higher loads, followed in 1926; the Mk.IV applied to Fighters Mks.II and III that had Handley-Page slots, a revised upper fin and balanced rudder, and a stronger undercarriage.

At an early post-war stage some thought was given to the possibility of using the Bristol F.2B as a carrier-borne aircraft. An engineless airframe had been

Above: *Possibly a SABCA-built Bristol F.2B, this was No. 45 of l'Aeronautique Militaire Belge, with 300-h.p. Hispano-Suiza engine, oleo undercarriage and horn-balanced rudder.* Below: *One of twelve new-built Bristols supplied to Spain in 1924 with 300-h.p. Hispano-Suiza, oleo undercarriage and Frise ailerons.* (Photo: Bristol Aeroplane Co., Ltd.)

subjected to immersion trials off the Isle of Grain on 9th November 1918, and *F4453* was later used in a series of deck landings, apparently aboard H.M.S. *Eagle.*

In the years following the armistice, many war-surplus Bristol F.2Bs were sold to foreign countries. In 1922 Norway bought five reconditioned F.2Bs from the Bristol company. Eight standard Falcon-powered aircraft were bought by the Irish Free State from the Aircraft Disposal Co., followed in 1925 by six new F.2Bs from Bristol. Belgium purchased fifteen aircraft with the 300-h.p. Hispano-Suiza from the Aircraft Disposal Co., and sixteen new aircraft with the same engine, Frise ailerons and oleo under-carriages, in 1923; finally the Société Anonyme Belge de Constructions Aéronautiques (SABCA) obtained a licence for the manufacture of the F.2B. They built forty in 1925; these had the 300-h.p. Hispano-Suiza, oleo undercarriage and horn-balanced rudder

After buying a number of Hispano-powered Bristols from the A.D.C., Spain ordered a dozen new aircraft from Bristol in 1924; these last had Frise ailerons. The ten aircraft delivered to Mexico in 1928 had these ailerons, balanced rudders and oleo under-carriage. Others went to other places by devious ways: one was reported to be on the strength of Sun Yat Sen's rebel air force in China; at least two found their way on to the U.S. civil register.

Oddly, very few went to Commonwealth air forces. In addition to *F4336* (*G-CYBC*) only *D7869* went to Canada to become *G-CYDP*. Under the Imperial Gift scheme *H1557* and *H1558* went to New Zealand, where they were used by the N.Z. Permanent Air Force. Five more Falcon F.2Bs were ordered by New Zealand; they were flown wearing their Bristol works sequence numbers (6856–6857 and 7120–7122) as serial numbers. No. 7122, a Mk.III, was delivered in July 1927.

Many variants and derivatives of the remarkable Bristol appeared in the 1920s, but in British and Commonwealth military service the Falcon-powered version was, fittingly, the last to remain. The R.A.F. finally relinquished its greatest two-seat fighter in 1932. Last of all were those of the R.N.Z.A.F., which were withdrawn in 1936 and scrapped in 1939.

Two examples of the Bristol F.2B survive. The Imperial War Museum, London, houses *E2581*, the more authentic of the two; this aircraft bears markings that suggest it may have been used by a Home Defence squadron in 1918. The other is the well-known *D8096*, which was with No. 208 Squadron in Turkey in the mid-1920s, was allotted the civil identity *G-AEPH* in 1936, and was restored to airworthy condition with its original serial number in 1951.

Specification

Power: 190-h.p. Rolls-Royce Falcon I; 220-h.p. Falcon II; 275-h.p. Falcon III; 150-h.p. Hispano-Suiza (*A3304* only); 200-h.p. Hispano-Suiza; 200-h.p. Sunbeam Arab; 230-h.p. Siddeley Puma; 290-h.p. high-compression Puma; 200-h.p. Wolseley W.4A Viper; 300-h.p. Hispano-Suiza; 200-h.p. R.A.F. 4d; 290-h.p. Liberty 8; 400-h.p. Liberty 12 (in U.S.A. O-1); 300 h.p. Wright H (in U.S. XB-1A); experimental installations of 350-h.p. Packard 1A-1327 and 400-h.p. Curtiss D-12 in U.S. XB-1As.
Dimensions (standard F.2B, Falcon III): Span 39 ft. 3 in.; length 25 ft. 10 in.; height 9 ft. 9 in.; chord 5 ft. 6 in.; gap 5 ft. 4½ in.; stagger 18·1 in.; dihedral 3° 30'; incidence 1° 45'; span of tail 12 ft. 10 in.; airscrew diameter (P.3045, four blades) 9 ft. 4 in., (two blades) 9 ft. 8 in.; wheel track 5 ft. 5¼ in. (tyres, Palmer 750×125 mm. on wartime F.2B). Span of the F.2A prototypes was 39 ft. 2½ in., of the U.S. XB-1A, 39 ft. 4⁷⁄₁₆ in.

Bristol F.2B Mk. II with oleo undercarriage, enlarged tyres, flare brackets and post-war radiator shutters, 1920. This air-craft, J6790, was tested at Martlesham Heath, later became G-ACCG, and survived until 1939.
(Photo: Bristol Aeroplane Co., Ltd.)

In service in India, F4349 displays some of the impedimenta with which the post-war Bristol F.2B was encumbered. This aircraft has the underslung auxiliary tropical radiator, an adjustable-pitch airscrew and navigation lights. (Photo: D. P. Woodhall)

The prototype Mk. IV, H1417, had square-tipped upper wings and its upper ailerons were linked to the slats.
(Photo: Bristol Aeroplane Co., Ltd.)

Areas: Wings (F.2A) 389 sq. ft. (F.2B) 405·6 sq. ft., ailerons, each 13 sq. ft.; tailplane (F.2A) 26 sq. ft. (F.2B) 22·25 sq. ft.; elevators (F.2A) 22·5 sq. ft. (F.2B) 23·25 sq. ft.; fin, upper 6·9 sq. ft., lower 3·8 sq. ft.; rudder 7·2 sq. ft.
Production: Under wartime contracts more than 5,500 Bristol Fighters were ordered, but not all were delivered; official statistics indicate that 3,101 had been accepted for service with the R.F.C. and R.A.F. up to the end of 1918. The Bristol company received post-war contracts for a total of 378 Bristol Fighters for the R.A.F. and supplied 49 new aircraft to foreign govern-ments. It is difficult to determine precisely how many new Bristol Fighters were built altogether, but the following blocks of serial numbers were allocated.
British & Colonial Aeroplane Co. Ltd., Filton and Brislington (later the Bristol Aeroplane Co. Ltd.): For Bristol F.2A: A3303–3354. For Bristol F.2B: A7101–A7300; B1101–B1350; C751–C1050; C4601–C4800; C4801–4900; D7801–D8100; E2151–E2650; F4271–F4970; H1240–H1739 (H1708–H1739 cancelled); J1231–J1430 (cancelled). For Bristol F.2B Mk.II: J6586–J6800; J7617–J7699. For Bristol F.2B Mk.III: J8242–J8291; J8429–J8458. Additionally the Bristol company supplied F.2Bs to other governments as follows: New Zealand, 5 (works sequence numbers 6856–6857, 6120–6122); Greece, 6 reconditioned aircraft (s/ns 6156–6161); Spain, 5 reconditioned (s/ns 6140–6144) and 12 new F.2Bs (s/ns 6510–6521); Belgium, 16 (s/ns 6223–6238); Mexico, 10 (s/ns 7222–7231); Irish Free State, 6, I.F.S. Army Nos. 17–22 (s/ns 6858–6863).
Sir W. G. Armstrong, Whitworth & Co. Ltd., Gosforth, Newcastle-on-Tyne: E1901–E2150; H3796–3995 (cancelled).
Austin Motor Co. (1914) Ltd., Northfield, Birmingham: H6055–H6058 known; Puma engines fitted.
Gloucestershire Aircraft Co. Ltd., Sunningend, Cheltenham: C9836–C9985; E9507–E9656; H926–H1060 (known part of larger batch).
Harris & Sheldon Ltd., Stafford Street, Birmingham: F5074–F5173.
Marshall & Sons, Gainsborough: D2626–D2775; J2292–2391 (cancelled).
National Aircraft Factory No. 3, Aintree, Liverpool: D2126–D2625.
Angus Sanderson & Co., Newcastle-on-Tyne: E2651–E2900.
Standard Motor Co. Ltd., Cash's Lane, Coventry: E5179–E5428 (E5253–E5308 were completed by British & Colonial Aeroplane Co., E5253–E5258 with Puma engines; E5309–E5428 were cancelled Co., E5253–E5258 with Puma engines; E5309–E5428 were cancelled).

Production in the U.S.A.

Curtiss Aeroplane & Motor Corporation, Buffalo, N.Y.: Two prototypes of U.S.A. O-1 and 25 production aircraft.

The standard Bristol F.2B Mk. IV had automatic slots on mainplanes of standard plan-form, strengthened undercarriage and fuselage, an enlarged upper fin and horn-balanced rudder.

Dayton-Wright Airplane Co., Dayton, Ohio: Forty U.S. XB-1A, including *A.S.64115* (P-171), *A.S.64156,* *A.S.64158* (P-179), *A.S.64160* (P-181), *A.S.64161* (P-182), *A.S.64177* (P-205), *A.S.64300* (P-180), *A.S.94107* (P-150), *A.S.94108* (P-151).
Engineering Division of the Bureau of Aircraft Production, McCook Field, Dayton, Ohio: Prototype U.S. XB-1A, S.C.40125 (P-90).

Production in Belgium

Société Anonyme Belge de Constructions Aéronautiques, 13 rue de Brederode, Brussels: Forty F.2Bs with 300-h.p. Hispano-Suiza 8Fb for l'Aéronautique Militaire Belge.

Wartime A.R.D. Rebuilds

B883, B7947, B8915, B8925, B8928, B8947, E9971, F5811, F5817, F5821, F5995, F5997, F5999, F6042, F6116, F6235, F9616, H7061–H7065.

Armament: One fixed 0·303-in. Vickers machine gun with Constantinesco C.C. synchronising gear, Aldis and ring-and-bead sights, Hyland Type B loading handle. One 0·303-in. Lewis machine gun, or a double-yoked pair, on Scarff No. 2 ring mounting with Norman sight or Hutton illuminated sight. Up to twelve 20-lb. Cooper fragmentation bombs could be carried on racks under lower wings; Negative Lens bomb sight.
Service use—wartime
Western Front: Bristol F.2A. No. 48 Squadron, R.F.C. Bristol F.2B. Squadrons Nos. 11, 20, 22, 48, 62 and 88; one or two Bristols attached to Squadrons Nos. 4, 10, 12, 15, 16 and 35 and to No. 3 Squadron, Australian Flying Corps; Long Range Artillery Spotting Flights L, M, N, O and P.
Home Defence: Squadrons Nos. 33, 36, 39, 76 and 141.
Palestine: No. 67 (Australian) Squadron, R.F.C. (later No. 1 Squadron, Australian Flying Corps); part of No. 111 Squadron, R.F.C.; one Bristol F.2B with "X" Flight at El Gueira and 'Azraq, September 1918.
Italy: One Flight of No. 28 Squadron, March 1918, detached and transferred to No. 34 Squadron as "Z" Flight end March, finally expanded to become No. 139 Squadron on 3rd July 1918.
Post-war service, Royal Air Force.
Home-based squadrons: Nos. 2, 4, 13, 16, 24. *Ireland:* Nos. 100,

105, 106. *Germany:* Nos. 5, 11, 12. *Iraq:* Nos. 6 and 8. *India:* Nos. 5, 20, 27, 28, 31. *Palestine:* No. 14. *Turkey:* Nos. 4 and 208. *Egypt:* Nos. 47 and 208.
Belgian use: Bristol F.2Bs equipped four *escadrilles* of l'Aéronautique Militaire Belge.
Examples of Bristol F.2Bs used by operational squadrons.
Wartime: No. 11 Sqn.—A7127, A7171 (aircraft "3"), B1332, C775, C797, E2215.
No. 20 Sqn.—A7144, B1307, C859, D7919, E2407, F6116.
No. 22 Sqn.—A7223, B1209, C795, C961, D7896, E2408.
No. 48 Sqn.—F.2As A3320, A3322 ("5"), A3323, A3330, A3336 ("I"), A3343, F.2Bs A7213, B1124, B1299, C814 ("12"), C943, F5995.
No. 62 Sqn.—B1207, C796, C4633, D7945, E2468, F5168.
No. 88 Sqn.—B7947, C785, D8064, E2263 ("Q"), E2459 ("12"), F5997.
No. 67 Sqn.—A7198, B1128, B1129 (Capt. Ross Smith, M.C., D.F.C., A.F.C.), B1146, C4624, C4840.
No. 139 Sqn.—C916, C997, D2185, D7972 (Maj. W. G. Barker, D.S.O., M.C., flew Maj. H.R.H. The Prince of Wales as passenger, 16th September 1918), E2284, E2285.
No. 141 Sqn.—C820, C977, C4822, D2245, D2535, D7987.
"L" Flight—F4306.
Post-war. No. 2 Sqn.—F4490, F4854, J6669, J6794, J7699, J8267.
No. 4 Sqn.—E2624 ('4A').
No. 5 Sqn.—C801 ("A"), C1039 ("B"), D8035 ("A"), F4320 ("D"), J6613, J6654 ("B").
No. 6 Sqn.—C766, DR8056, E2629, FR4744, H1493, J8281.
No. 8 Sqn.—D7823, D7852, D7881, D7901.
No. 12 Sqn.—C9982 ("A1"), D8059 ("B5"), E2533 ("C6"), F4414 ("B2"), H1568 ("C6"), J6600.
No. 13 Sqn.—F4503, F4957, H1440, J6743, J7660, J8290.
No. 16 Sqn.—F4513.
No. 24 Sqn.—F4688.
No. 31 Sqn.—E2297, F4494 ("F"), F4658.
No. 40 Sqn.—C4879.
No. 208 Sqn.—D8096, FR4583, F4950, H1678, J6767, JR6788.

The author acknowledges his indebtedness to the researches of
C. H. Barnes and L. E. Opdycke.

Weights and Performance

Aircraft	A3303	A3304	C4808	A7183	B1201	B1204	B1206	C4654	B1200	E2400	P-30	U.S.A. O-1	U.S. XB-1A	U.S. XB-1A P-180
Engine	Falcon I	150-h.p. Hispano-Suiza	Falcon II	Falcon III	200-h.p. Hispano-Suiza	Arab	230-h.p. Puma	290-h.p. Puma	Viper	300-h.p. Hispano-Suiza	300-h.p. Hispano-Suiza	400-h.p. Liberty 12	300-h.p. Wright H	350-h.p. Packard 1A-1327
Weights (lb.):														
Empty	1,727	1,474	—	1,934	1,733	1,866	1,918	1,944	1,867	2,067	—	—	2,010	—
Military load	180	160	—	185	192	185	185	185	185	185	—	—	283	—
Crew	360	360	—	360	360	360	360	360	360	360	—	—	360	—
Fuel and oil	486	479	—	300	345	373	347	344	394	408	—	—	341	—
Loaded	2,753	2,473	2,860	2,779	2,630	2,804	2,810	2,833	2,806	3,020	2,910	2,937	2,994	3,988
Max. speed (m.p.h.):														
At ground level	110	—	—	—	—	—	—	—	—	—	—	—	124	—
At 6,000 ft.	105	99	—	119	—	—	—	—	100·5	—	113·6	138	121	121·5
At 10,000 ft.	101	95	111·5	113	105	104	104	110	95	107	—	—	118·5	—
At 15,000 ft.	76	—	103·5	105	97·5	94	99	103·5	—	101	—	—	112	—
Climb to:	m. s.	m. s.	m. s.	m. s.	m. s.	m. s.	m. s.	m. s.	m. s.	m. s.	m. s.	m. s.	m. s.	m. s.
6,500 ft.	7 30	10 30	— —	6 30	8 40	8 5	7 40	7 00	12 20	7 10	— —	— —	7 50	— —
10,000 ft.	14 30	19 00	13 15	11 15	15 5	14 25	13 30	11 55	22 20	12 20	— —	8 30	13 20	— —
15,000 ft.	31 00	— —	— —	21 20	28 50	29 45	25 10	22 10	— —	24 50	10 45	— —	24 00	15 20
Service ceiling (feet)	16,000	14,500	20,000	20,000	20,000	19,000	20,000	20,500	14,500	18,250	—	—	20,900	—
Endurance (hours)	3½	6	3	3	—	—	—	—	—	—	—	—	—	—

The Fiat C.R.32

The Fiat C.R. 32
by Gianni Cattaneo

Fiat C.R.32s of the XVI° Gruppo "Cucaracha" (Cockroach Group) over Spain. Note two different styles of command pennants on nearest and farthest aircraft.
(Photo: via R. Ward)

CHARACTERISED by superlative manoeuvrability, the Fiat C.R.32 came to be regarded, during the five years preceding the Second World War, simply as the "Italian Fighter". This small aeroplane, designed by Ing. Rosatelli, represented the climax of a ten-year development of a formula deep-rooted in illustrious forebears.

The peculiar array of wing struts, arranged in the form of a Warren truss, appeared for the first time in the well-known S.V.A. scout of 1917 vintage —one of the best aircraft designed by the First World War Italian team which included the young Rosatelli.

The birth of the new family of fighter aircraft can be dated in about 1923, when the prototype Fiat C.R. with 300-h.p. Hispano-Suiza 42 engine first flew. With few changes the new biplane was produced in quantity as the C.R.1 and was forthwith adopted by the first aerobatic teams of the Italian

Air Force, and was further destined to achieve great popularity both in Italy and abroad.

From the fundamental C.R.10 prototype, identified by the installation of the 400-h.p. Fiat A.20 engine, were derived the more refined C.R.20 and C.R.20 Asso (the latter with 450-h.p. Issotta Fraschini "Asso" engine), and eventually, in 1932, the C.R.30 with 600-h.p. Fiat A.30. In the C.R.30 were apparent all the aerodynamic and structural characteristics that were to re-appear one year later in the C.R.32.

The Fiat C.R.30, manoeuvrable and fast for its day, achieved immediate success in July 1932 by winning the important "Dal Molin Cup" for fighter aircraft at the respectable average speed of 215 m.p.h. The C.R.30 was accepted in limited quantity by the *Regia Aeronautica*, but was superseded only one year later by the C.R.32. Exceptional qualities were nevertheless demonstrated by the C.R.30 and, in July 1934, a

The Fiat C.R.30, predecessor of the C.R.32, served with the Regia Aeronautica *in limited numbers.* (Photo: via Col. Cesar Milani)

A two-seat trainer conversion of the C.R.30: note the tri-coloured elevators.　　　　(Photo: via Col. Cesar Milani)

squadron of twelve aircraft performed the first European tour by a fighter unit in formation. On the Bruxelles-to-Paris leg the speed of the formation was a remarkable 230 miles per hour. The C.R.30 was also exported in small numbers to Austria, China and Paraguay.

Notwithstanding the direct similarity to its precursor, the C.R.32 was smaller and more compact, its fine handling qualities even further enhanced; it was destined not only to gain international renown but to fight a bitter, bloody war in Spanish skies. The small fighter began to arrive in first line units late in 1933, first with the *1st Stormo* based at Campoformido, then with the *2nd Stormo* (Turin), the *4th Stormo* (Gorizia), the *3rd Stormo* (Milan), and subsequently with practically every fighter unit in the I.A.F.

THE C.R.32 DESCRIBED

It was a biplane of sesquiplane configuration with considerably greater span in the upper wing. The wing structure consisted of two aluminium alloy tubular spars with ribs of aluminium square tube. Only the top wing carried ailerons, balanced by outrigged "bench-type" tabs supported by steel struts. The covering was fabric and the two wings were rigged with a stagger of 9° 30′ by a system of steel primary struts and two secondary N-struts between the top wing and the fuselage. The main fuselage structure was an aluminium and steel tubular frame faired externally by a superstructure of U-section longerons and aluminium sheet formers. The covering was of metal panelling from the nose to the cockpit, on the aft decking and in the area round the tailwheel; the remainder was fabric-covered. The cockpit was equipped with an in-flight adjustable seat with parachute incorporated in the squab.

The empennage structure was of aluminium tube, with variable incidence tailplane, and statically- and dynamically-balanced elevator.

The fixed undercarriage was of the split-axle and independent wheel type, and incorporated two main legs with wheel fairings, hydraulic shock absorbers and pneumatic wheel brakes.

The Fiat C.R.32bis mounted two additional 7·7 mm. guns in the lower wings and was powered by an improved version of the Fiat A-30RA engine.　　　　(Photo: G. Cattaneo)

The military equipment included a fire extinguisher, a gun camera, an optional survey camera, the pilot's oxygen system and an optical tubular gunsight.

Power was provided by a Fiat A30 R.A.-geared and liquid-cooled 12-cylinder upright-V in-line engine, developing 600 b.h.p. at 10,000 feet and at 2,750 r.p.m. The metal two-blade propeller incorporated ground-adjustable pitch setting.

Two fixed synchronised Vickers or Breda machine guns (0·303-in. or 0·5-in. calibre respectively) constituted the armament, located on the nose decking and firing through the propeller. Later variants mounted two attachment points under the fuselage for twelve light bombs each of 5 lb., one 200-lb. or two 100-lb. bombs.

The main fuel tank, situated in the fuselage about the centre of gravity, was of 75 Imp. gal. capacity and an auxiliary 6-gal. tank was mounted in a streamlined fairing in the top wing on the aircraft centreline.

Exceptionally robust, the C.R.32 weighed 4,225 lb. fully loaded with 1,160 lb. of disposable load—including the reconnaissance camera and 350 rounds of ammunition for each gun. At this all-up weight the take-off run was 880 feet and the climb to 10,000 feet occupied 5 minutes 25 seconds; at this height the maximum speed was 237 m.p.h. Still air range was 485 statute miles at 15,800 feet at an airspeed of 200 m.p.h.

The fighter's outstanding quality was its manoeuvrability: the Fiat C.R.32 was undoubtedly one of the most manoeuvrable fighters ever built. Highly praised by its pilots and by them long remembered with affection, the C.R.32 was responsible for the persistence of the biplane formula in I.A.F. design concept —even after the adoption of the monoplane fighter—

*This C.R.32*ter *displays a three-shade segment camouflage scheme. Approximately one hundred examples of this version were built.* (Photo: G. Apostolo)

*The final production variant in the series was the C.R.32*quater, *which remained in production until the autumn of 1939.* (Photo: G. Apostolo)

and created the premises for a dangerous over-confidence in an already obsolete design philosophy.

FIATS OVER SPAIN

It is not intended here to recall the political events that led to the outbreak of the Spanish Civil War, nor the causes, already provoking argument between historians, that brought about Italian and German

C.R.32s of the XVI° Gruppo "Cucaracha" served with distinction with the Italian air component in the Spanish Civil War.
(Photo: G. Cattaneo)

intervention alongside the Nationalist forces against the Republicans, soon to be assisted by massive Russian aid.

When the Nationalist forces began their insurrection in the summer of 1936, they lacked even an embryonic air force; and the 214 aircraft left in the Republican sectors were also obsolete. Between 1936 and 1939 the Nationalists received 730 aircraft from Italy as the equipment of the "Aviacion del Tercio"; this total was made up of Fiat C.R.32s, S.M.81s, S.M.79s, B.R.20s, Ro.37s, Ba.65s and, late in the Civil War, a squadron of G.50s. Germany supplied some 400 aircraft (He 51s, Bf 109s, Ju 87s, Do 17s and He 111s) with the "Condor Legion".

The Republicans received a total of 1,947 aircraft from various foreign powers during the war, in addition to the 214 elderly machines with which they began hostilities, the 40 civil types operated by the Government and 55 aircraft built in the Red Zone during 1937–38. Of this force, 400 were destroyed during training and in accidents and no less than 1,520 machines fell in combat with Nationalist pilots. To the Italian and mercenary aviators of the "Tercio" 943 victories were credited, about 60 per cent of these being achieved by the fighter units which were almost exclusively equipped with Fiat C.R.32 variants.

The activities of the Italian air component in Spain between August 1936 and March 1939 may be summarised by the following figures:

Note the underwing markings displayed by this Aviacion del Tercio Fiat C.R.32.

Aircraft sent to Spain	..	..	..	..	730
Engines sent to Spain	..	..	..	..	700
Sorties flown	..	..	..	..	86,420
Bombing sorties flown	..	..	..	..	5,318
Enemy a/c destroyed on ground		..	..		40
Total aircraft lost		..	..	..	186
Aircraft lost on operations		..	..	..	86
Hours flown on operations		..	..	..	138,265
Aerial engagements	..		..	..	266
Enemy a/c destroyed in air		..	..	..	903
Flying personnel lost	..		..	..	175

C.R.32s of the XVI° Gruppo escort an Aviacion del Tercio S.M.81 on a bombing mission over Government lines in Spain.

(Photo: G. Apostolo)

Of the 1,947 aircraft received by the Republicans, 1,409 were sent from Russia (including 550 I-15 "Chato" fighters and 475 I-16 "Rata" fighters), 260 from France (including 70 Dewoitine D.371, D.500 and D.510 fighters; 20 Loire Nieuport 46 and 15 Bleriot-Spad S.510 fighters), 72 from the United States (no fighters), 72 from the Netherlands (including 26 Fokker D.XXI fighters), 57 from England (no fighters) and 47 from Czechoslovakia (no fighters).

The first Fiat C.R.32 fighters arrived by sea at Melilla in August 1936 and gained their first air victory over Cordoba one week later. This first contingent of 12 aircraft was soon reinforced and before many weeks the four famous fighter units of the "Aviacion del Tercio" appeared in Spanish skies; the VI° *Gruppo* "Gamba di Ferro" (Iron Leg): the XVI° *Gruppo* "Cucaracha" (Cockroach): the X° *Gruppo* "Baleari": and the XXIII° *Gruppo* "Asso di Bastoni" (Ace of Clubs). All these units were equipped with the Fiat C.R.32, of which 380 examples were received by Italian and Spanish units during the Civil War.

The C.R.32 soon established its superiority over the mixed equipment of the Republican Air Force; and Rosatelli's nimble fighter continued to acquit itself well in the late autumn of 1936 when more modern types began to appear with Red units. Successes were achieved not only against biplanes of comparable performance such as the I-15 but also against faster monoplanes such as the "Rata" and the pride of the Russian bomber units, the SB-2 "Katiuska". These latter aircraft were at first erroneously identified as American Martin bombers; although faster than the Fiat, their speed was neutralised when patrolling C.R.32s were able to take advantage of height to making diving interceptions.

The appearance of the first I-15s over Madrid took the Italian aviators by surprise and two C.R.32s were lost in the initial encounter; the following day, however, they destroyed seven "Chatos" over the capital.

A more formidable opponent of the "Tercio's" C.R.32s was the I-16 "Rata", the most widely used fighter in Government units after the reorganisation of the Republican forces in March 1937. Usually flown by Soviet aircrew on six-month tours of duty, the I-16, with its retractable undercarriage and cantilever wing, represented an advance in design philosophy of a complete generation over the C.R.32. However, although slower than the "Rata" the Fiat was a superior gun platform and enjoyed advantages in manoeuvrability, diving speed and turning radius. By the end of hostilities in Spain 496 of the 550 "Ratas" supplied to the Government forces had been destroyed; of the 475 I-15s and 210 SB-2s sent from Russia, 415 and 178 respectively had also been lost.

Foremost among the Spanish pilots who flew the C.R.32 was the leader of the famous "Patrulla Azul" (Blue Patrol), Garcia Morato. This legendary pilot died in a flying accident after the Civil War, having gained many of his 35 air victories while flying the "Chirri", as the Spaniards affectionately christened the C.R.32.

Between 1938 and 1942 the C.R.32*quater* was

Aviacion del Tercio C.R.32 in segment camouflage scheme.
(Photo: G. Cattaneo)

The 163 Squadriglia of the Regia Aeronautica operated C.R.32s from the Aegean island of Rhodes in 1940. (Photo: G. Cattaneo)

Formation of "Cockroach Group" C.R.32s.
(Photo: G. Apostolo)

licence-built as the HA-132-L by the Hispano Aviacion company. Small numbers were used as aerobatic trainers as late as 1953, with the official designation C.1.

The practical combat experience gained by C.R.32 pilots over Spain confirmed the high opinion of the aircraft already earned in many countries in the more peaceful context of demonstration flying by aerobatic teams of the Italian Air Force. The perfect co-ordination of the controls, small turning circle and excellent

Emulating the angles of their Warren truss interplane struts; this zig-zag formation was a familiar sight at pre-war international air meetings. (Photo: G. Apostolo)

general handling qualities made the C.R.32 the ideal aircraft for such displays, the pilots involved attaining a highly sophisticated level of flying skill at the same time as providing an impressive spectacle. A team consisting of five pilots from the I Stormo and five from the II Stormo gained particular renown during a Latin American tour in 1938, performing in Peru, Argentina and Brazil. The C.R.32 also appeared with considerable success at various international military aviation meetings in Europe, including appearances at Zurich and Budapest.

Four principal versions of the C.R.32 appeared between 1933 and 1938. The standard C.R.32 of which some 350 were built, was powered by the Fiat A-30RA engine and mounted two 12·7 mm. machine guns. The C.R.32*bis* had an improved powerplant, the Fiat A-30RA*bis* and carried two additional 7·7 mm. guns in the lower wing at the junction of the outboard interplane struts. The *bis* saw some service in Spain; but the increased weight (4,350 lb.) had an adverse effect on its performance. The C.R.32-*ter* and -*quater* reverted to the original armament, but with improved sights and instrumentation; radio installations were fitted to some C.R.32*quater* machines.

EXPORT SALES

Small numbers of the C.R.32*bis*, -*ter* and -*quater* variants were exported to Venezuela and Paraguay, the latter country employing them during the final stages of the brief but violent "Gran Chaco" war between Paraguay and Bolivia. A further batch were purchased by China and participated in combat over Shanghai with Japanese intruders. One dozen C.R.30 and C.R.32 fighters were acquired by Austria, and following the *Anschluss* of 1938 they were taken over by the Luftwaffe, marked with standard black crosses and swastikas and employed as training machines.

The other main foreign operator of the Fiat C.R.32 was Hungary. Several aircraft were purchased during the expansion of the Hungarian Air Force in preparation for possible conflict with the states of the "Little Entente". After the re-annexation of Carpatho-Ruthenia in 1939 a squadron of Hungarian C.R.32s

destroyed without loss nine intruding Avia and Letov aircraft of the Slovak Air Force. With the arrival of the more modern C.R.42 and Reggiane Re.2000 on Hungarian squadrons, the C.R.32 was relegated to the training rôle.

THE C.R.32 IN W.W. II

Early in November 1939 the Fiat C.R.32 was still numerically the most important fighter equipping the Italian Air Force, a total of 292 aircraft being on the strength of first line squadrons as compared to 143 C.R.42s, 19 G.50s, 29 Macchi-Castoldi M.C.200s and 31 Ro.44s. Four complete *Stormi*, an autonomous *Gruppo* and an autonomous *Squadriglia* were equipped exclusively with the type, and another *Stormo* operated a mixed strength of C.R.32s and C.R.42s. Nevertheless, the little Spanish veteran was undeniably obsolete and during the period of Italian non-belligerence (November 1939 to June 1940) a programme of progressive replacement of the C.R.32 in squadron service was carried out.

When Italy entered the Second World War in the second week of June 1940, the C.R.32 was in first line service with the following units: *22nd Gruppo* of the

"Cockroach Group" squadron commander's C.R.32 over Spain.

This C.R.32, photographed in the grounds of an Italian museum, is finished in a Spanish camouflage pattern.   (Photo: G. Cattaneo)

52nd Stormo, based at Pontedera; *2nd Gruppo*, based at Grottaglie; *1st Stormo* based at Palermo (some C.R.42s also on strength); *3rd Gruppo*, based at Monserrato. In Libya were based the *13th Gruppo* at Castelbenito and the *8th Gruppo* at Benina. The *160th Gruppo* was based at Tirana in Albania, the *136th Squadriglia* in the Aegean and the *410th* and *411th Squadriglie* in Italian East Africa.

Some use of the C.R.32 was made in North Africa during the first offensive in the summer of 1940, which led to the conquest of Sidi Barrani. The Fiat was mostly active in the ground-strafing and light attack rôle, supplementing the Ba.65s of the *50th Stormo*

Assalto, of limited usefulness in the desert war. It also saw some action in the opening stages of the campaigns in Greece and the Aegean; and because local conditions made its replacement by the C.R.42 a difficult operation in the case of the units in Italian East Africa, the C.R.32 bore the brunt of the operations of the *410th* and *411th Squadriglie*. Notwithstanding their marked inferiority to the enemy's equipment, C.R.32s had the fortune on two occasions to shoot down aircraft of such superior performance as the Hawker Hurricane. Some success was obtained in the early fighting in Somaliland, but conditions worsened and soon only miracles of ingenuity and

C.R.32 fighter trainer of the Hungarian Air Force in late-scheme markings.   (Photo: G. Cattaneo)

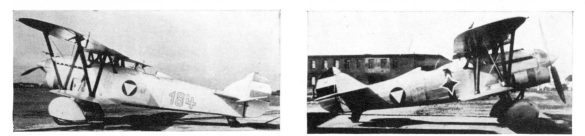

The Austrian Air Force operated C.R.30s (left) and C.R.32s (right) until the Anschluss of 1938; subsequently they were used by the Luftwaffe as trainers.
(Photos: G. Cattaneo)

improvisation sufficed to keep the weary C.R.32s operational, lacking fuel, ammunition and spares and opposed by machines of the calibre of the Gloster Gladiator and the Hawker Hurricane.

The first line service of the C.R.32 was over, and the remaining machines were relegated to the training schools where they gave reliable and popular service until the end of the Second World War. For a short time some trials were carried out concerning the Fiat's possible use as a night fighter, involving the installation of a long exhaust pipe with flame damping fittings; but little success was achieved and the project was dropped.

The story of the C.R.32 would not be complete without reference to the four prototypes which linked the aircraft with its successor, the Fiat C.R.42 (*Profile* No. 16). The prototype C.R.40 first flew in 1934, powered by a Bristol Mercury IV radial engine of 550 h.p.; the upper wing was connected directly with the fuselage in a gull-wing configuration, giving better pilot visibility. The same year saw the appearance of the C.R.40bis, in which the British power-plant was replaced by a 700 h.p. Fiat A-59R. The

C.R.41 was powered by a Gnome-Rhone K-14 engine of 900 h.p., and tested two armament systems, the first involving two 20 mm. Oerlikon cannon and the second comprising four 12·7 mm. machine guns. Maximum speed was 265 m.p.h. The C.R.33 reverted to the wing arrangement of the C.R.32 and was powered by a 700 h.p. Fiat A-33 engine, driving a three-bladed airscrew. This last prototype, which mounted four guns, flew in 1937.

The C.R.32 was for five years the mainstay of *Regia Aeronautica* fighter units, and with its excellent service record in Spain to support the affection held for it by all who flew it the agile and aggressive fighter represented the zenith of conventional biplane design. It is interesting to note that both the C.R.32 and its British contemporary, the Gloster Gauntlet (*Profile* No. 10) were eventually replaced in service by fighters of biplane configuration which nevertheless displayed many features characteristic of the generation of monoplanes which was to follow—the Fiat C.R.42 and the Gloster Gladiator. The C.R.32 may thus be said to have been in the forefront of the last of the world's true biplane fighters.

Only known photograph of a Fiat C.R.32 of the Chinese Air Force. These aircraft fought in the defence of Shanghai against Japanese bomber attacks.
(Photo: G. Apostolo)

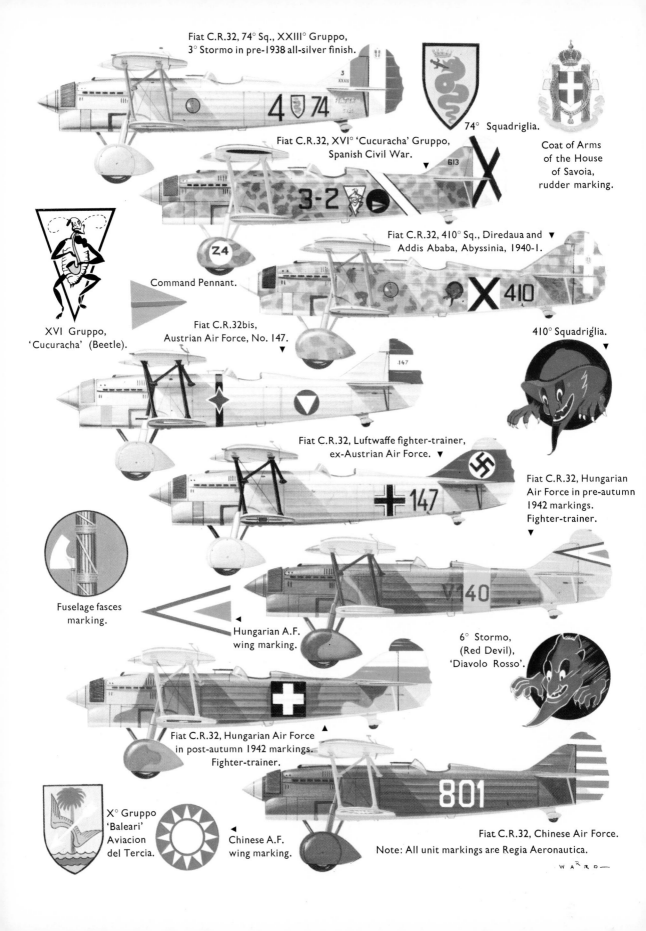

Fiat C.R.32, 74° Sq., XXIII° Gruppo, 3° Stormo in pre-1938 all-silver finish.

74° Squadriglia.

Coat of Arms of the House of Savoia, rudder marking.

Fiat C.R.32, XVI° 'Cucuracha' Gruppo, Spanish Civil War.

XVI Gruppo, 'Cucuracha' (Beetle).

Command Pennant.

Fiat C.R.32, 410° Sq., Diredaua and Addis Ababa, Abyssinia, 1940-1.

410° Squadriglia.

Fiat C.R.32bis, Austrian Air Force, No. 147.

Fiat C.R.32, Luftwaffe fighter-trainer, ex-Austrian Air Force.

Fuselage fasces marking.

Fiat C.R.32, Hungarian Air Force in pre-autumn 1942 markings. Fighter-trainer.

Hungarian A.F. wing marking.

6° Stormo, (Red Devil), 'Diavolo Rosso'.

Fiat C.R.32, Hungarian Air Force in post-autumn 1942 markings. Fighter-trainer.

X° Gruppo 'Baleari' Aviacion del Tercia.

Chinese A.F. wing marking.

Fiat C.R.32, Chinese Air Force.
Note: All unit markings are Regia Aeronautica.

WARD

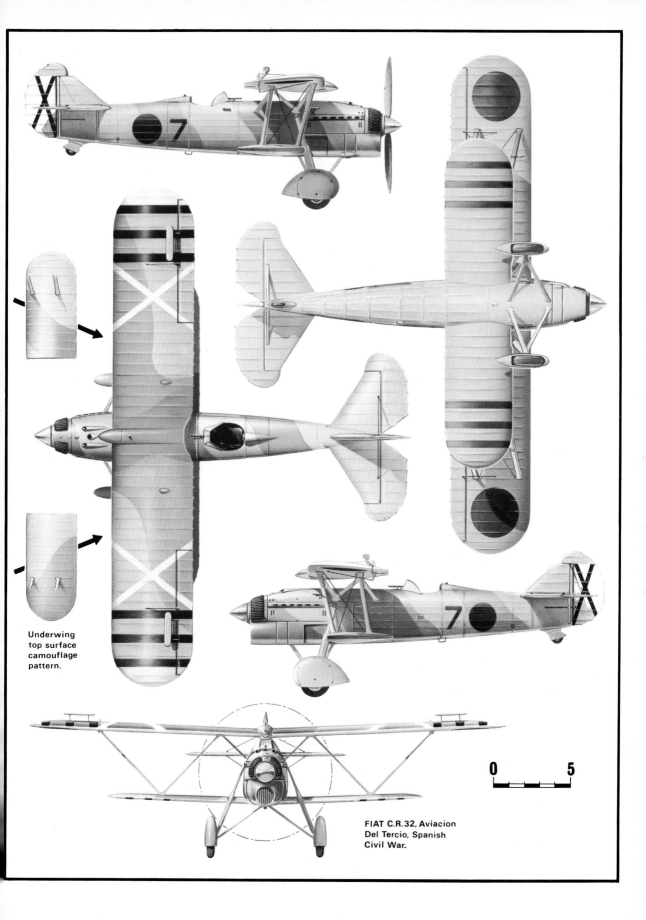

Underwing
top surface
camouflage
pattern.

FIAT C.R.32, Aviacion
Del Tercio, Spanish
Civil War.

0   5

A Hungarian Air Force C.R.32 displaying pre-autumn 1942 tail flash and post-autumn 1942 fuselage marking. (Photo: G. Cattaneo)

Fiat C.R.32ter—Specification
(Data from Technical Manual C.A. 351 of "Ministero dell 'Aeronautica".)

Powerplant: One FIAT A.30 R.A. bis, in line, liquid cooled, 600 h.p. rated at 2,750 r.p.m. FIAT two-bladed propeller, with adjustable pitch, diameter 9·242 ft.

Dimensions: Wing span (upper) 31·168 ft.; Wing span (lower) 20·160 ft.; Length 24·294 ft.; Height 8·634 ft.; Wing area 237·880 sq. ft.

Weight (lb.): Empty 3,205; Useful load 1,015 of which—Pilot 176; Rounds 129 (350 each gun); Various 48; Fuel 573; Oil 53; Camera 36. Total loaded 4,220.

Performance: (at 600-h.p. and 2,750 r.p.m.); Maximum speed: sea level 206 m.p.h.; 10,000 ft. 220 m.p.h.; 20,000 ft. 208 m.p.h.; Landing speed: 65 m.p.h.; Climb to: 3,000 ft. 1 min. 35 sec.; 10,000 ft. 5 min. 25 sec.; 20,000 ft. 14 min. 25 sec.; Combat ceiling 25,250 ft.; Take-off run 890 ft.; Landing run 755 ft.; Range (15,800 ft. and 196 m.p.h.) 485 miles.

Armament: Two 12·7 mm. calibre SAFAT machine guns. Provision for under-fuselage rack for light bombs.

Representative Units of the Italian Air Force Equipped with the Fiat C.R.32

Units			Based at	Date
1° *Stormo*	6° *Gruppo*	*Sq.* 79–81–88	Campoformido (Italy)	1936
4° *Stormo*	9° *Gruppo*	*Sq.* 73–96–97	Gorizia (Italy)	1936
	10° *Gruppo*	*Sq.* 84–90–91	Gorizia (Italy)	1936
3° *Stormo*	18° *Gruppo*	*Sq.* 83–85–95	Milan (Italy)	1937
	23° *Gruppo*	*Sq.* 74	Milan (Italy)	1937
6° *Stormo*	2° *Gruppo*	*Sq.* 150–151–152	Campoformido (Italy)	1936
	3° *Gruppo*	*Sq.* 153–154–155	Campoformido (Italy)	1936
52° *Stormo*	22° *Gruppo*	*Sq.* 539–362–369	Pontedera (Italy)	1939
	24° *Gruppo*	*Sq.* 354–355		1939
51° *Stormo*	20° *Gruppo*	*Sq* 351–352–353	Ciampino (Italy)	1938
	160° *Gruppo*		Tirana (Albania)	1940
		Sq. 163	Rhodes (Aegean)	1940
		Sq. 410 (ex 150)	Dire-Dana (Italian East Africa)	1940
		Sq. 411	Addis Ababa (Italian East Africa)	1940
	13° *Gruppo*	*Sq.* 167	Castelbenito (Libya)	1940
	8° *Gruppo*		Tobruk (Libya)	1940

Note: The location indicated is related to a specific date, since in the pre-war period the units were often moved to different bases. The fighter *Stormo* was made up of two *Gruppi*; each *Gruppo* comprised three *Squadriglie* of 12 a/c (officially) each.

Tab and bracing detail is visible in this photograph of a Hungarian C.R.32quater trainer in early-style markings. (Photo: via R. Ward)

The Messerschmitt bf 110

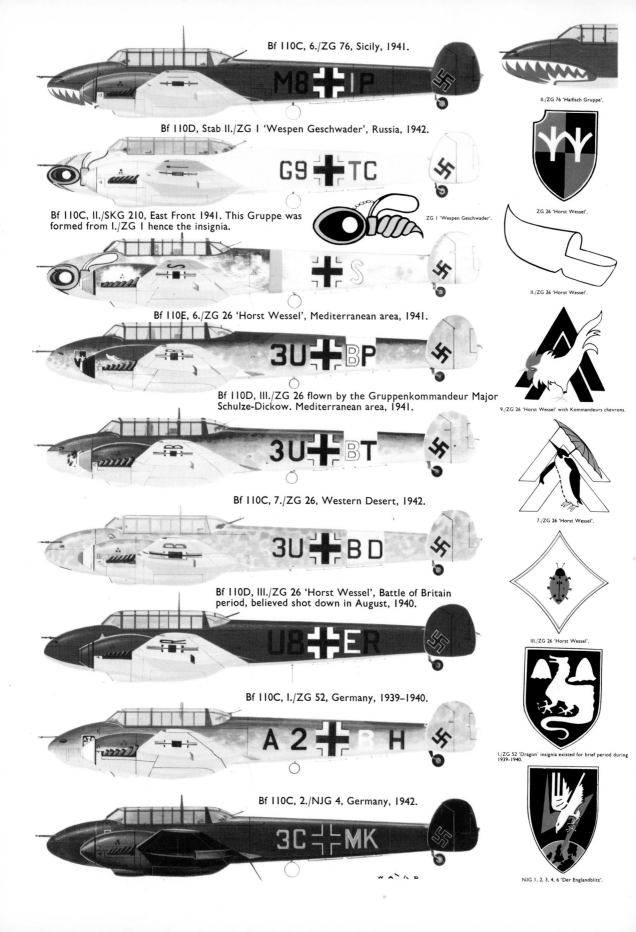

Bf 110C, 6./ZG 76, Sicily, 1941.

II./ZG 76 'Haifisch Gruppe'.

Bf 110D, Stab II./ZG 1 'Wespen Geschwader', Russia, 1942.

ZG 1 'Wespen Geschwader'.

Bf 110C, II./SKG 210, East Front 1941. This Gruppe was formed from I./ZG 1 hence the insignia.

ZG 26 'Horst Wessel'.

II./ZG 26 'Horst Wessel'.

Bf 110E, 6./ZG 26 'Horst Wessel', Mediterranean area, 1941.

9./ZG 26 'Horst Wessel' with Kommandeurs chevrons.

Bf 110D, III./ZG 26 flown by the Gruppenkommandeur Major Schulze-Dickow. Mediterranean area, 1941.

7./ZG 26 'Horst Wessel'.

Bf 110C, 7./ZG 26, Western Desert, 1942.

III./ZG 26 'Horst Wessel'.

Bf 110D, III./ZG 26 'Horst Wessel', Battle of Britain period, believed shot down in August, 1940.

Bf 110C, I./ZG 52, Germany, 1939–1940.

I./ZG 52 'Dragon' insignia existed for brief period during 1939–1940.

Bf 110C, 2./NJG 4, Germany, 1942.

NJG 1, 2, 3, 4, 6 'Der Englandblitz'.

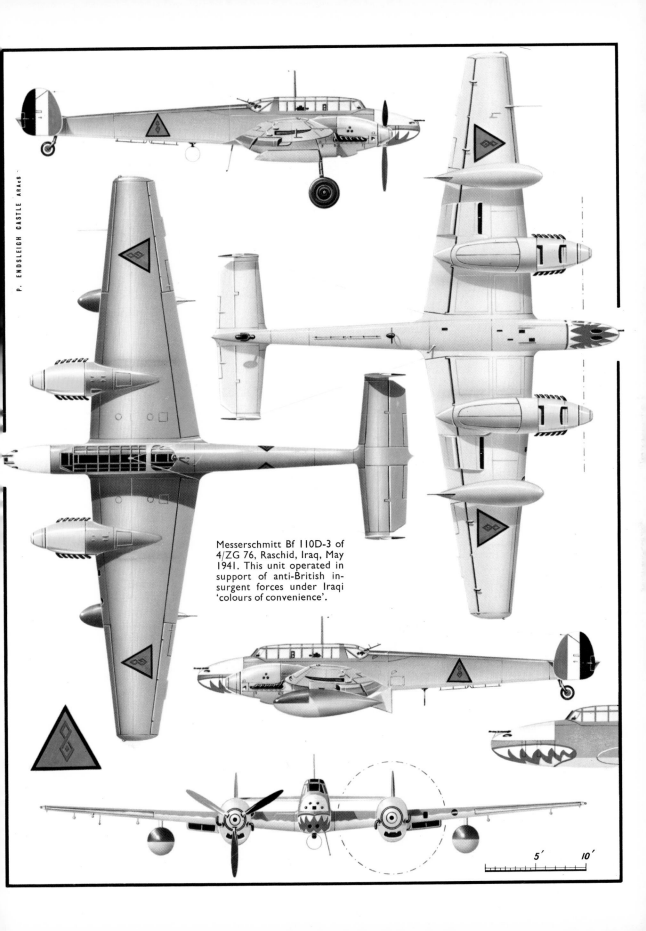

Messerschmitt Bf 110D-3 of
4/ZG 76, Raschid, Iraq, May
1941. This unit operated in
support of anti-British in-
surgent forces under Iraqi
'colours of convenience'.

5'   10'

The Messerschmitt Bf 110

by Martin C. Windrow

A Messerschmitt Bf 110C-5 (5F+CM) of the 4th Staffel, Close Reconnaissance Gruppe 14. Note patched bullet-holes in tail and wing roots.
(Photo: Imperial War Museum)

THE Messerschmitt Bf 110 provides for aero historians the classic example of an aircraft of indifferent quality which was for political and bureaucratic ends hailed with unrealistic enthusiasm by the authorities responsible for its adoption. Consequently, the inevitable failure of the type when exposed to combat was doubly unexpected and humiliating, and many fine airmen were sacrificed on the altar of national pride and political expediency before the counsels of common sense triumphed to any extent.

The strategic fighter, or *zerstörer* as it was melodramatically christened in Germany, was to be an aircraft capable of cutting a path for bomber formations through enemy airspace, eliminating fighter opposition and accompanying the bombers to and from the target, and it is important to bear the essentials of this concept in mind if the full measure of the Bf 110's failure is to be appreciated. Such an aeroplane represents an obvious conflict between the demands of range and manoeuvrability; nevertheless, this conception was realised in at least one effective aircraft during World War II—the Lockheed P-38 Lightning which, although not strictly a product of this line of thought, demonstrated a successful solution to comparable problems of range, weight, speed and control response.

It was inauspicious that the design team to which the *zerstörer* contract was allotted was in all probability never intended to succeed in producing a worthwhile aeroplane. Willy Messerschmitt's office at the *Bayerische Flugzeugwerke* in Augsburg had been out of favour with the Secretary of State for Air, General Erhard Milch, for more than five years before the development contract was placed late in 1934. It seems more than likely that originally Milch and his supporters saw the *zerstörer* theory, which they had accepted with less than unbounded enthusiasm anyway, as a convenient means of destroying Dipl.Ing. Messerschmitt's reputation for good. Similarly, when less prejudiced elements came to power in the Technical Department of the R.L.M., their determination to give the designer a fair hearing may have caused them to turn an indulgent eye on some of the more glaring inadequacies of the aeroplane which eventually emerged from this jungle of petty politics and jealousy.

During the summer of 1935 construction of the Bf 110V1 was begun. It was a slim, low-wing, cantilever monoplane with an attractive, shark-like silhouette, and when two pre-production DB 600 engines of 900 h.p. were earmarked for the prototype by the *Daimler-Benz Aktiengesellschaft*, the designers were relieved of their main problem. Previously, the 610 h.p. Junkers Jumo 210B had been the most potent German powerplant available.

Maiden flight of the Bf 110V1 took place on 12th May 1936; the pilot was Rudolph Opitz, who later played such a part in the development of the Me 163 rocket fighter. The prototype achieved 316 m.p.h. in level flight early in the trials programme, a speed comparable to that of contemporary single-engined fighter projects. The second and third prototypes flew in October and December of 1936, but when the *Luftwaffe* took over the Bf 110V2 for a series of evaluation flights at Rechlin the following January, it quickly became apparent that this satisfactory speed was offset by extremely poor acceleration and manoeuvrability.

Disregarding the reports of the experienced service pilots at Rechlin, the R.L.M. authorised the construction of four more airframes under the designation

The aircraft of II/ZG 76 were emblazoned with "shark's teeth" from the earliest months of the war. This Bf 110C (M8+EP) of the 6th Staffel displays its individual letter "E" on the upper wing surfaces, a practice discontinued in the winter of 1940/41.
(Photo: Real Photos Ltd.)

The Bf 110V1, first flown in May 1936; the pilot was Rudolph Opitz.   (Photo: Imperial War Museum)

Bf 110A-0, to be (inadequately) powered by Jumo 210B engines due to a delay in DB 600 production. Two further machines were initially engined with slightly improved Jumo 210Gs as 110B-0s. These airframes, completed in the spring of 1938, were re-engined with DB 600As a year later. In the autumn of 1938 Bf 110B-1 production commenced. The DB 600A engine was now available, and the B-1, with a nose armament of two 20 mm. MG FF cannon and four MG 17 rifle-calibre machine guns, was undeniably a formidable unit of flying artillery—if its guns could be brought to bear.

Goering (who was, predictably, an enthusiastic champion of the romantic-sounding *zerstörer* theory) had already instituted—prematurely—the formation of *Zerstörergeschwader*. Like the machine destined to be its weapon and its death-warrant, the organisation was born in bitterness. Of the limited manpower available to the still-young *Luftwaffe*, the majority were fighter pilots, and the Fighter Arm strongly resented seeing its best personnel drained off to equip one new unit after another. In the case of the *Zerstörergeschwader*, this resentment was aggravated when the "stolen cream" of the Fighter Arm, once integrated into the Reichsmarschall's new toy, were in fact equipped with Bf 109Cs and Bf 109Ds while continued attempts were made to perfect the Bf 110. Thus the Bf 110B-1 never saw true *Luftwaffe* service, the few examples built being employed almost exclusively on trials programmes of one type or another. Two results of these trials were the repositioning of the radiator baths outboard of the engine nacelles and the strengthening of the rear fuselage, to reduce turbulence round the nacelles and tail vibration respectively.

The Bf 110C-0, the next sub-type produced, was the B-1 variant re-engined with the new DB 601 powerplant; this engine had been adopted in preference to the DB 600 because it offered better supercharging and direct fuel injection. It is at this point in the life of the Bf 110 that its career in the true operational configuration began. The Bf 110C-1, essentially a strengthened C-0, is described below.

STRUCTURE OF THE Bf 110

Fuselage: Light alloy monocoque structure, oval section; comprising two halves joining longitudinally along the upper and lower centre-lines. Spar with fuselage between the wing attachment points had tubular steel upper boom and T-section lower boom.

Hat-section transverse frames, Z-section stringers, and flush-riveted stressed-skin covering.

Wings: All-metal single-spar structure with light alloy stressed-skin flush-riveted covering. The inner wing, containing the self-sealing petrol tanks, had not ribs but closely-spaced inverted hat-section stringers and chordwise stiffeners. The outer wing had light lattice ribs at 18-inch intervals, Z-section stiffeners and hat-section stringers. Slotted, fabric-covered ailerons with external horn-type mass balances. Handley Page-type leading edge slots. Slotted, metal-skinned trailing-edge flaps.

Tail: Light alloy cantilever unit. Twin fins and rudders, adjustable tailplane. Metal stressed-skin fixed surfaces; fabric-covered movable surfaces.

Undercarriage: Backwards-retracting, the main wheels enclosed within the engine-nacelles by hinged doors. Fixed tail-wheel.

The nose battery of the Bf 110C-5 comprised four MG 17 machine guns.   (Photo: Imperial War Museum)

Bf 110Cs of 10/ZG 26 in Sicily.   (Photo: Collection R. Ward)

An aircraft graveyard in the North African desert. Behind a wrecked Ju 87B/Trop of 5/St.G 5 stands a Bf 110E-1 (3U+DT) of 9/ZG 26 "Horst Wessel"; W.Nr.2354.
(Photo: Imperial War Museum)

ZERSTÖRER DEVELOPMENT

The further development of the Bf 110 in its day fighter, reconnaissance and ground-attack configurations may be traced through the following variants:

Bf110C-2. Revised electrical system. New Telefunken *Funke Geräte* (FuG) 10 radio.

Bf 110C-3 and *C-4.* These versions were similar to the C-1 and C-2 apart from their improved MG FF cannon.

Bf 110C-4/B. Racks for two 550 lb. bombs under fuselage. Powered by 1,200 h.p. DB 601N engines.

Bf 110C-5. Reconnaissance variant. Cannon omitted.

Bf 110C-6. Bomber-interceptor version with additional 30 mm. MK 101 cannon in ventral fairing.

Bf 110C-7. Strengthened undercarriage to allow for carrying of two 1,100 lb. bombs.

(Several late production Bf 110C variants were re-engined with the DB 601N powerplants as they became available.)

Bf 110D-0. The emphasis in the Bf 110D series was on improved range. The pre-production D-0 model dispensed with the MG FF cannon and featured a large faired fuel tank under the forward fuselage. This non-jettisonable supplementary tank brought the total fuel capacity up to 907 Imp. gal., provision being made for two drop-tanks of varying size.

Bf 110D-1. The considerable aerodynamic penalty imposed by the belly fairing of the pre-production model led to the abandonment of the project, and production D-1 versions reverted to the cannon armament while retaining drop-tank capability.

Bf 110D-2. Racks for two 1,100 lb. bombs under fuselage. Rear armament increased to two MG 17s.

Bf 110D-3. Bombs and drop tanks could be carried simultaneously.

Bf 110E-0 and *E-1.* These variants were fitted with racks for two 110 lb. bombs under each wing, outboard of the radiators, in addition to the fuselage racks.

Bf 110E-2. The increased power of the DB 601N engines, which became standard with this version, raised the bomb load capacity to 4,410 lb.

Bf 110E-3. A reconnaissance variant similar to the Bf 110C-5. Two 198 Imp. gal. drop-tanks could be carried.

Bf 110F-0. DB 601F engines rated at 1,300 h.p. Apart from this change, the *F-0, F-1* and *F-3* variants were similar respectively to the *E-0, E-1* and *E-3.*

Bf 110F-2. Bomber-interceptor with provision for two 21 cm. WG 21 "Dodel" rocket tubes under each wing.

Bf 110G-0. The introduction of the 1,475 h.p. DB 605B engines allowed an increase in weights and thus in war load. The *G-0* and *G-1* variants could carry two 1,100 lb. and four 110 lb. bombs and any of a wide variety of combinations of 550 lb., 1,100 lb. 2,205 lb.,

"The Belle of Berlin", a damaged Bf 110D-2 abandoned in Libya by the Luftwaffe and reconditioned by the R.A.F. The aircraft retains ETC 500 bomb racks; it probably served with SKG 210, which was based at Tobruk in August 1942.
(Photo: Imperial War Museum)

The unusual method of access to the rear cockpit was modified on late Bf 110 variants, a side-hinging canopy section replacing the Bf110C's folding hood. (Photo: Imperial War Museum)

Bf 110Ds of 8/ZG 26 and 9/ZG 26 over North Africa. Note the finned 198 Imp. gal. drop tanks.

and 110 lb. general-purpose, high penetration or fragmentation bombs and incendiary containers.

Bf 110G-2. This variant saw the introduction of a number of improvements. The MG FF cannon were replaced by two faster-firing MG 151s, and a further two MG 151s could be carried in a ventral tray in place of the bomb racks. The rear armament was increased to twin 7·9 mm. MG 81s. Other changes included strengthened oleo legs, a re-set fin and enlarged rudder surfaces, and modifications to the ignition systems, engine bearers and oil tankage.

*Bf 110G-2/R1. MG 151s and fuselage bomb racks discarded to accommodate faired 37 mm. BK 3.7 (Flak 18) cannon under centre section.

Bf 110G-2/R2. Similar to *G-2/R1*, with GM-1 engine boost (nitrous oxide injection) and no rear armament.

Bf 110G-2/R3. MG 81s re-installed; forward-firing battery of two MK 108 and four MG 151 cannon. Fuselage bomb racks discarded to accommodate ventral installation of two MG 151s.

Bf 110G-2/R4. Forward-firing armament two MK 108s, one Flak 18 cannon.

Bf 110G-2/R5. Similar to *G-2/R4* with no rear armament. GM-1.

Bf 110G-3. Long range reconnaissance variant. Forward-firing armament decreased to four MG 17s. One Rb 75/30 camera and one Rb 50/30 camera. Rear armament increased to twin MG 81s and one fixed MG 151 cannon. No bomb racks.

Bf 110G-3/R3. Similar to *G-3*; MG 17s replaced by two MK 108s.

Bf 110H-2. First H-series variant to reach production. Similar to *G-2*; retractable tail-wheel.

Bf 110H-2/R1. Similar to *G-2/R4*; extra armour protection for Flak 18 ammunition stowage.

*Rüstsatz, meaning the complete kit of parts necessary for modifying an aircraft to a special configuration.

Luftwaffe personnel prepare a Bf 110D of III/ZG 26 for a night sortie in North Africa.

Bf 110F-1s of SKG 210 information. (Photo: Collection R. Ward)

Bf 110H-2/R2. Similar to *H-2/R1*, with GM-1.

Bf 110H-3. Long range reconnaissance variant. Similar to *G-3* apart from nose battery of two MK 108s.

Minor variants included the Bf 110C-1/U1 glider-tug, converted from early C-1 fighter models; and the C-2/U1 test-bed for the remote-control gun barbettes of the Messerschmitt Me 210 series.

NIGHT FIGHTER DEVELOPMENT

The various Bf 110 night fighter models evolved as a parallel but separate line of development. Progress in this field may be traced through the following variants:

Bf 110F-4. The first Bf 110 night fighter. Powered by DB 601F engines of 1,300 h.p. and carrying two 30 mm. MK 108 cannon in a ventral tray in addition to standard armament, the F-4 was employed on G.C.I. operations. It was also the first variant to carry three crew members.

Bf 110G-4. Powered by two 1,475 h.p. DB 605B engines, this type carried forward-firing armament comprising four MG 17s and two MG 151s. Twin MG 81s were mounted in the rear of the cockpit and FuG 212 radar was installed. The forward fuselage was more heavily armoured than previously. Two 66 or 198 Imp. gal. drop-tanks could be carried; provision for bomb armament was two 550 lb. racks under the fuselage and two 110 lb. racks under each wing (if drop-tanks were not carried).

Bf 110G-4/U7. No rear armament. The GM-1 booster, of 968 lb. capacity and 45 minutes' duration, was fitted to this version. FuG 212.

Bf 110G-4/U8. Fuselage bomb racks omitted. No rear armament. Third crew member's position occupied by 119 Imp. gal. fuel tank. FuG 212.

Bf 110G-4/R3. Twin MG 81 re-installed in rear cockpit. Fuselage and wing bomb racks. Forward-firing armament improved by replacement of MG 17 battery by two MK 108s. FuG 212.

Adjusting the camera of a Bf 110 reconnaissance aircraft in the Western Desert. (Photo: Collection R. Ward)

A captured Bf 110G-4/R7 night fighter. Note drop tanks, fuselage bomb racks and radar array. (Photo: Imperial War Museum)

Bf 110G-4/R6. No rear armament. GM-1 installed. FuG 212.

Bf 110G-4/R7. Similar to *G-4/R3* except for lack of rear armament and installation of 119 Imp. gal. fuel tank in third crew member's position. FuG 212.

Bf 110H-4. Twin MG 81 re-installed. Optional fuselage and wing bomb racks. Forward-firing armament of four MG 17s, two MG 151s and two additional MG 151s in ventral tray if fuselage bomb racks were omitted. Improved armour protection for crew. FuG 212.

Bf 110H-4/U7. Similar to *H-4*, with GM-1 booster.

Bf 110H-4/U8. No GM-1; 119 Imp. gal. fuel tank in third member's position. FuG 212.

Bf 110G and Bf 110H-4 night fighters often carried both FuG 212 and FuG 220 radar arrays; the rapidly changing demands for radio aids and counter measures in the final year of the war make a rigid tabulation of the radar carried by night fighter variants impossible.

THE Bf 110 IN SERVICE

It had been intended to test the Bf 110B-1 under operational conditions in the Spanish Civil War, but that conflict ended before the *zerstörer* was ready, and the Bf 110 fired its guns in anger for the first time in Poland. Almost exclusively engaged on ground support operations during this "Eighteen Day War", the Bf 110 faced no realistic fighter opposition. As far as is known, the Bf 110 first exchanged shots with the Royal Air Force on 18th December 1939, when a force of 22 Wellington bombers attacking shipping off Wilhelmshaven were intercepted by elements of III/JG 77, equipped with Bf 109Es, and Bf 110Cs believed to have been attached to JG 1. Against the unescorted bombers the Bf 110s acquitted themselves well, a Hptm. Falk, later a night fighter ace, destroying two Wellingtons and damaging a third in this action.

When *Operation Weserübing*, the German invasion of Norway, was launched on 8th April 1940, the fighter strength of the *Luftwaffe* component included II/ZG 76. Fighter opposition was minimal, and apart from one or two sharp skirmishes with the Gladiators of 263 Squadron R.A.F. over Bodo the Bf 110s may be said to have won another "walk-over".

During the invasion of France and the Netherlands in the spring of 1940 some 350 Bf 110C-1s were on the strength of *Luftflotten* 1 and 3. For the first time the *zerstörer* units were opposed by a vigorous, if outgunned, fighter defence and losses were higher than had been anticipated. When attacks on Channel ship-

A Bf 110 in flight during manufacturers' trials. The rear guns have not been fitted and the aircraft bears a radio call-sign code on the fuselage sides. (Photo: Collection R. Ward)

A pilot of 7/ZG 26 changes sun helmet for flying helmet before a desert flight.   (Photo: Collection R. Ward)

The MG 81Z (*Zwilling-Twin*) *machine gun, standard late model defensive armament.*   (Photo: J. L. E. Maskall)

ping led the Bf 110 into its first equal combats with R.A.F. Spitfires and Hurricanes, the loss statistics began to alarm certain *Luftwaffe* officers who placed more reliance upon known facts than upon their own propaganda.

The Battle of Britain began in earnest in July/August 1940, and some 220 Bf 110C-1s were committed to the campaign. The units involved were two *Gruppen* of ZG 2; three *Gruppen* of ZG 26 "*Horst Wessel*"; two *Gruppen* of ZG 76; and one *Gruppe* of *Lehrgeschwader 1*, an operational training wing. In September *Erprobungsgruppe* 210, an experimental unit which operated Bf 110s alongside Bf 109Cs and Me 210s, joined the battle and thus launched the Bf 110 on its career as a fighter-bomber.

The Bf 110 displayed in the great air battles over Kent and Sussex all the shortcomings which had been built into it, and the *zerstörer* dream was shattered at last. It was easily identifiable from long distances; its acceleration and speed were insufficient to allow it the luxury of avoiding combat; it was sluggish in evasive manoeuvres; its turning circle was wide, and with its large wing and tail surfaces it presented a good target. The single rear gun was inadequate as a defensive weapon, and the formidable battery of nose guns was useless if the Messerschmitt was trying to rid itself of fighters attacking from the rear, as was so often the case. The "destroyer" became the "destroyed"; the strategic fighters which were to have carved a path for the avenging *Kampfgeschwader* through the Spitfires and Hurricanes were reduced to forming defensive circles and waiting for the overworked Bf 109Es to extract them from their perilous position.

Early in 1941 the mauled *Zerstörergeschwader* were withdrawn from first-line service in Europe. ZG 26 was disbanded and reformed; *Erprobungsgruppe* 210 became *Schnelles Kampfgeschwader* 210. Reconnaissance and ground support duties were allotted to the ex-*élite* fighter units, and they were dispersed over other fronts where it was hoped they would not encounter first-class fighter opposition. The Bf 110C, Bf 110D, Bf 110E and Bf 110F series served in a variety of rôles in the Balkans, Finland, Russia, North Africa and Southern Europe, mainly as "twin-engined Stukas". In Iraq, II/ZG 76, the "*Haifisch Gruppe*", were painted in rough Iraqi Air Force markings and operated in support of the insurgents who threatened the R.A.F. base at Habbaniyah. Two Messerschmitts masquerading in this fashion were destroyed at Raschid airfield on 17th May 1941 by Sgt. Smith and Sgt. Dunwoodie of 94 Squadron, R.A.F., flying Gladiators.

The last pure *Zerstörer* formations, ZG 76 and the reformed ZG 26 "*Horst Wessel*", were used as inter-

The Bf 110C-4/B was one of the most widely used variants in the first three years of the war.

129

ceptor units during the daylight operations over Germany of the 8th U.S.A.A.F. The range and heavy armament of the Bf 110 were invaluable in these actions, and a variety of rocket weapons were tested against the huge formations of B-17s and B-24s. Naturally, the survival of the Bf 110 interceptors depended on their avoiding the attentions of the Allied escort fighters, but even when forced to remain out of range of the American formations they were of use as "shadow" planes, relaying information ahead to single-engined fighter forces. The Bf 110 *staffeln* were heavily committed as interceptors during the aerial slaughters of 17th August 1943, the day of the great Schweinfurt-Regensburg raids.

Gunners' position in the Bf 110G-4/R3, with MG 81Z machine guns. (Photo: J. L. E. Maskall)

The DB 605B engine which powered Bf 110G night fighters Note special exhaust shrouds. (Photo: J. L. E. Maskall)

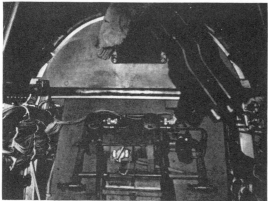

Luftwaffe armourers feeding belts of 7·9 mm. ammunition into the nose magazines of a Sicily-based Bf 110D before a mission over Crete. (Photo: Collection R. Ward)

Vulnerable during the daylight hours, the Bf 110 was an obvious choice when the *Luftwaffe* began the expansion of night fighter defences in 1940/41. The 1st Night Fighter Division, which actually only consisted of three *Gruppen* drawn from survivors of *Zerstörer* units, was founded in Holland late in 1940. Two years later, largely due to the energy of *Luftwaffe* General Josef Kammhuber, this force had grown to six (albeit under-strength) *Geschwader*. By the end of that year the first properly co-ordinated G.C.I. radar service had been set up, based on the control bunkers at Arnheim, Doberitz, Metz, Schleissheim and Stade. Previously the night fighters had been largely dependent upon pre-arranged co-ordination with searchlight batteries. By March 1943, the *Nachtjagdgeschwader* had attained a high degree of efficiency, claiming some 1,600 R.A.F. night bombers destroyed. These claims are the more impressive when one considers that the Night Fighter Arm seldom exceeded 350 pilots, and that the Bf 110 night fighter was a death-trap if crucially damaged. Vast quantities of fuel were carried, and abandoning the aircraft was virtually impossible for at least one member of the crew. The radar-operator, cramped in the centre of the narrow cockpit on a seat which consisted of a tubular metal frame covered with a square of cord netting, could only leave or enter the aircraft through the gunner's hatch. If the gunner were killed or injured, the radar operator was completely trapped. It was physically impossible for a man in flying clothes to crawl over or round the gunner and open the cockpit. It was hard enough to get in when the aircraft was standing on the tarmac.

Two factors began to reduce the high level of effectiveness of the Night Fighter Arm in the spring and early summer of 1943. The crews and aircraft of the *Nachtjagdgeschwader* were ordered into the air by day to help the day fighters in their struggle against the 8th Army Air Force. This increased the strain on men and machines, and losses rose due to night fighter pilots, accustomed to the cover of darkness, pressing home lone-wolf attacks too vigorously by day.

It was also in this period that the "radio war" of radar counter-measures began in earnest; and until the end of the war the record of the night fighters was subject to sharp fluctuations as the British and German scientists fought out their own long range war with

Cockpit of the Bf 110G-4/R3 night fighter.
(Photo: J. L. E. Maskall)

such exotically named weapons as "Ground Grocer", *Lichtenstein*, *Neptun*, "Piperack", *Flensburg*, "Serrate" and *Naxos*.

LUFTWAFFE UNITS AND MARKINGS

The basic *Luftwaffe* tactical unit was the *Geschwader*. The units which employed the Bf 110 series of aircraft were named *Zerstörergeschwader* (Destroyer Wings), *Schnelles Kampfgeschwader* (Fast Bomber Wings), *Nachtjagdgeschwader* (Night Fighter Wings) or *Aufklärungsgruppen* (Reconnaissance Squadrons). Other types of units flew the Bf 110 for specialised tasks or as communications or "hack" machines at one time or another, but the majority of the machines produced were assigned to the above-mentioned types of formation.

Each *Geschwader* was made up of a number of *Gruppen*, each of which was in turn made up of three *Staffeln*. These sub-units were numbered independently thus, for instance, II/ZG 26 (the second *Gruppe* of *Zerstörergeschwader* 26 "*Horst Wessel*") was made up of 4/ZG 26, 5/ZG 26 and 6/ZG 26 (the fourth, fifth and sixth *Staffeln* of ZG 26).

The operational strengths of these formations varied greatly; but an average *Staffel* mustered between ten and 16 aircraft, thus giving a *Geschwader* an establishment of some 90 to 120 machines. Unfavourable loss/replacement ratios often rendered these "paper strengths" very inaccurate.

All *Luftwaffe* operational units except *Jagdgeschwader* (Fighter Wings) and some *Schlachtgeschwader* (Ground Attack Wings) used a four-symbol code on the fuselage sides of aircraft for identification purposes. On the left-hand side of the national insignia on each side of the machine appeared a numeral/letter code identifying the *Geschwader*, e.g., 2 S—ZG 2; and F 1—KG 76 (Bomber Wing No. 76). From 1943 onwards this code tended to be painted in very small characters by some units, or omitted altogether. In the case of *Nachtjagdgeschwader* unit codes and even national insignia were often considered superfluous and were obscured by sprayed camouflage finishes.

On a Russian airfield, a snow-camouflaged Bf 110 starts a minor blizzard with its slipstream. The wasp motif of ZG 1 "Wespen Geschwader" can just be seen on the nose.
(Photo: Collection R. Ward)

Two 550-lb. bombs can be seen on the fuselage racks of this white-painted Bf 110 of ZG 1 in Russia.
(Photo: Collection R. Ward)

On the right-hand side of the national insignia two letters appeared. The first was the identification letter of the individual machine, and was painted or outlined in the *Staffel* colour (see organisation table below). This practice was abandoned by NJGs late in the war. The second letter identified the *Staffel* within the *Geschwader* in accordance with a rigid schedule which applied throughout the war (see table).

Various combinations of this four-symbol code were marked on the wings. Early in the war, all four symbols were often applied to wing undersurfaces. It was observed that the individual and *Staffel* letters were sometimes painted outboard of the national insignia under starboard and port wingtips respectively. In the Battle of Britain several types of German aircraft, notably Bf 110s and Dornier Do 17s, carried the individual letter outboard of the national insignia on the wing upper surfaces. Probably the most common practice, however, was the repetition of the individual letter in black under both wing tips.

Each *Geschwader* and *Gruppe* had a Staff Flight, varying in size but always marked in accordance with the following schedule. The Flight colour was green, and the appropriate letter replaced the fourth, or *Staffel*, symbol.

Geschwader Staff = A	III Gruppe = D
I Gruppe = B	IV Gruppe = E
II Gruppe = C	V Gruppe = F

Thus, 2 S + (white E) R was machine "E" of 7/ZG 2; R 4 + T W was machine "T" of 12/NJG 2; and M 8 + (green L) D was machine "L" of *Gruppe Stab*/III/ZG 76.

Two important exceptions to the above should be noted. Reconnaissance units were organised around the *Gruppe* rather than the *Geschwader*. Consequently, the *Aufklärungsgruppen* often mustered up to six *Staffeln*, and the individual letter immediately to the right of the national insignia on the fuselage sides was not coloured. The *Gruppen* were coded as if they were *Geschwader* for identification purposes, being allotted two-symbol codes. Thus, 5 F + C M was machine

The Bf 110G-2/R4 mounted one 37 mm. Flak 18 cannon, with 72 rounds of ammunition, in a large belly fairing. The aircraft illustrated was operated by ZG 1.

"C" of Reconnaissance Squadron 14's 4th *Staffel.* (See photograph on page 268.)

When engaged on bomber-interceptor operations towards the end of the war, ZG 76 applied fighter-style markings to their Bf 110s. The four-symbol code was either abandoned or supplemented by fighter identification numbers of one or two digits, and staff aircraft were marked with the various chevron/bar symbols employed by *Jagdgeschwader* staff flights.

Units known to have operated the Bf 110 during their service include:

ZG 1 (6 U, later G 9, later 2 J); ZG 2 (2 S); 6/ and 7/(Z) JG 5 "*Eismeer Geschwader*" (L N); 10/ and 13/ (Z) JG 5 (1 B); ZG 26 "*Horst Wessel*" (U 8 until 30th June 1941, later 3 U); ZG 76 (M 8); E.Gr. (later SKG) 210 (S 9); LG 1 (L 1); LG 2 (L 2); Aufkl.Gr.(H)14 (5 F); Aufkl.Gr.(F)33 (8 H); NJG 1 (G 9); NJG 2 (R 4); NJG 3 (D 5); NJG 4 (3 C, later G 9); NJG 6 (3 C until 30th July 1943, later 2 Z); St.G 1 (A5).

It will be noted that certain *Staffeln* of the *Zerstörer* element of JG 5 "*Eismeer Geschwader*" did not conform to the usual pattern of *Geschwader* codes; it will also be seen that owing to the disbandment and re-formation of several units, the code G9 was carried by three distinct *Geschwader* at various times.

Specification

Bf 110C-4 Two-seat Day Fighter
Dimensions: Span 53 ft. 4⅞ in.; length 39 ft. 8½ in.; height 11 ft. 6 in.; wing area 413 sq. ft.

Powerplants: Two 1,100-h.p. Daimler-Benz DB 601A twelve-cylinder inverted Vee liquid-cooled engines; V.D.M. three-blade controllable-pitch airscrews.
Armament: Four 7·9 mm. MG 17 machine guns with 1,000 rounds per gun in upper half of nose. Two 20 mm. MG FF cannon 180 r.p.g. in lower half of nose. One rearward-firing 7·9 mm. MG 15 machine gun with 750 r.p.g. in cockpit.
Weights: Normal loaded 15,300 lb.
Fuel Tankage: 279 Imp. gal. in wing cells.
Performance: Maximum speeds—349 m.p.h. at 22,965 ft.; 294 m.p.h. at sea level. Maximum cruising speeds—301 m.p.h. at 22,965 ft.; 263 m.p.h. at sea level. Range on 279 Imp. gal.—481 miles at 262 m.p.h. at sea level; 528 miles at 304 m.p.h. at 16,400 ft.; 565 miles at 301 m.p.h. at 22,965 ft.; operational ceiling 32,000 ft.

Specification

Bf 110G-4/R3 Three-seat Night Fighter
Dimensions: Span 53 ft. 4⅞ in.; length 41 ft. 6¼ in.; height 13 ft. 1¼ in.; wing area 413 sq. ft.
Powerplants: Two 1,475 h.p. Daimler-Benz DB 605B twelve-cylinder Vee liquid-cooled engines; V.D.M. three-blade airscrews.
Armament: Two 30 mm. MK 108 cannon with 135 rounds per gun in upper half of nose. Two 20 mm. MG 151 cannon with 300 and 350 r.p.g. respectively in lower half of nose. Two rearward-firing 7·9 mm. MG 81 machine guns in twin mounting with 400 r.p.g. in cockpit. (Alternative cockpit armament was the "Schräge Musik" installation of twin 20 mm. MG FF cannon mounted to fire obliquely upward from the rear cockpit bulkhead.) Bomb load 1,540 lb.
Weights: Empty 11,220 lb.; normal loaded 20,700 lb.; maximum loaded 21,800 lb.
Fuel Tankage: 279 Imp. gal. in wing cells; two 198 or 66 Imp. gal. drop tanks.
Performance: Maximum speeds—342 m.p.h. at 22,965 ft.; 311 m.p.h. at sea level. Range on 675 Imp. gal.—1,305 miles. Operational ceiling 26,000 ft. Maximum climb rate—2,306 ft./min. to 18,000 ft.

Bf 110 production: By 31st December 1939, approx. 573 machines had been delivered. Subsequent production totalled: *1940* 1,083 machines; *1941* 784 machines; *1942* 580 machines; *1943* 1,580 machines; *1944* 1,525 machines. Between 1st January 1945 and the cessation of hostilities, 45 machines were produced.

Bf 110s of Schlachtgeschwader 1 dispersed in a Russian clearing. The two nearest machines, A5+EB and A5+HB, are aircraft of the 1st Gruppe staff flight The yellow belly-band near the tail indicates service in the North and Central Russian zones. The under wing-tips were also painted yellow.

The Hawker Hurricane IIc

The Hawker Hurricane IIC

by Francis K. Mason, 1965.

Bearing the presentation inscription "United Provinces—Cawpore 1", this night intruder Hurricane IIC (LK-A) of No. 87(F) Squadron was flown by Sqdn. Ldr. D. C. Smallwood, D.F.C.
(Photo: Imperial War Museum)

AS the summer of 1940 drew to a close, the sadly depleted ranks of the R.A.F.'s victorious Fighter Command started the laborious but vital task of building up and re-equipping its interceptor squadrons; the lessons learned had been hard-won, and peacetime fighter tactics had long since gone by the board. The Spitfires and Hurricanes had earned their keep and been found little wanting, while the surviving pilots—now sadly bereft of their professional hardcore—had assumed the responsibilities of seasoned veterans.

As the tactical advances came to be written into the Service training, so the characteristics of the British fighters acquired an essential scrutiny. Under wartime conditions—and especially those prevailing in Britain in 1940—there could be no question of replacing the Hurricane or Spitfire on account of obsolescence and it was no less than a foregone conclusion that many years' service lay before these magnificent designs. Indeed, any major advance in British fighter design that could be expected was already being anticipated in the Hawker Typhoon.

So far as the Hurricane was concerned, there can be no denying that although it had represented the numerically superior element of Fighter Command's defence, it *was* regarded as "half-a-generation older" than the Spitfire, and only the tremendous demands being made upon the aircraft factories for standard fighters had delayed the introduction of the more advanced Hurricane II.

Fundamentally the airframe of the Hurricane was entirely satisfactory; its performance, on the other hand, had been something of a handicap, and it was

in this direction that design attention was turning during the summer of 1940. On 11th June that year a Hurricane I, *P3269*, was flown at Langley powered by the new Rolls-Royce Merlin XX with a Rotol R.X.5/2 constant-speed propeller. Armed with eight Browning guns, this aircraft achieved a level speed of 348 m.p.h. at a weight of 6,689 lb. in the hands of Philip Lucas—and was thus the fastest armed Hurricane ever flown. This Merlin, delivering 1,185 b.h.p. in its early form, was a two-stage supercharged engine and had been developed with mass production and widespread subcontracting uppermost in mind.

As already mentioned, preoccupation with replacements occasioned by the vital battle raging delayed introduction of the new Merlin and also any serious attempts to increase the Hurricane's gun armament. No marked shortage in Browning guns was felt during the battle, yet allocations to various new aircraft were being drawn up many months ahead of production, so that the first Hurricane IIs to reach the Royal Air Force—on 4th September 1940—were Mark IIAs with standard 8-gun wings. Twelve-gun wings started moving down the Langley lines shortly afterwards and were delivered to home squadrons as Hurricane IIBs at the end of the year.

HEAVY GUNS

As if any proof had been necessary, the Battle of Britain well illustrated the lack of penetrative power of the rifle-calibre Browning. German aircraft shot down displayed much evidence of damage to soft-skinned components—control surfaces and cockpit

134

An early series Hurricane IIC of No. 3(F) Squadron in North Europe day camouflage of 1941. The exhaust shield was an "optional fit".

transparencies—whilst even relatively thinly armoured fuel tanks, engines and crew positions had resisted penetration. Such shortcomings had been foreseen as far back as 1935 and the various compact 20 mm. gun designs were assessed and were incorporated in a number of Air Ministry Specifications—resulting in the Westland Whirlwind and Bristol Beaufighter twin-engine fighters. It did not occur to the Air Staff that such guns could reasonably be accommodated in single-engine aircraft—despite a design tender by Hawker to Spec. F.37/35 for a Hurricane to be armed with four 20 mm. guns! Preoccupation with the Whirlwind and delays in negotiating licences to manufacture the Oerlikon and Hispano guns thus fore-stalled an early advance in the Hurricane's armament.

In 1939 a Hurricane I (*L1750*) was "lashed-up" with a pair of Oerlikons *under* the wings as part of the armament flight trials for the Whirlwind, but this aeroplane remained impotently on Air Ministry experimental charge and safely locked-up in a hangar at Martlesham Heath through the Battle of Britain! More serious 4-cannon proposals were made by Hawker in May 1940, but in view of the massive losses being suffered by Hurricane squadrons in France that month, official support was—probably justifiably—absent. Hawker did, however, gain per-

mission to adapt a pair of battle-damaged wings to mount four drum-fed Oerlikons, and these were flown by Dick Reyell on *P2640* on 7th June. Top speed of this aircraft was probably as low as 290 m.p.h., yet it was delivered for trials with No. 151 Squadron at North Weald on 19th August (although no record of combat by the aircraft can be found).

Service evaluation of the cannon installation encouraged Hawker to persevere, and as more sets of guns became available, semi-tooling methods were used to fit these in Mark I airframes (e.g. *V7260*, *V7360* and *W9324*). Due to the lack of power in the Merlin III, the 4-cannon Hurricane I did not enter service with the R.A.F., but did so in large numbers with the Royal Navy as the Sea Hurricane IC.

Towards the end of the semi-tooled conversions, numerous Merlin XX-powered airframes became available and four of these—*V2461*, *Z2588*, *Z2885* and *Z2891*—represented prototypes of the Hurricane IIC. The first was flown by Seth-Smith on 6th February 1941.

Of all Hurricane versions, the Hurricane IIC was built in greatest numbers, 4,711 being constructed in the U.K.—the majority at Langley. Others were built by Gloster and Austin and some by the Canadian Car & Foundry at Fort William. Many Hurricanes, start-

Close-up of 20 mm. gun installation of Hurricane IIC.

Re-arming and servicing a Hurricane IIC.

A formation of tropical Hurricane IICs. The three aircraft farthest from the camera are presentation machines commemorating the three MacRobert brothers, and outboard cannons of the nearest aircraft have been deleted in the interests of performance.

ing life as Mark IIAs and IIBs, acquired 4-cannon wings according to the availability of repaired battle-weary components. Both Hispano and Oerlikon guns were used and although early installations used the Chattelerault belt feed (due to delays in satisfactory de-icing protection for the drum-feed), the drum-feed became standard.

Hurricane IICs entered operational service with the R.A.F. at the end of May 1941, but already the Hurricane had been superseded as a metropolitan day interceptor on account of performance shortcomings. Instead, with the benefit of its heavy weight of fire, the aircraft joined in the growing tide of offensive sweeps over the French Channel ports, attacking the many targets of opportunity that were presented—the light coastal craft, invasion barges, railway and road vehicles that disintegrated under the storms of cannon shells.

Bombs came to be added to the Hurricane (as did 44-gallon underwing fuel tanks) but such was the reduction in performance—top speed of 220 m.p.h. with four cannon and two 250-lb. bombs—that the daylight sweeps fast became regarded by Hurricane pilots as suicidal, especially with regard to the presence of Fw 190s and extensive *flak* defences in Northern Europe.

By the autumn of 1941, therefore, Hurricanes were operating for the most part by night or in half-light conditions. By October no fewer than fifty-seven home-based squadrons flew Hurricane IIs, usually a mixed complement of IIBs and IICs. Perhaps the most famous of all R.A.F. Squadrons was No. 1, operating from its traditional base at Tangmere, and this Squadron led the van of night intruder operations, carrying the battle back to the *Luftwaffe's* night bomber bases in France. The cloak of darkness concealed the Hurricane's performance deficiencies and enabled many a pilot to lurk in the path of returning raiders and to shoot down the weary and unwary.

Taking off from Tangmere on 4th May 1942, Flt. Lt. K. M. Kuttlewascher, star of No. 1, set course for Fécamp on the French coast in Hurricane IIC *JX-E (BE581)* with two 44-gallon drop tanks. Flying on south he came upon St. André airfield, lit with a flarepath for bombers returning from raids over England. Several aircraft were already in the circuit when the intruder arrived, and, having made these out as He 111s, Kuttlewascher slipped in behind one and destroyed it with a two-second burst from his 20 mm. guns. Twice more the Czech fired his guns and, on circling the airfield, noted three enemy aircraft blazing furiously on the ground.*

Hurricane IICs went into action over the ill-starred Dieppe landings of 19th August 1942. No. 43 Squadron, also of the Tangmere sector, were the first into the attack having come to readiness at four that morning. In the first raid twelve pilots, led by Sqdn. Ldr. de Vivier, carried out a beach-level sweep, attacking with guns and bombs the coastal gun positions, machine gun nests and radio buildings. They flew through a storm of *flak* and one pilot was

* *Kuttlewascher's aircraft on this occasion is the subject of the 5-view drawing on page 2.*

Close-up of tail-armed 250-lb. bomb on Hurricane II.

Hurricane IIC carrying two 90-gallon fixed ferry tanks.

Late-series presentation Hurricane IIC "British Prudence" with two 44-gallon drop tanks.　　　(Photos: Hawker Siddeley Aviation)

lost; another baled out to be picked up at sea and a third crash-landed at Tangmere. Four other aircraft sustained damage from ground fire. 43 Squadron flew three further raids over Dieppe that day. . . .

These were typical offensive sorties performed by Hurricane IIs in those frustrating years of 1941 and 1942. Frustrating was the description of another task performed by Hurricane IICs of Nos. 1 and 43 Squadron—that of Turbinlite collaboration. Powerful miniature searchlights mounted in twin-engine aircraft (notably Havocs of No. 1460 Flight) were intended to illuminate enemy raiders to that accompanying Hurricanes could close in for the kill. Hundreds of flying hours were spent in fruitless patrols and exercises before the scheme was abandoned.

During 1942–43 Hurricane IICs added a long list of external stores to their combat inventory. Small (anti-personnel) Bomb Carriers were used against road vehicles in France and the Low Countries; smoke screen dispensers were used to cover the various isolated amphibious attacks on the continent, and a few IICs acquired rocket projectiles—though operational rocket-equipped Hurricanes were of the Mk.IIB and IV variety. 500-lb. bombs were occasionally used at night but seldom in the presence of *flak*

or defending night fighters as the Hurricane IIC thus loaded scarcely achieved 180 m.p.h.!

By D-Day the Hurricane IIC had disappeared from the R.A.F.'s front line strength in Northern Europe, the aircraft still being built by Hawker (until September 1944) equipping the numerous training and communication units supporting the fighting echelons.

AT WAR OVERSEAS

First Hurricane IICs to be shipped overseas were those that joined the stream of aircraft allocated to the Middle East in mid-1941. IIAs and IIBs had been arriving at Canal Zone Maintenance Units since the spring that year and experience showed the absolute necessity to equip the Merlin XX engines with sand filters over the carburettor intakes. These filters effectively prolonged engine life but severely reduced performance; and although the IIC still retained an adequate speed margin over the radial-engined Italian fighters, the appearance of modern German fighters over the Mediterranean in 1941 prompted some Hurricane IIC squadrons to reduce the armament by removal of two guns. By mid-November 1941, out of forty British fighter squadrons in the Middle East, twenty-five flew Hurricanes and, of these, eighteen flew IICs.

With guns removed this Hurricane IIC of the Northolt Air Despatch Letter Service carried despatches to France after D-Day 1944.

This Hurricane IIC of 83 O.T.U. is the subject of a drawing on page 286

A four-cannon Sea Hurricane IIC conversion, NF717.

Seldom documented among the many Hurricane variants were the Mark IIs converted in the Middle East to carry reconnaissance cameras both in the wings and in a ventral fairing. Often aircraft which were returned for repair at Egyptian M.U.s were thus converted and among them were several Mark IICs, though with the removal of their gun armament they were simply termed P.R.IIs. Such aircraft served with a number of units, including 451 Squadron of the R.A.A.F. and No. 208 Squadron, R.A.F.

Despite their suspected performance handicaps, IICs achieved many notable victories in the desert war. For example, No. 274 Squadron, flying a composite formation of twelve Hurricane IIAs and IICs on a patrol near Gazala early in December 1941, joined combat with twenty Bf 109Es and Fiat G.50s. Three Messerschmitts were shot down for the loss of one Hurricane. The latter aircraft collected a bullet in the glycol coolant tank and caught fire, forcing the pilot, Lt. Hoffe of the S.A.A.F., to bale out. Another pilot, Flt. Lt. Tracey, seeing Hoffe reach the ground in no-man's-land, landed his Hurricane beside the South African, picked him up and brought him home, seated in his lap! A week later 274 was again in action near El Adam when eight Hurricane IICs met a formation of fifteen Ju 87s escorted by eighteen Bf 109Fs, Fiat G.50s and Macchi C.202s. Three Ju 87s, two Macchis and a Fiat were destroyed for the loss of three Hurricanes. One of the Hurricane pilots, Sgt. Parburvry, spotted a Ju 87 landing to pick up the pilot of another which had force landed, and proceeded to destroy both aircraft. Two evidently couldn't play that game!

Malta was a happy hunting ground for Hurricane IICs during 1941, these aircraft being taken on strength by the three Squadrons, Nos. 126, 185 and 251, based on the Island in June that year. Initially vested with purely defensive duties, No. 126 Squadron achieved its first victories on 30th June, destroying two Macchi C.200s without loss. No. 185 shot down two and damaged three more, again without loss, four days later.

About a fortnight later Italy carried out an E-Boat attack on Valletta's Grand Harbour. Nos. 126 and 185 took off to attack the enemy ships and were set upon by escorting Macchi C.200s. Flt. Lt. Lefebre, by singling out one ship and carrying out repeated attacks, so unnerved the crew that it ran up the white flag. Plt. Off. Winton of No. 185 Squadron had to bale out of his Hurricane and, landing in the water, swam to the nearest E-Boat only to find the entire crew dead. "No. 185 Squadron thus captured the E-Boat and kept the Italian marine flag as a souvenir." Between them the Squadrons destroyed or captured all the E-Boats and shot down one of the escorting Macchis.

During those critical weeks when Rommel's *Panzers* were halted at El Alamein scarcely forty miles from the vital Suez Canal, another Hurricane IIC squadron, No. 73, was called upon to provide night defence of British installations around Alexandria and Cairo, and during July 1942 alone destroyed twenty-three enemy raiders for the loss of six Hurricanes.

The "Torch" landings on the French Algerian and Moroccan coasts opened up further fields of operations for the Hurricane. One of the initial objectives of the landings was the capture of Maison Blanche airfield near the port of Algiers. This was quickly captured by an American combat team and it was

One of a number of tropical Hurricane IICs supplied to Turkey from R.A.F. Maintenance Units in the Middle East in 1942.
(Photo: Imperial War Museum

(Above and below): *The story behind these two rare pictures of Hurricanes in U.S. markings is obscure. They were taken on a beach at St. Leu, Algeria, on 8th November 1942 shortly after the Torch landings. The aircraft above is a four-cannon Canadian Sea Hurricane X still bearing the serial AM277; that below is a twelve-gun Canadian Sea Hurricane XII, JS327. Being deck-equipped, it seems possible that they had been brought from Canada aboard a U.S. Carrier and on flying-off ran out of fuel, force landing on the beaches of Algeria. Examination of rutting and the position of broken propeller blades suggest conventional wheels-up "dead-stick" landings.*
(Photos: via R. Ward)

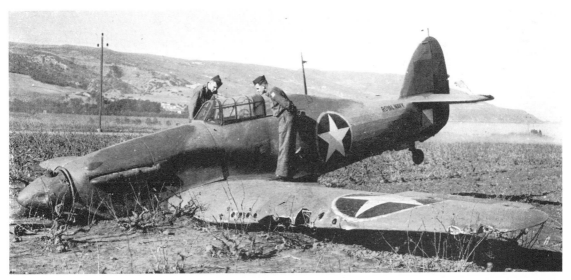

A late-series Hurricane IIC of the Yugoslav Partisan Forces.

No. 43 Squadron with Hurricane IICs that were the first Allied fighters to land, having flown from Gibraltar non-stop.

By the eve of the Sicilian landings the number of Hurricane squadrons had dropped to twenty, of which the thirteen IIC squadrons were deployed over the entire Middle East theatre, ranging from No. 74 in Northern Persia to No. 32 performing defensive patrols over Algeria and Tunisia. It is not generally known that at about this time U.S. Navy detachments, newly-arrived from America aboard U.S. Carriers, were also flying Hurricanes. These aircraft— Canadian-built Sea Hurricanes and 4-cannon Mark XIIs—were later left on French North African territory as the tide of battle ebbed away, and it is believed that a few were restored and taken over by the French Navy towards the end of the War in Europe. Though most of these American-flown Hurricanes appear to have retained their drab "British" camouflage throughout their life, at least one is believed to have been flown from South Italy in 1944 on communications duties, repainted silver overall and displaying the American "star and bar" insignia.

RUSSIA AND THE FAR EAST

Bearing in mind that the Hurricane IIC was introduced into R.A.F. service in mid-1941, it is ironic to reflect that Britain was supplying these aircraft in relatively large numbers to Russia some months before British and Commonwealth forces were crying out for modern fighters with which to combat the Japanese attacks in the Far East. While home-supplied Hurricane IICs continued to occupy deck space on convoys to North Russia, it was not until May 1942 that the first IICs arrived on squadrons in India and Ceylon. By then they were too late to participate in the defence of Burma.

Throughout the remainder of 1942, a steady flow of Hurricane IICs continued to equip squadrons sadly depleted during early Japanese onslaughts, and by June 1943 Hurricane IIBs and IICs were being flown by sixteen Squadrons in India, Northern Burma and Ceylon. No. 11 Squadron, having been moved from the Middle East the previous October, was now stationed with No. 261 at Baigachi in East Bengal. Nos. 30, 258 and 273 constituted the defence of

Ceylon, based at Colombo, China Bay and Ratamlana. In all, 670 Hurricanes were on charge in India, available for the forthcoming campaigns in Burma, and 200 were turned over to the slowly-expanding Indian Air Force.

By 1944 twenty-nine Hurricane squadrons had been

Above: *Bomb-carrying tropical Hurricane IICs on a Burmese airstrip in 1943.* (Photo: Imperial War Museum)

Below: *Hurricane IICs served with various training units in the I.A.F. and R.A.F. in India towards the end of World War 2 The unarmed aircraft seen here over Bengal served with the G.A.T.U. until 1947 when it was struck off charge.*

Camouflage and marking schemes of the Yugoslav and American Hurricanes (see pages 286 and 287).

equipped, of which seven were Indian. It would be wrong, however, to imply that the Hurricane bore the sole responsibility for tactical support and defence in Eastern India and Burma; yet it was the Hurricane that performed the lion's share of the close support duties throughout the critical Kohima and Imphal operations and accompanied the army on its advance southwards through Burma, while the Spitfires provided the principal cover for these and many other bombing operations.

One of the more specialised duties performed during the campaign was that of tactical reconnaissance, carried out by the Hurricane IICs of No. 1 Squadron, I.A.F. Fitted with a forward-facing camera inboard of the starboard cannon, this version was used for low altitude photography, gunnery spotting and message dropping. An example of this good work was afforded

by Sqdn. Ldr. Arjan Singh who, on a late evening patrol, reported the approach of a Japanese battalion moving on Imphal. Forthwith thirty-three cannon and bomb-armed Hurricanes took-off in the gathering dusk and presently arrived over the area of the reported enemy forces. Turning on their landing lights, the leading Hurricane pilots could discern the Japanese column and straightaway went into the attack. There was no immediate result visible in this foray, but no attack materialised on Imphal—later it was learnt from captured papers that fourteen Japanese officers and over two hundred other ranks perished that evening.

Relatively little is known of the thousands of Hurricanes shipped and flown to Russia's aid. In August 1941 the first Hurricanes (actually IIAs and IIBs) were sent to North Russia as the equipment of

Hurricane IIC "The Last of the Many" in the royal blue and gold racing colours of H.R.H. Princess Margaret, c. 1950. Civil lettering and trim were gold, the aircraft blue and race numbers white.

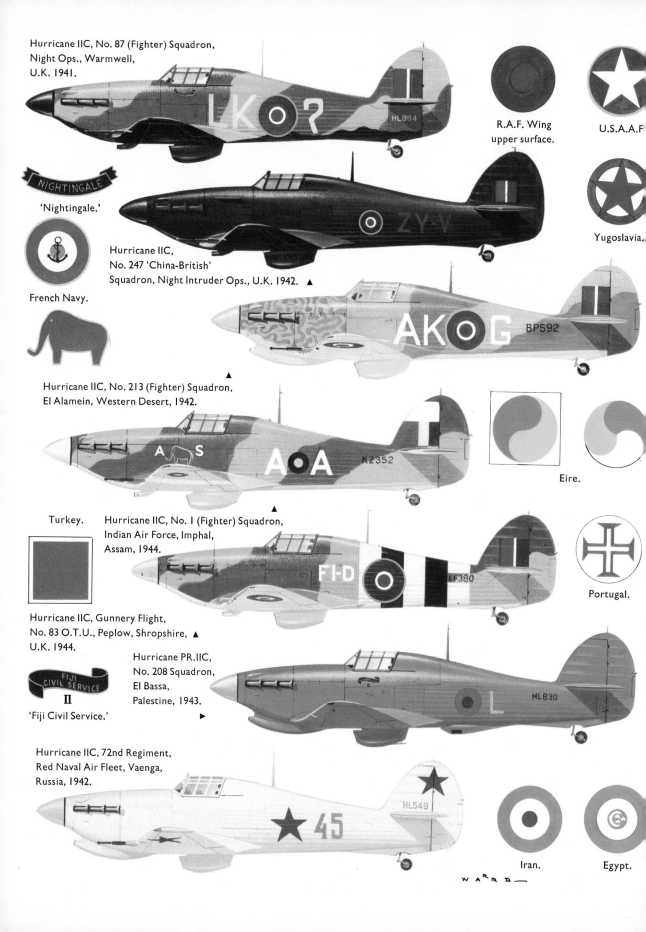

Hurricane IIC, No. 87 (Fighter) Squadron,
Night Ops., Warmwell,
U.K. 1941.

R.A.F. Wing
upper surface.

U.S.A.A.F

NIGHTINGALE

'Nightingale.'

French Navy.

Hurricane IIC,
No. 247 'China-British'
Squadron, Night Intruder Ops., U.K. 1942. ▲

Yugoslavia.

Hurricane IIC, No. 213 (Fighter) Squadron,
El Alamein, Western Desert, 1942.

Eire.

Turkey.

Hurricane IIC, No. 1 (Fighter) Squadron,
Indian Air Force, Imphal,
Assam, 1944.

Portugal.

Hurricane IIC, Gunnery Flight,
No. 83 O.T.U., Peplow, Shropshire, ▲
U.K. 1944.

FIJI
CIVIL SERVICE
II

'Fiji Civil Service.'

Hurricane PR.IIC,
No. 208 Squadron,
El Bassa,
Palestine, 1943.
▶

Hurricane IIC, 72nd Regiment,
Red Naval Air Fleet, Vaenga,
Russia, 1942.

Iran.

Egypt.

WARD

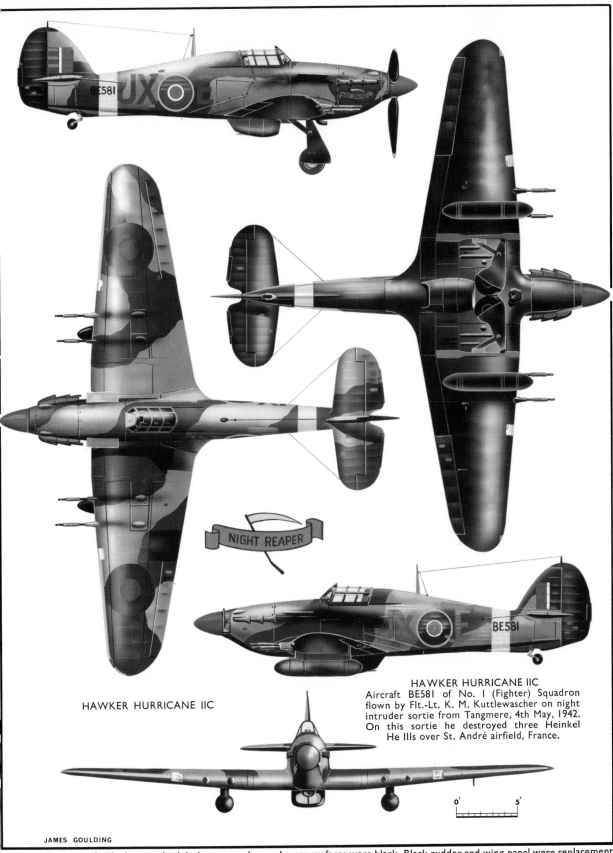

NIGHT REAPER

HAWKER HURRICANE IIC

HAWKER HURRICANE IIC
Aircraft BE581 of No. 1 (Fighter) Squadron flown by Flt.-Lt. K. M. Kuttlewascher on night intruder sortie from Tangmere, 4th May, 1942. On this sortie he destroyed three Heinkel He IIIs over St. André airfield, France.

JAMES GOULDING

Upper surfaces were finished in standard dark green and grey. Lower surfaces were black. Black rudder and wing panel were replacement components from Turbinlite flight Hurricane BD770. Aircraft displayed red doped patches over previous battle damage on port aileron, rear fuselage and tail unit.

Portuguese Hurricane N.F.IIC of the Lisbon Defence Flight, 1948.

(Photo: Comando Geral da Aeronautica Militar)

an R.A.F. Wing, consisting of Nos. 81 and 134 Squadrons. Withdrawn before the onset of the Russian winter, the R.A.F. pilots left their aircraft behind, these already being joined by the cannon-armed IIC. IICs reached Russia by several routes, the majority sailing in the North Cape convoys. Others were flown direct from Middle East M.U.s and some were even transferred from spare stocks in North West India.

SEA HURRICANES AND OTHERS

At first glance, designation of 4-cannon Hurricanes was straightforward—and within the spheres of R.A.F. operations all such aircraft *were* Mark IICs. As already remarked, however, the Royal Navy used cannon-armed Sea Hurricane ICs with Merlin III engines. These were superseded in March 1942 by Hurricane IIBs and IICs converted for naval use by the addition of deck equipment; though not strictly Sea Hurricanes, they were nevertheless adorned with

Above: *Persian Hurricane T.IIC with rear cockpit enclosed.*

Below: *The same aircraft in flight with both cockpits "un-hooded".* (Photos: Hawker Siddeley Aviation)

ROYAL NAVY on their rear fuselage sides. Later, true standard Sea Hurricane IICs entered service with the Royal Navy, but the vast majority of these served at shore stations.

As the Hurricane came to be withdrawn from R.A.F. service at the end of the war, numbers were sold abroad and Mark IICs found their way in many guises into the air forces of Eire, Portugal and Persia. The last Hurricane ever built—a Mark IIC—has been preserved in flying condition by Hawker Aircraft Ltd., and, as if to emphasise the reluctance of a great aircraft to vacate its place in history, this aircraft was used as observation "chase plane" during the transition trials of Hawker's Kestrel vertical take-off fighter prototype in 1960!

Hurricane IICs in Service
Representative Aircraft with R.A.F. Units
No. 1 (F) Sqdn., Hawkinge, convoy patrols, and Tangmere, 1941: *Z3778* ("Y"); Intruder Ops., 1942, *HL603* ("I").
No. 3 (F) Sqdn., *BD867* ("W"), *BN188* ("A").
No. 17 (F) Sqdn., Burma, *BN462, HV798.*
No. 43 (F) Sqdn., Acklington, Turbinlite patrols, *BD715*; Intruders, *HL460* (damaged in Dieppe attacks, 19/8/42).
No. 73 (F) Sqdn., Heliopolis, 6/42, *BN538* (shot down over Cairo 29/8/42); *BP518* (destroyed Ju 88, El Alamein, 31/8/42).
No. 174 (F) Sqdn., *BN795* (presentation aircraft in memory of Sqdn. Ldr. John Gillan).
No. 208 (AC) Sqdn., Tac R Mk.IIC, *BN156* (missing, 24/8/42).
No. 1413 (Met.) Flt., Met. Mk. IIC, Ryak, Damascus, Aqir and Lydda, 1943–45, *BN974.*
Aircraft supplied to Turkey from Middle East stocks, *HV551.*
Aircraft supplied to Russia, *KX113, KZ234.*

Hurricane II C Specification
Powerplant: Rolls Merlin XX developing 1,260 b.h.p. at 3,000 r.p.m. at 11,750 ft. in MS gear, and 1,160 b.h.p. at 3,000 r.p.m. at 20,750 ft. in S gear. Sea level take-off power: 1,300 b.h.p. at 3,000 r.p.m.
Propeller: Either 3-blade Rotol R.S.5/2 with Schwarz blades or Rotol R.S.5/3 with Jablo blades. Gear ratio: 0·42. Airscrew diameter: 11 ft. 3 in.
Dimensions: Wing span, 40 ft. 0 in. Overall length, 32 ft. 2¼ in. Maximum height (one airscrew blade vertical, tailwheel on ground), 13 ft. 1 in. Gross wing area, 257·6 sq. ft. Aspect ratio, 6·2. Wing incidence, +2°. Dihedral, 3·5° on datum. Undercarriage track, 7 ft. 10 in.
Weights: (Temperate version) Tare weight, 5,658 lb. Normal loaded weight, 7,544 lb. Overload combat weight, 8,044 lb. (Tropical version) Tare weight, 5,785 lb. Normal loaded weight, 7,707 lb. Overload combat weight 8,207 lb.
Performance: Temperate version. 329 m.p.h. at 18,000 ft. Rate of climb, 2,750 ft./min. at sea level. Time to height, 12½ min. to 30,000 ft. Range (clean aircraft), 460 statute miles at 178 m.p.h., or 920 miles with two 44-gallon auxiliary tanks.
Armament: Four 20 mm. Hispano or Oerlikon guns with total of 364 rounds of ammunition.